International Crafts

With 460 illustrations in color

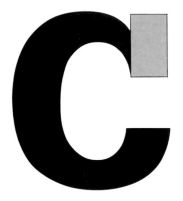  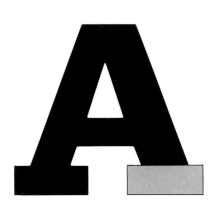

C R A

Advisers   **Lois Moran**
Editor/Publisher, *American Craft*, New York

Mitsuhiko Hasebe
Chief Curator, Crafts Gallery, National Museum of Modern Art, Tokyo

Miharu Ando
Director, Miharudo Gallery, Tokyo

John McPhee
Senior Curator, Australian Art, Australian National Gallery, Canberra

Yvonne Brunhammer
Director, Musée des Arts Décoratifs, Paris, and the curators

Karl-Günter Nicola
Editor-in-Chief, *Kunst+Handwerk* and *Neues Glas*, Erkrath, Germany

International

F T S

Edited by **MARTINA MARGETTS**

THAMES and **HUDSON**

Assistant editor: Lucinda Gane

Administrative assistant: Melanie Cox

Designed by Richard Hollis
by arrangement with Trolley Enterprises

Assistant designer: Celia Stothard

First published in the United States in 1991 by
Thames and Hudson Inc., 500 Fifth Avenue,
New York, New York 10110

Library of Congress Catalog Card Number 91-65323

Printed and bound in Singapore

Acknowledgments

The Editor would like to thank most warmly:
everyone who sent material to be considered
for the book;
the Advisers, Dan Klein, Paul Derrez, Annemie Boissevain;
Junko Ando, Kyoko Ando, Gretchen Adkins, Juliana Barrett,
Anita Besson, Thierry de Beaumont, Eleonoor van Beusekom,
Chantal Bizot, Mecky van den Brink, Alison Britton,
Floris van den Broecke, Pauline Burbidge, Veronica Burtt,
Canada House, London, Centre des Métiers d'Arts, Paris,
Emma Dent Coad, Garth Clark, Chloë Colchester,
Liesbeth Crommelin, Dick Dankers, Guillemette Delaporte,
Peter Dormer, Helen Drutt, Richard Edgcumbe, Rupert Faulkner,
Jenny Fell, Robin Fior, Jacqueline Ford, Anne French,
Griselda Gilroy, Gaynor Goffe, Tomo Hirai, Makoto Ito,
Janis Jefferies, Yvonne Joris, Peter van Kester, Maria van Kesteren,
Elizabeth Kodré-Defner, Atsuko Koyanagi, Yvette Lardinois, Morris Latham,
Eileen Lewenstein, Ingrid Lie, Frances Lord, Susan McCormack,
Les Manning, Tatjana Marsden, Jasper Morrison, Gunnel Myhrberg,
Steven Newell, John Odgers, Jean-Luc Olivié, Jennifer Opie,
Anatol Orient, Linda Parry, Caroline Pearce-Higgins, Tom Perkins,
Marie-Laure Perrin, Tessa Peters, Polish Cultural Institute, London,
Alan Poole, Helmut Ricke, W. J. Roeterink, Andrea Rose, Michael Rowe,
Geraldine Rudge, Helen van Ruiten, Terry Sandell,
Romilly Saumarez-Smith, Colette Save, Sissel Ree Schjønsby,
Linda Seckelson, Masaaki Sekiya, Isobel Sinden,
Galerie Smend, Cologne, Philip Smith, Tomio Sugaya,
Swiss Crafts Council, Biel, Sissy Thomas, Cathy Tragaris,
Vladimir Tsivin, John Vedel-Rieper, Birthe Warnolf,
Oliver Watson, Rüdiger Wiese;
also Richard Hollis, Lucinda Gane, Melanie Cox,
Celia Stothard, Philomena Munzer, Moira Swayne, Kay Henderson,
Anne Barbour, Karin Hofer,
and my family.

A note on selection

This book is a distillation of
thousands of recent slides and transparencies
submitted during late 1990.
As a first attempt to present
the international crafts world in book form,
its pages, like maps of the world
by the earliest explorers,
can offer only a partial record
of all the wonderful things to be seen,
and yet to be discovered.
Those whose work is not included
will be the first to agree that
several volumes would be needed to do full justice
to the variety and quality of current work
in the crafts.
What I have tried to do is
highlight themes within the main craft disciplines
which at this time have emerged
as common ground for craftsmen and women
in different parts of the world.

Most of the works illustrated were made in 1989/1990.

Measurements are given in centimetres and inches in the order of height, width, depth.
Where only one measurement is given, this is the height, unless otherwise stated.

CONTENTS

FOREWORD

Brooch
by Shinya Yamamura
Japan

This book is both a review and a celebration of crafts now, in the Western world and Japan. For the first time, an international selection of current work in all the main craft disciplines is presented in one volume. The scale of the Information section of the book, the most comprehensive available, reinforces the fact that the art of craft is firmly established on our Western cultural agenda.

The following pages show work principally from North America, Japan, Australia and all the countries of Europe. They connect in sensibility, and in forms and use of materials, not only to the world's rich decorative and applied arts traditions but also to the concerns of contemporary artists of all kinds, to architects and designers. Conversations among the greatly increased number of crafts students round the world indicate the range of influence and inspiration (just one seminar in London took in Rei Kawakubo, Jean Baudrillard and Tom Wolfe, Jim Morrison, Anselm Kiefer, Alessi and the Beaubourg).

Within a context of spiritual *glasnost* (politics struggles behind), the Soviet Union and the countries of Eastern Europe enter the international, consumerist crafts arena. Their arts infrastructure is underdeveloped and visual stimulus, raw materials and tools are harder to come by, but the work is impressive, with its different perspective on the human condition. Czech glass, of course, stands out as a sophisticated and long-established movement, supported by the state, continuing and extending its Bohemian glass tradition into sculpture. Polish textiles also have a distinctive pedigree.

If there is any blessing in Postmodernism, it is its inclusive spirit, which promotes no moral or aesthetic orthodoxy and allows myriad creative ideas to be more objectively assessed. Works elide: craft = applied art = design, while the so-called ethnic crafts are at last acknowledged as important in their own right, rather than as mere tribal source material for 'real' Western artists. The Aboriginal and Maori works in this book, now avidly collected, attest to a changed perception by the West.

Stoneware vessel
by Karl Scheid
Germany

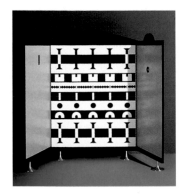

Cupboard
for Studio Alchimia
by Giorgio Gregori
Italy

Silk ikat-woven scarves
by Mary Restieaux
UK

Forged-steel gates
by Christoph Friedrich
Switzerland

The danger of an eclectic climate, to paraphrase the critic Robert Hughes, is that style mutates into styling ('Plus ça change, plus c'est la même pose') and that, while Postmodernism ebbs and flows, the tidemark of Modernism finds itself 'defended as archaeology and derided as a failed Utopia'.

This book applauds Modernists as much as Postmodernists – and all countries, including Scandinavia and Japan, now have both: those who construct, who deal with new tools and new materials and who distil their reflections on the present age into an essence of pure form, as much as those who assemble, collage or synthesize memory, sensation, ornament, narrative, symbols, myths and complex references into a potent cocktail.

While the word 'crafts' embraces a spectrum of meanings and object types, including the most basic utilitarian artefacts of everyday living, the works here are all made with an exceptional degree of personal commitment. Each stage in the making process is a matter of individual choice – tools, materials, techniques, colours, surface treatment, textures, scale, concept, function. The resolution of all these elements into a unique piece, whether intuitive or deliberately planned on the part of the maker, is what gives each work a compelling presence.

Those who collect crafts, individuals, corporations or museums, and those who write about them, recognize the importance of a confluence of factors in a given craft discipline at a particular time. Key ideas, materials, techniques, together with certain exhibitions and reviews, coalesce across national boundaries to form movements. Examples over the past two decades have been the non-utilitarian vessel, whether in ceramic, glass, metal, cloth, wood or paper; glass art; furniture and domestic objects made of metal and found materials; jewelry made of non-precious materials whose aesthetic provokes debate about the purpose of adornment; and fiber art, the transmutation of traditional textile techniques into dramatically new forms. Such movements are reflected in the pages of this book.

While growing collections, retail galleries, awards schemes, residencies, administrative organizations and publications have been supporting the increasing number of craft practitioners and consumers, scholars and historians have only just begun to explain this 'crafts revival' in objective terms. But if the crafts world is at last becoming institutionalized in contemporary culture, there are many who will lament the loss of innocence and freedom that entry into the cultural mainstream denotes.

Alison Britton writes in her Introduction of the crafts as a creative field which excitingly offers a tangible alternative to this mainstream. Perhaps

Lettercutting
by Tom Perkins
UK

the crafts are now on the horns of a dilemma: the range and quality of contemporary work will inexorably propel it and its creators into the cultural and media spotlight; but at the same time, the status stakes, the superficial categorizations and the need for ever-changing styles of work at keener prices to satisfy demand, may suck the crafts into a vortex akin to the contemporary art world. The result may damage its independent, free-radical spirit which at the moment gives the work and its makers their remarkable quality. It is my hope that this book will assist in casting the spotlight on such deserving creators while indicating that the work they make is unlikely to continue seeding and flourishing if the pressures of the commercial climate are too harsh.

Martina Margetts

Handbuilt vessel
by Rudy Autio
USA

Glass and metal table
by Danny Lane
UK

Bookbinding
by Monique Mathieu-Frenaud
France

The breadth and ambiguity of the craft field is what has always attracted me to it. You can be concerned with basic practicalities or with elusive ideas; feet on the ground or head in the clouds, or both. Work in the crafts today covers a very wide spectrum from the traditional to the invented, and from the functional to the abstract. All kinds of qualities can be manifested from the raggedly hewn to the meticulously detailed, from the brash to the restrained. It all depends on the object.

The crafts sit in the middle of art and design, but they are not a refuge or a backwater. The idea that the crafts are *safe*, a haven from the commercial guile of designed mass-production on the one hand and the provocative dangers of fine art on the other, is denied by the range of unforeseen and experimental work made by some of the artists shown here. The last twenty years have seen great developments in this middle field. Good craft work can be exhilarating, tactile, reassuring, stunning, disconcerting – the whole gamut of feeling can be evoked. The response to a craft object can be physical, emotional or intellectual. The narrative, the useful and the purely formal all have a place in the crafts.

Objects can tell us a great deal about the people that made, used, displayed and owned them. Museums collect doorhandles as well as heroic paintings. (And museums now are buying contemporary craft work.) New thinking in museum studies, and the development of the writing of design and craft history, are making greater and deeper sense of the objects that have been gathered into museums over the centuries. In this enriched context the new craft work has found an audience and a place.

But why do we still have the crafts? They are no longer essential to our existence in the modern world – there are other ways of doing things. The props of daily life are more quickly and cheaply made in factories. The crafts are needed and wanted for a complicated variety of reasons. These include nostalgia, aesthetic accessibility, notions of individuality and – what is more surprising – an ideology of opposition. In a succession of waves, the crafts have functioned as a small but serious cross-current against the drift of development in industrialized society.

Cork necklace
by Paul Derrez
Holland

Engraved and
sandblasted bowl
by Eva Vlasáková
Czechoslovakia

Wooden 'leaf' dish
by Peter Niczewski
UK

What might be called the self-conscious crafts, things which are made by hand, by choice, as a deliberate alternative to mass-production, are about a century old. The ideas of William Morris and John Ruskin are still a point of reference. While the Arts and Crafts Movement in Britain saw the crafts as a bastion against dehumanizing industry, on the Continent the instigators of the Modern Movement believed the opposite. They took great interest in the socialist aspects of Arts and Crafts theory, but they had a positive view of industry. They thought that by engaging with it, and harnessing craft practice to it, they could make things in mass-production which contained the values of beauty, utility, etc. and which really were available to everyone. These early design pioneers were not ostriches, they were open to technology. A new synthesis of art and design and craft, collaborating with industry, was seen to be the answer to social needs of the time. Artists, architects, sculptors and craftspeople of all kinds could work together. This was the spirit of the Bauhaus school in Germany (1919-1933).

Bauhaus theory embraced craft as a very important part of the training of designers, but not as an end in itself. Craft was there to re-energize art and design, to put manual and material understanding back into an effete drawing-board approach. But Modernist design, though it was rational, sensible, democratic and accessible, brought a uniformity and standardization that was not ultimately what people wanted. (One of the ironies of Modernism has been that the crafts were marginalized in an area where they could have made such a helpful contribution, in the humanizing of the details of the built environment. In recent times this role is being recovered; both in building and in some areas of product design an input from the crafts is now more welcome.)

In the 1960s, I can remember Pete Seeger singing a song about houses that were 'Little boxes, all the same'. This conjures up the atmosphere of frustration with uniformity in which the crafts, like folk-singing, had a place in reaffirming people's difference, their individuality, their do-it-yourself independence. People with Ph.Ds became carpenters, grew onions, travelled vast distances, wore homemade clothes. *Making* things (perhaps badly) was revalidated. Making something yourself can be a gesture of protest in a technological world of increasing creative powerlessness and passivity. It is not possible to separate the roots of this amateur phenomenon distinctly from the craft revival that we are currently still experiencing, although now we are at a very different stage in its progress, with established professional practitioners leading the various fields.

Signorina Così
Earthenware vessel
by Aldo Rontini
Italy

Mystery Woman
Painted glass
by Ulrica Hydman-Vallien
Sweden

1. Elizabeth Fritsch,
Pots about Music,
Leeds 1978

■ I think it would be a surprise to the early Modernists to learn of the survival of the craft approach. It does seem that the decades of impeccable, streamlined, regular manufactured objects have left people with a hunger for contradiction; for things that show signs of having been made by a human, with unrepeatable qualities. Made things communicate defiance of the machine, and express 'difference' clearly and instantly.

■ The philosophy and literature of this century often have been concerned with the idea of man as a separate being, an individual. People can express their sense of self through the things they use, own and wear, as well as by what they say and do. The choosing of something that is evidently not run-of-the-mill can be self-revelatory in a satisfying way. This is why the one-off object has held its place in our desires.

■ Craft work does nothing to threaten industry, but it does in a quiet way subvert the norms, in both the objects that it produces and in the peculiar kinds of living it provides. The idea of making things to sell and surviving in a hand-to-mouth fashion is one that has gained momentum in the last thirty years. Like many of the other arts practices, it is now an aspect of the 'alternative' culture. Craftspeople, in common with other artists and some of the self-employed, choose to work in a way that means they have maximum control over what they produce. They are stubborn, determined and independent, and usually put up with difficult working conditions and low and erratic pay to achieve this ideal mode of work. They need to feel convinced about what they make, or it wouldn't be worth it. Whether they live in a rural idyll or in the middle of a crowded terrace, the decision to be a maker is some sort of statement; an interruption of the mainstream.

It is this that drives me to turn each pot into something improvised and different and to squander days, even weeks, on the making and painting of one vessel. I suspect that the making of art at all in this society has to be in defiance of economic pressures and psychic repressions; a kind of insistence on some measure of freedom and magic.[1]

■ But the craft world is not a random one of disconnected expressive spirits. Craft work is inevitably linked to strong aesthetic traditions, and to proven techniques. There are times when reminders of past values are useful and times to push on and overturn the rules. I would not want to suggest that craft production has only opposed Modernism and not brushed with it. Modernism, after all, is a principle and not a style. It is not just concerned with mass-production, it seeps into painting and novel writing as much as blocks of high-rise flats. The Modern Movement wanted to clothe the values of a new era in a different language, and who could complain about that?

The spirit of enquiry, without preconceptions, into new forms and relevant new materials has been very much a part of recent crafts history. This has been particularly noticeable in jewelry, lighting and furniture. Many areas of the crafts have been questioning whether or not function is obligatory, and whether an *idea* of function is an interesting subject, as it is to the still-life painter of pots and pans. The catalogue to *The Maker's Eye* exhibition in 1982, for which a very mixed group of craftspeople chose objects that were important to them from the previous decade, is one that becomes increasingly interesting as time passes.[2] I wrote in it about 'two-faced' objects that were both functional and self-questioning, poised between real life and still-life. Having made my choices and written my statement, I realized that this was an area of concern at the time to a whole group of artists making objects across several different media. In a previous generation they might have been making sculpture; but now they were keen to look closely into the characteristics of ordinary useable things – the chair, the jug, the box.

Besides looking around the house, the crafts have looked far afield for sources of interest and excitement too. They have inhaled the primitive and the exotic, which bring a powerful narrative of 'elsewhere', and the types of early Modern art such as Cubism whose exponents were so impressed with these strange forms. The last half of this complicated century has seen on many fronts a great reaching out to be surprised, refreshed and stimulated by unfamiliar non-Western traditions. Craft works from distant places, from other very different societies, have had great appeal to the jaded Western public. The development of a multi-cultural eye has broadened the range of what is made here, and what is wanted. The quest for new forms is not something that comes to an end.

The fascination for makers in coming across craft work from far afield is partly to do with the way it is made; a desire to understand different kinds of skill. Skill is an issue at the moment in the crafts, the crafts having developed such new forms over the last twenty years. The generation that trained at art colleges in the early Seventies found their own paths with new approaches to techniques and unconventional materials, and a general quest for colour in all sorts of substances. They usually had traditional skills behind them. The following generation is missing some of the basics.

In my experience of teaching graduates, fewer and fewer students of ceramics are able to throw, for instance, or understand much about glaze. The tendency in ceramics has been towards irregular and handbuilt forms

2. Crafts Council, London 1982

From the Red Forest
Stoneware sculpture
by Johanna Rytkölä
Finland

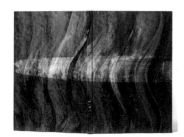

Bookbinding
by Gotthilf Kurz
Germany

Calligraphy
by Jovica Veljovič
Czechoslovakia

Pomegranate Girdle
by Esther Knobel
Israel

Soft Bag
Bark paper, caning
by Lillian Elliott
USA

Environmental ceramic
sculpture
by Michel Kuipers
Holland

and dry, unreflective painterly surfaces. Exciting new ground is gained, but there are potential losses in the breadth of the body of standard potters' knowledge. People become skilled in more personal and diverse ways, evolving specific means to suit a particular imagined form. There is great skill and ambition in some of the new ways of handbuilding, piecing together a thin skin of clay, keeping the plastic and immediate, unworked qualities. I know there are equivalent examples of innovative technique in other craft fields.

I am not convinced that we are facing a crisis in the disappearance of traditional skills. At present many of them are still in reach and I think that we should offer them in teaching while we can, where there is a sensible context and not just for the sake of preservation. The pursuit of personal expression will inevitably take up new threads of skill and drop some old ones. I believe that the critics who are mourning the diminution of skill forget that a culture has its own pace. At any one time, not everything is potently interesting enough to raise the energy and conviction to get on and *do* it. With subject matter and with the necessary skills, some things are in the air and others aren't. To ignore this is to opt for dead work.

Certainly I know that I always have the same reaction of dismay when I see something that is made perfectly, a virtuoso triumph, but has no thinking behind it, no point to it, no relevance or life. Where the use of the skill in itself has been a justification. There is plenty of that sort of slick and empty work about. It is one of the most disappointing culs-de-sac of the craft world. Such work proliferates in a climate where great emphasis is placed on *how* things are done, often as a sort of entertainment. Popular interest in the crafts may well begin with the practicalities, watching demonstrations and so on. While this is not to be discouraged, it is a pity that so often people fail to get past an appreciation of skill into questions of context or meaning.

In contrast to the respect for 'polished' skill, sometimes we particularly value craft work for its roughness and spontaneity. Ruskin was fully aware of this. He thought that liveliness and vigour and the positive mark of humanity were manifested in rough work. He cherished the unprecious handling of the carving in Gothic churches, the irregularities and the imperfections. The sense of the carvers having been happy in their work was part of the visual pleasure. This has echoes for us today: the direct gesture, collage, assembly, interest in used materials, evidence of making as a kind of decoration – all these have been seen in art and craft in modern times. They could all be described as kinds of roughness.

3. *Five Furniture Pieces*,
London 1985

Rosella box
Varnished card
by Pini Brockmann
Germany

Conditions for Ornament No.11
Brass/copper, tinned finish
by Michael Rowe
UK

Stoneware vessel
by Kazuo Takiguchi
Japan
Victoria and Albert Museum
Collection

'Craft' means many different things to different ears. I must say that I do not find the word an easy one to use. Some people are put off by it altogether, it smacks to them of frumpiness and a retreat from the modern world. Paradoxically, that is exactly what others are looking for: comfort in the crafts. Writing in an exhibition leaflet in 1985 I tried to do without it. 'Craft is a means to an end and is not really anything in itself. It consists in doing something properly, and it is a basis of recognition of values and skills and methods and knowledge of materials. It has no real substance or meaning without one or other of these leanings: the design world and the art world have equal need of it.'[3] None of the terms – decorative art, applied art, design art, craft – do quite the whole job in delineating the territory. Some craft work, in furniture for instance, is indistinguishable in its aims from design, but is made perhaps in smaller quantities and by slower means. Some craft work blurs with fine art in its cerebral intentions, but may be made of materials unauthenticated by the conventions of fine art practice. A book like this may suggest that the crafts are a category with distinct edges, but this is not the case. It is quite fruitless to try and draw clear dividing lines between the three parts of the continuum, and it doesn't matter.

There is pleasure and freedom in the condition of being loosely defined. Ambiguity is the mother of invention. Makers have thrived on the variety of possibilities, the overlaps between disciplines, and the provisional atmosphere. Some makers have stuck to a narrow path, others have crossed media, synthesized and accumulated. The conventions of the past have been of great interest in the search for meanings outside the functional. Figurative work, animal and human, is a current preoccupation among many younger artists. Perhaps the state of the world's ecology is the cause. It is also noticeable that artists are recycling pieces of wood, metal or cloth. The choice of already-used materials can be metaphorical, or may express the conservational mood of the times. Work like this is triggered by the artist's attraction to the found object. It is a question of personality. Some people like to fill empty spaces, start from scratch, control everything, others can only respond to a different kind of creative pressure and take their cue from something that is picked up, or something that happens, a clue towards subject matter. Some of the endless options are curtailed.

In the course of travelling to exhibit and to talk in North America, Australia, Japan, Czechoslovakia and other parts of Europe, I have had the chance to see a great variety of practice in craft work. The more I have seen, the less inclined I am to make a qualitative judgment.

Carb
Silkscreen-printed
and painted hanging
incorporating found materials
by Rushton Aust
UK

The differences, and the background reasons for those differences, have amazed me. But I think that a common thread could be seen to be that many people choose to work in the crafts because close involvement with a material brings a set of limitations that are stimulating to work with. I would suggest that pleasure in limitations is a characteristic that distinguishes craft practice from that of fine art or design.

What I cherish in the crafts besides this quality of blossoming through the constraints is the celebration of the hybrid. Pieces of textile that are *like* painting but not confused with it; free-hanging, like tapestry also. Jewelry that can easily be worn, but looks intact when it is by itself hung on the wall. The chairs or pots or sheet-metal containers that tantalizingly echo the shapes of other ambiguous objects. Beautifully-finished brooches made from tin cans; intriguing touches of the incongruous. Makers may need to ignore conventions to get closer to an accurate realization of an idea or a feeling. They have been doing this for centuries – that is how a culture moves along. Like an amœba unconsciously gathering up little gestures of advance.

To me the value and importance of the crafts exist in their refusal to be completely one thing or another. It may be middle class and middle ground, but the crafts territory as it is now encourages some dazzling and subtle subversions of our expectations. This sort of work is worth doing and worth writing about.

Alison Britton is
an internationally-acclaimed potter,
writer on the crafts and
teacher at the Royal College of Art,
London.
*Alison Britton:
Ceramics in Studio*
by Tanya Harrod
(Bellew, London 1990)
accompanies her major
retrospective currently touring
the UK and Holland.

(Opposite)
Double horn F/B 'Model R'
(unique design and methods)
by Max and Heinrich Thein
Germany

Ceramics is practised in virtually every country of the world, its vessel forms rooted in the most basic concerns of survival and ritual, its sculptural forms a commentary on society's preoccupations at any given time. Today's inheritors of ceramic traditions stretching back thousands of years can fuse their inspiration of every conceivable clay form, surface treatment and symbolic meaning with their experience of contemporary life.

As the following pages reflect, the majority of ceramic artists continue to explore the potential of the vessel, both literally and metaphorically, orchestrating form and surface in a great variety of ways. Some exploit the intrinsic link with the earth and nature, pinching, punching, cracking the clay to dramatic effect; others transform the material into colourful objects of sophistication and wit, figuration and narrative.

The Americans are so diverse and prolific that only a sampling can be shown here. The alignment of Peter Voulkos with the Abstract Expressionist movement in the 1950s proved a catalyst for new directions in ceramic art in the USA. Its bravura stance, in terms of imagery, of technical, formal and colour combinations, and often of scale, is matched only by the so-called Second and Third Generation of Japanese potters such as Kimpei Nakamura and Yo Akiyama. It could be said that this radicalism is counterbalanced by Europe's comparatively Modernistic approach, with the Eastern Europeans evident in a reflective mood.

The works shown demonstrate a mastery of the techniques and methods available to the potter, including throwing, handbuilding, slabbing, coiling, pinching, mould-making, slipcasting, painting, glazing and mark-making with tools. These, together with the magical, alchemical process of firing and the possibility of bringing together in one piece the concerns of both the painter and the sculptor, give ceramics a unique position in contemporary art.

Belgium
Carmen Dionyse
Charon (details)
Grogged white stoneware clay, biscuit-fired to 1150°C. Four glaze firings between 1080 and 1225°C (black, turquoise, green, brown)
67 x 47 cm / 26 x 18½ in

◄ Japan
Jozan Yamada
Thrown teapot with pear-peel
surface
5 x 8.5 cm / 2 x 3½ in

Australia
David Pottinger
Tall Lidded Pot
Soft-paste porcelain slabbed
and coiled, matt glaze,
high-fired
c.23 x 11 cm / 14 x 4½ in

France
Catherine Vanier
Thrown, glaze-painted plate
3.5 cm / 9 in diameter

UK
Walter Keeler
Thrown stoneware jug,
joined, top altered and cut,
saltglazed at 1300°C
53 x 14 x 26 cm / 21 x 5½ x 10 in

■ The Japanese teawares are archetypal ceramic objects,
combining utility with beauty and offering
an active as well as contemplative relationship
with the user.

European domestic pottery traditions,
as well as those of other cultures, are also
being re-explored by contemporary potters.

◄ Japan
Kyusetsu Miwa
Thrown and glazed white *hagi*
teabowl
11.9 x 14.9 cm / 4½ x 6 in

Holland
Monique Middelhoek
Part of *'Sjampian'* tableware,
slipcast stoneware, engobe
coloured, glazed and fired
to 1200°C. Batch production
9x18cm / 3½x7 in

Denmark
Alev Ebüzziya Siesbye
Bowls, handbuilt (large) and
thrown (small) stoneware,

electric-fired to 1280°C
26x43 and 9x15cm / 10x17
and 3½x6 in

Australia
Gwyn Hanssen Pigott
Still Life
Thrown porcelain, woodfired
to 1300°C with reduction
27 cm / 10½ in tallest

USA
Karen Karnes
Thrown, flattened, glazed and
woodfired vessel
28 cm / 11 in

Germany
Thomas Naethe
No.2 Vessel
Turned stoneware, slip, salt
and oxide colourings,
glaze-fired at 1250°C with
reduction
13 x 35 cm / 5 x 14 in

USA
Ruth Duckworth
Untitled Vessel
Porcelain
15 x 23 cm / 6 x 9 in

■ Many ceramics combine a refined sculptural presence
with everyday function, the emphasis decided on
as much by the owner as the maker.

UK
Lucie Rie
Thrown porcelain
23 cm / 9 in diameter

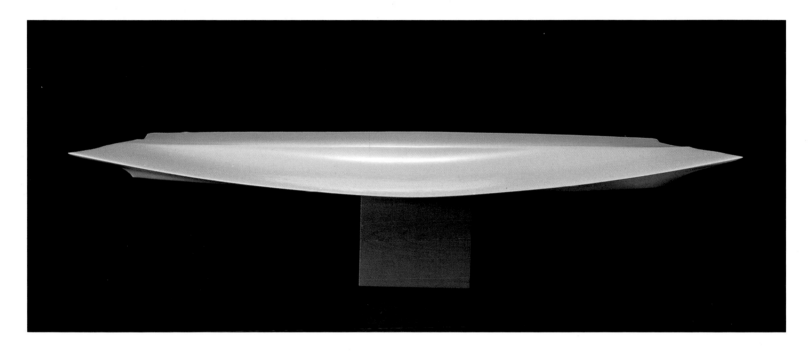

Japan
Sueharu Fukami
Slipcast and carved porcelain
with celadon glaze
c. 100 cm / 39 in long

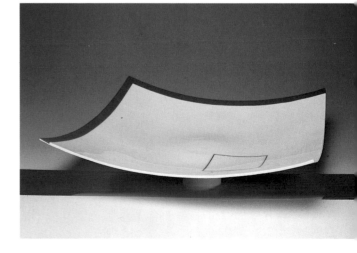

Austria
Kurt Spurey
Porcelain dish
c. 30 cm / 12 in wide

◀ USA
Rudolf Staffel
Light Gatherer
Porcelain, slabbed and
constructed
23 cm / 9 in

◀ Norway
Arne Åse
Unglazed porcelain, relief
patterning inside and out
13 cm / 5 in diameter

■ Porcelain, beloved for its delicacy and translucence,
has attracted many of the world's great potters.
(Lucie Rie, born in 1901, made the pot illustrated in 1990.)
But assumptions about the material, especially Sung celadon,
can be subverted by new formal treatments.

USSR
Vladimir Gorislavtsev
Vessel, chamotte, metallic
salts, fired to 1000°C
50 cm / 20 in

▶
UK
Carol McNicoll
(Opposite, left inset)
Slipcast and painted
earthenware jug, batch
production
38 x 28 cm / 15 x 11 in

USA
Adrian Saxe
(Opposite, right inset)
Black Patty Pan Teapot
Porcelain
18 x 25.5 cm / 7 x 10 in

UK
Kate Malone
(Opposite)
Lidded Starfish Jar
Press-moulded and coiled
'T' material (biscuit-fired
to 1180°C). Earthenware
glaze-fired eight times from
1100°C to 1020°C
43 x 41 x 41 cm / 17 x 16 x 16 in

USA
Betty Woodman
Still Life Vase No. 6
Glazed earthenware
77 x 70 x 25.5 cm /
32 x 27 x 10 in

■ Clay, the perfect
Postmodernist medium,
lends itself to
camouflage,
transformation
and illusion.
The juxtaposition of
two-dimensional and
three-dimensional
forms, of handbuilt
and thrown parts,
of glazed, painted,
slipcast textured
areas, produces works of
ambiguous function,
playing on the history
and traditions of art
and ceramics.

Germany
Heike Mühlhaus at Cocktail
Ceramic, copper, steel drinking vessels, limited edition of 120
45 cm / 18 in

■ The heightened colours, surface patterning and ritual forms of some 'tableware' give it an air of ceremonial treasure. Janice Tchalenko works with versatility in the functional realm, also designing for production.

UK
Janice Tchalenko
High-fired reduction stoneware platter with coloured glazes (and detail)
40.5 cm / 19 in long

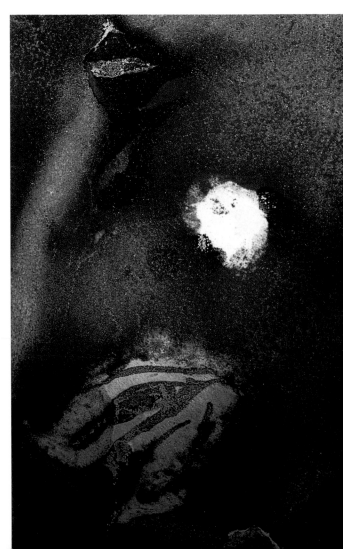

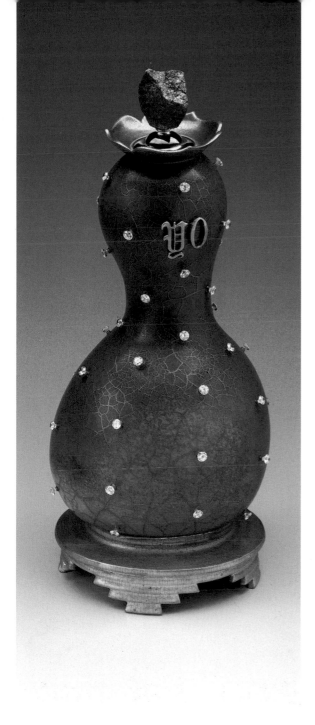

USA
John Donoghue
Thrown plate, clear-glazed
earthenware with coloured
slips
51 cm / 20 in

USA
Adrian Saxe
Yo
Porcelain
55 x 25.5 cm / 22 x 10½ in

USA
Ralph Bacerra
Earthenware teapot
38 x 28 cm / 16½ x 11 in

USA
Roseline Delisle
Série pneumatique
Thrown porcelain,
wheel-trimmed, painted,
assembled
30.5 x 13 cm / 12 x 5 in

UK
Elizabeth Fritsch
Spiral Vase from Tlon (1984)
Lachrymatory (1987)
Music Vase 'Green in Blue'
(1989)
Coiled and handbuilt
stoneware
30 cm / 16 in (left pot)

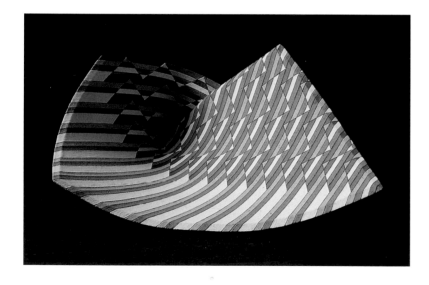

Germany
Rita Ternes
No. 1 Folded Slab
Slip-coloured stoneware,
reduction gas-fired at 1600°C
48 cm / 19 in wide

Japan
Tatsusuke Kuriki
Primeval Vase III
Stoneware sculpture, Tsurui
Museum Collection
41.5 x 56 x 40 cm / 16½ x 22 x 16 in

■ The techniques of incising, painting,
cutting, slabbing and coiling create geometric patterning
with musical eloquence.

■ Part of the ceramic cycle is to consign glazed forms to the fire, producing crackled and pitted surfaces of perfect imperfection, like earth itself.

Germany
Martin Mindermann
Raku vessel
42x53cm/16½x21in

USA
Richard DeVore
Untitled (#622)
Glazed stoneware
34 x 30 x 35 cm / 13½ x 12 x 13 in

Finland
Outi Leinonen
Kota
Press-moulded stoneware
with copper oxide
30 x 27 cm / 12 x 11 in

Hungary
Karoly Szekeres
Vase III
Porcelain coloured with salt,
fired at 1400°C
40 cm / 15½ in diameter

Switzerland
Edouard Chapallaz
Asymmetrical Vase
Thrown, copper glazed,
reduction-fired at 1800°C
26 x 27 cm / 10½ x 11 in

■ The dense, smoothly polished texture of burnished pots, epitomized by the works of the great Pierre Bayle, is contrasted with the pot by Mutsuo Yanagihara, who mixes stylized Japanese patterning with American-style funk.

France
Pierre Bayle
Burnished vase
c.51 cm / 20 in

France
Pierre Bayle
Burnished vase
c.60 cm / 24 in

Japan
Mutsuo Yanagihara
Cosmic Pattern Pot
52 x 46 x 30 cm / 20½ x 18 x 12 in

Norway
Fritz Harstrup
Slab and thrown earthenware,
black slip layers burnished,
red slip, burnished again
48cm / 19 in

UK
Magdalene Odundo
Handbuilt red firing clay,
burnished, low-fired and
reduced
46.5 x 26.5 cm / 18 x 11 in

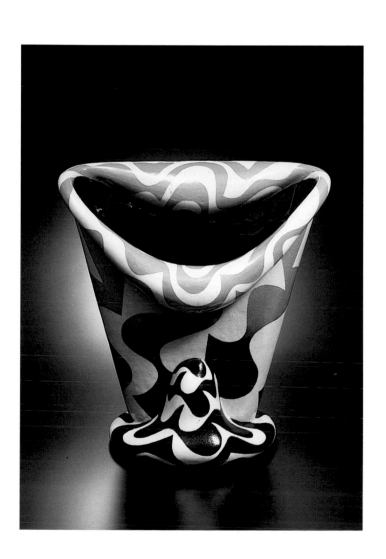

Holland
Irene Vonck
Blue Rhythms
Solid soft lump of clay,
opened up and shaped, slips
and pigment applied
38x42x45cm / 15x15½x18in

▲
Spain
Enrique Mestre
(Inset)
Spiritual Square No.1
Stoneware
60x46x95cm / 23½x18x37in

USA
Anne Currier
(Above)
Waughbrook
Hollow form, handbuilt slabs,
rolled, cut, scored,
high-temperature biscuit,
spray-glazed and low-fired
48x94x51cm / 19x37x20 in

UK
Martin Smith
(Above right)
Vessel 1/90
Red earthenware and
sawdust, pressmoulded,
jigger and jollied, underglaze
colour, assembled in epoxy
adhesive after firing
30cm / 12 in wide

■ Pots as architecture,
their interior and
exterior structures,
whether organic
or constructed,
delineated with
only minimal surface
treatment.

USA
William Daley
Taos Revisited
Fire clay, ball clay, flower pot
clay, slab-built over and in
preforms, fired at Cone 6 in
oxidation, unglazed.
Collection Everson Museum,
USA
43x76x61cm / 17x30x24 in

UK
Gordon Baldwin
Large Round Vessel
Buff clay with engobes,
oxides, stains and glazes
43 x 43 cm / 17 x 17 in

Sweden
Ingrid Olsson
Blue Pot
Slab-built stoneware,
low-fired and painted with oil
colours
41 x 45 x 22 cm / 13 x 16 x 8½ in

■ A European Modernist theme is
the exploration of the essence of a vessel form.
The constructed forms and brush-marked surfaces
give the arts of sculpture and painting
a third dimension.

UK
Alison Britton
Pot with Two Spouts
Handbuilt and slip-painted
earthenware, underglaze and
clear matt glaze
34 x 37.5 x 24 cm / 13½ x 14½ x 9½ in

UK
Ken Eastman
Slab-built grogged white
stoneware pot, painted with
coloured slips and oxides and
fired several times to 1180°C
32 x 40 x 31 cm / 13 x 16 x 12 in

Italy
Nino Caruso
Archivaso
Low-fired clay, slipcast
and fired at 1500°C
30 x 38 cm / 12 x 15 in

Germany
**Christina Kluge
Haberkorn**

Handbuilt red clay, white matt
glaze, painted with coloured
oxides, oxidized at 1160°C in
electric kiln
40 x 35 cm / 16 x 13½ in

USA
Wayne Higby
Nightfall Bay
Raku-fired earthenware
32 x 50 x 40.5 cm / 12¾ x 19 x 16¼ in

Germany
Beate Kuhn
Thrown red stoneware, clay
elements assembled when
leather hard, oxidizing electric
firing at 1240°C
36 x 60 x 60 cm / 14 x 23½ x 23½ in

USA
Peter Voulkos
Thrown, pierced, assembled
jar, anagama firing
c.100cm / 39½ in

UK
Ewen Henderson
Inside/Outside Complex series
Bone china and porcelain
50/50 mixture laminated onto
stoneware, oxidized to 1200°C
55cm / 22 in

Greece
Theodora Chorafas
Conical 1
Red earthenware and fine
grog, handbuilt, 900°C
biscuit, 800°C pitfired and
fumed
c.56cm / 22 in

■ Peter Voulkos, a key ceramic artist,
broke the mould of American ceramics in the 1950s
with his Abstract Expressionist forms and working methods
and a reinterpretation of Japanese traditions.
His work epitomizes a genre
which marries a consciousness of art
with a consciousness of nature, its forms,
materials, colourings and surfaces.

41

Japan
Ryoji Koie
Glazed earthenware
34 x 28 x 5.8 cm / 13½ x 12 x 2 in

■ These three renowned potters
exemplify the dazzling impact of works
created within the Oriental and 'organic' traditions
in which the nature and potential of clay
and glaze are the subject.

▶
Spain
**Claudi Casanovas i
Sarsanedas**
Gerra No.14
Stoneware with O.F.E. glaze,
reduction-fired at 1280°C
71 x 77 cm / 29 x 31½ in

France
Claude Champy
Razor Clam Box
Glazed ceramic
24.6 x 96.5 x 61 cm / 9¾ x 39 x 24½ in

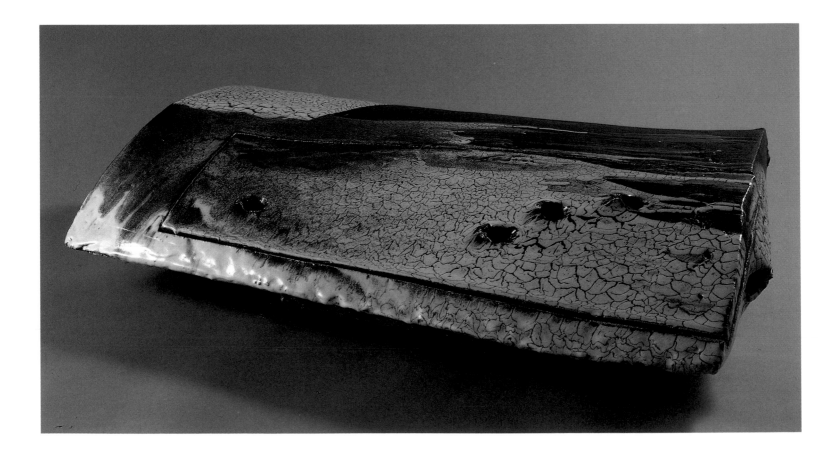

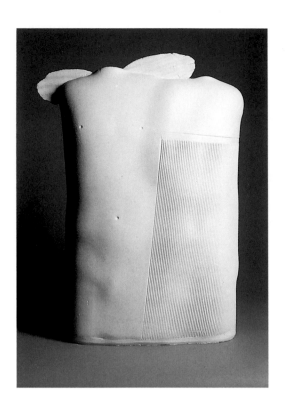

USSR
Vladimir Tsivin
Angel with Wing
China clay and grog
23.5 cm / 9 in

Poland
Anna Malicka Zamorska
Standing
Gold, wood, porcelain, part
slipcast, part handbuilt, part
glazed, fired at 1360°C
200x40cm / 78¾ x 15¾ in

USSR
Mikhail Kopylkov
Garden Clinic
Free-modelled chamotte,
salts, and glazes, airbrushed,
oxidized at 1250°C
220cm / 88 in

USSR
Alecsandr Zadorin
Seated Woman
Chamotte, glazes, wood
132cm / 53 in

■ The Eastern Europeans offer
a reflective, often ironical view
of the human condition.

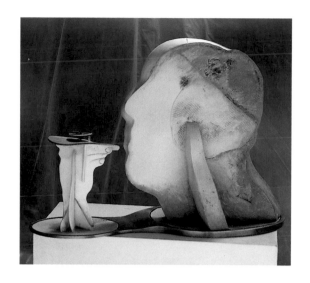

Czechoslovakia
Jindra Viková
Portrait With Compass
Brass, plastic and porcelain
slabs, over and underglazed,
oxidation-fired to 1300°C
75x30cm / 30x12in

Germany
Gertraud Möhwald
*Reclining Head, Sleep,
Companion of Death*
Handbuilt stoneware
42cm / 16½in long

Hungary
György Fusz
Figure
Press-moulded and handbuilt
stoneware mixed with grog,
reduction woodfired
at 1250°C
40x40cm / 15¾x15¾in

CERAMICS **45**

Australia
Bev Hogg
Holy Orders: House and Garden

Ceramic figure, birds and planter with metal stand and acrylic paintwork
200 x 155 cm / 72 x 60 in

▶
USA
Viola Frey
Untitled
Glazed earthenware
185 x 102 x 67 cm / 74 x 41 x 27 in

Holland
Maggi Giles
The Old Man and the Sea (Homage to Hemingway)
Handbuilt, biscuit-fired at 1020°C, alkalisch glazes brush-applied, fired at 1020°C
135 x 45 cm / 54 x 18 in

▶
Canada
Susan Low Beer
(Inset)
In the Hands of Memory and Expectation
Handbuilt, fired to cone 1, painted with encaustic (pigments and wax)
78.5 x 35.5 x 34.5 cm / 31½ x 14 x 13 in

USA
Anthony Natsoulas
Bus Ride
Handbuilt clay and antique bus seats
129.5 x 124.5 cm / 51 x 49 in

■ An increasing number of ceramic artists are working figuratively, some on a monumental scale creating tableaux about contemporary life and attitudes, others elaborating on the tradition of figurines.

Spain
Xavier Toubes
Descriptions Without a Place
series
Installation, handbuilt, glazed,
multifired

■ Kimpei Nakamura is one of Japan's
most influential ceramic artists of
the Second Generation breakaway group.
'I would like to rethink
traditional Japanese aesthetic concepts,
such as the elegance of *wabi* and *sabi*
(the beauty of decay and of desolate loneliness).'

Japan
Kimpei Nakamura
*Skin Shape with Wrinkles
Pattern*
Mixed clay, cone 10 and cone
017 oxidation firings
240x180cm / 84x70in

Japan
Kimpei Nakamura
An Exploration of Japanese Taste
Mixed stoneware clay, cone 10 reduction, cone 017 oxidation
7-piece installation, each 70x60x63cm/ 27½x23½x24 in

Finland
Pekka Paikkari
The Road of Antigone
Red tiles sagger-fired a
1260°C
190.5 x 304 cm /
75 x 120 in

Japan
Yoh Akiyama
Zone
Black ware, iron, aluminium.
Several cycles of slabbing
and cutting, gas-burner flame
applied to shrink clay and
crack surfaces
97 x 120 cm /
37½ x 47½ in

Finland
Kristina Riska
(Far left)
Fragile Time
Coiled and handbuilt
earthenware and stoneware
140 cm / 55 in each

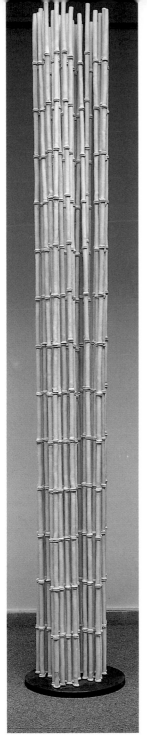

Italy
Pino Castagna
Canneto
Porcelain sculpture
360 cm / 144 in

■ Many installation works mimic the idioms of nature; some, like the witty mosaic pavement, mimic architecture.

Portugal
Eduardo Nery
Mosaic Pavement in Rua Da Mouraria, Lisbon
Black, white and red limestone, mosaic pattern reflecting the buildings
160 metres/525 feet

It is now almost thirty years since the first Lausanne Textile Biennale. Founded with the intention of moving tapestry away from the notion of being simply copied paintings in thread, Lausanne made the world aware of contemporary Polish weavers, especially Magdalena Abakanowicz. They not only combined the roles of designing and making but were also experimenting with three-dimensional sculptural forms that signalled a new freedom of expression in textile art. Since then, waves of activity have rippled across the globe, from Latvia to Bogota, Iceland to Australia and, notably in recent years, Japan.

While the Poles presented monochrome, monumental works, the Americans explored pattern, colour, structure, synthetic yarns and non-textile materials in a variety of works. The likes of Lenore Tawney, Ed Rossbach, Jack Lenor Larsen, Gerhard Knodel and Claire Zeisler have led what is now a nationwide fiber art movement, documented in magazines and landmark books and exhibitions such as *Beyond craft: the art fabric* , *The art fabric: mainstream* and *Fiber (R)Evolution*.

The key international exhibitions, at Lausanne, Kyoto, Lodz and Krefeld, attest to the diversity of current textiles. All the traditional techniques – knitting, lacemaking, printing, quilting, appliqué, embroidery, batik, felting, weaving – have been adapted to express abstract, metaphorical and narrative ideas. Textile techniques can be applied to non-textile raw materials: tripe, steel filament, sponge and rubber are to be found in works on the following pages.

While textile art is the dominant trend, supported by exhibitions and public and private commissions, there is a growing interest in handmade textiles for use in clothing and interior design. Now it is not just the *haute couture* customers and the richest interior design clients who are seeking out the remarkable structural and surface designs and varied textures and colours achievable in one-off and limited-edition textiles.

National characteristics have become difficult to identify. The same tendencies in contemporary textiles now appear in many countries.

Denmark
Jetta Valeur Gemøze
Karavi (and detail)
Woven from the raw straw of
Chinese *ramie*, then boiled,
pressed and painted
450x200cm/185x78in

Japan
Fukumi Shimura
Appreciation of 'No' Play
Kimono of *tsumugi* weave
c. 157 cm / 62 in

USA
James Bassler
Runner's Shroud
Wool, linen, brass
safety-pins, silk warp ikat,
woven, wrapped ends,
blue print, discharge on
runner's bib number
106.6x73.5cm / 42x29 in

■ Although a basic part
of our daily lives,
clothes can nevertheless
emit signs of ritual
and symbolic meaning
through their structure
and use of materials.

New Zealand
**Puti Rare
(Ngati Maniapoto tribe)**
Korowai
Maori ceremonial cloak of
prepared flax fiber and
feathers, handwoven without
a loom

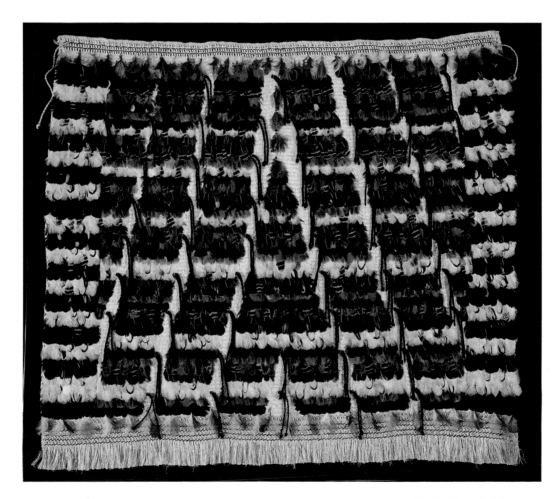

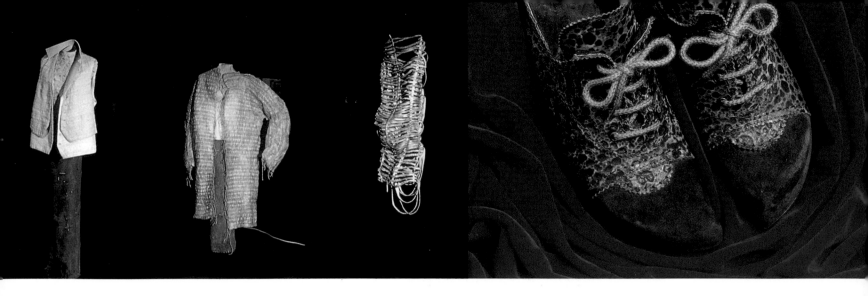

Portugal
Maria José Oliveira
Layered jacket, cotton,
silk and raw canvas; coat,
woven pig's tripe and
linen cord; 'carapace',
raw canvas, clay, gold and
silver leaf
70cm; 135cm; 150cm/
27;45;59in

Holland
Renate Volleberg
Halve Maan Pumps
Handmade ladies' shoes,
dyed leather and fabric

■ Concepts about the human form,
deploying unexpected materials such as wire and tripe,
as well as fresh interpretations of functional clothing,
are burgeoning areas of textile activity.

UK
Caroline Broadhead
Web
Stitched silk and wire
sculpture
168cm/66in

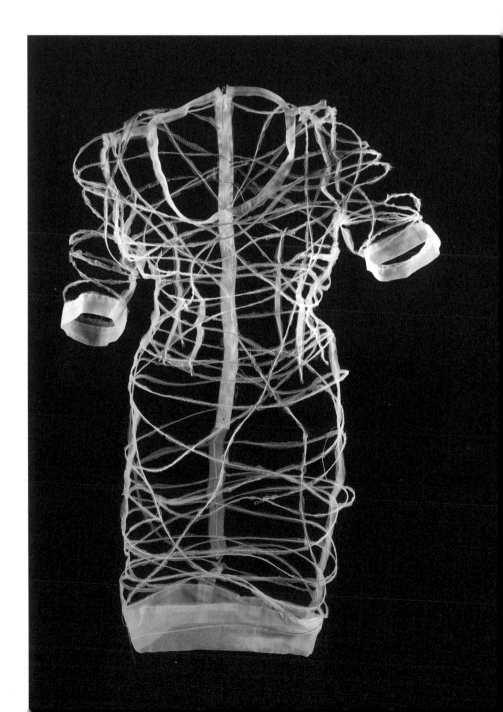

Australia
Liz Williamson
Crushed, handwoven,
fine wool wraps
Various sizes

UK
Jilli Blackwood
Stitched leather waistcoat
86 cm / 34 in chest

Germany
Maria Hössle
Machine-smocked and knitted
cotton velour skirt

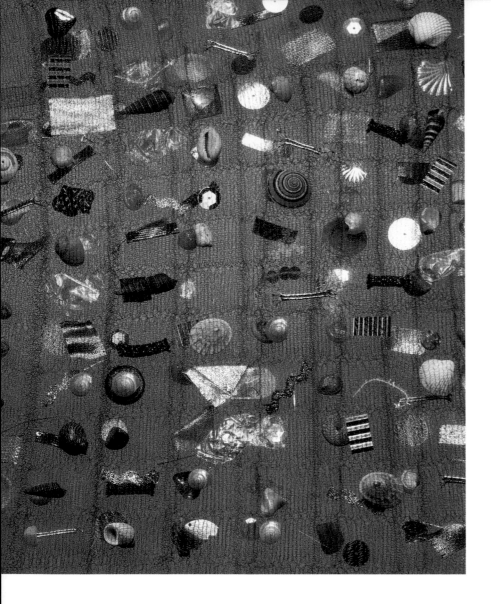

■ New technology assists experimentation
with knitted structures,
while traditional techniques,
such as painting, printing and *shibori*,
produce works reminiscent of Fortuny,
all illustrative of textiles' potential for exciting textures
and surface decoration.

Japan
Mitsugi Yamada
The Tide
Screen of *yuzen* dyework
c.180cm / 72 in

■ Surface imagery, achieved by various methods
of printing and dyeing, is in widespread use
for furnishings, interior design schemes and conceptual ideas.
Susan Bosence, in her late seventies, continues
the relatively rare art of blockprinting
with virtuoso technique.

Norway
Katrine Giæver
The Eye
Wallhanging, various printed
techniques on cotton canvas
216 x 138 cm / 86 x 56 in

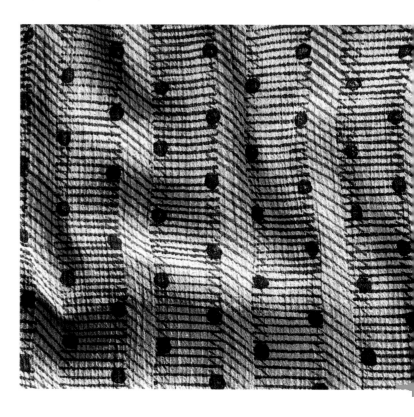

UK
Susan Bosence
Blockprinted length:
fine-cut linoleum blocks
(spot rubber printed),
Soledon fast-print dye
on Portuguese crepe
100 x 300 cm / 39 x 117 in

UK
Susan Bosence
Pattern panel kept
in workshop: print snippets,
colour tests, range of wood,
lino, cork and rubber
block prints
200 x 100 cm / 78 x 39 in

France
Patrice Hugues
Interférences (detail)
Handsewn book, 21 'pages',
thermo-impression,
polychrome motifs and
inscriptions, wooden case
(not pictured)
64 x 42 cm / 26 x 17 in

Australia
**Gloria Petyarre
(Anmatyerre language
group)**

Aboriginal silk batik length
made at Utopia Batik,
Northern Territory.
Australian National Gallery
Collection, Canberra
179x89cm / 70½x35in

Australia
**Angkuna Graham
(Pitjantjatjara tribe)**

Silk batik length made at
Ernabella Arts, an Aboriginal
group workshop in
South Australia.
Australian National Gallery
Collection, Canberra
376x93cm / 148x36½in

Holland
Philip Boas
Java Batik (and detail)
Handwoven mercerized
cotton, traditional batik *tulis*
method of Indonesia (Java)
50 cm / 19½ in

■ Batik and resist printing methods
allow for spectacular narrative patterning
on a large scale.
Aboriginal works are now collectors' items.

UK
Jacqueline Guille
La Nuit
(Left of two panels and detail)
Handpainted and stencilled
silkscreen. Drimarine dye
images, gum-transferred to
chataka satin silk.

Silk steam-fixed and
gum removed, then stretched
over padded frames
171 x 171 cm / 67½ x 67½ in

Germany
Monika Speyer
Grosses Weiches Gitter
(Big Soft Trellis)
320 pieces of silk, handsewn
225x300x50cm /
88½x118x20in

UK
Pauline Burbidge
Canopy II
Pure cotton fabrics,
machine-pieced,
appliquéd and quilted
247.5x127cm / 97½x50in

USA
Michael Olszewski
Mourning
Fabric collage
50x70cm / 20½x28¼in

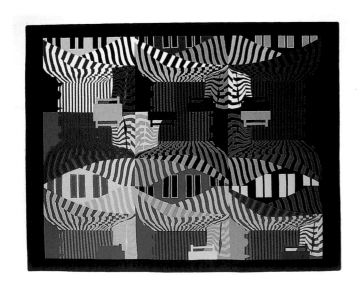

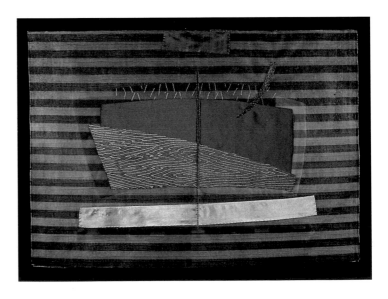

USA
Lia Cook
Leonardo's Quilt
Acrylics handpainted
on abaca and dyes on rayon,
handwoven, immersed in
water, pressed on
etching press.
Collaged
157.5 x 124 cm / 62 x 49 in

■ The *Quilt National* exhibitions in the USA
and the foundation of the Quilt Art group in the UK
attest to the current status and popularity of quilting.
Top practitioners express ideas in abstract,
collaged, pieced and appliquéd works.

USA
Jan Myers-Newbury
Running Rain
Cotton, machine-pieced and
quilted, tied and hand-tinted
with procion dye
104 x 101.5 cm / 41 x 40 in

USA
Michael James
Sky Wind Variations 2
Machine-pieced,
quilted cotton and silk
129 x 218 cm / 51 x 86 in

▶
USA
Faith Ringgold
Tar Beach
Appliqué made at
the Fabric Workshop,
Philadelphia
122 cm / 48 in wide

▶
USA
Risë Nagin
Gate
Silk, polyester, acetate,
cellophane, acrylic paint.
Stained, pieced, appliqué,
quilted, embroidery.
Handsewn
27.5 x 27.5 cm / 70 x 70 in

UK
Kaffe Fassett
English Garden Tapestry
Wool on canvas, handstitched
in random long-stitch
152 cm / 60 in square

■ The straightforward
techniques of stitching
and appliqué
allow free reign for
pictorial narrative and
(literally) layers of
meaning.

Germany
Ursula Rauch
Fan for Man
Various fabrics, wax painting,
stitched appliqué
128 x 200 cm / 49 x 78 in

■ Michael Brennand-Wood, conventionally trained in embroidery, exploded the cosy world of stitched samplers by applying the techniques to three-dimensional structures.
Marie-Rose Lortet has had a similar impact on lacemaking.

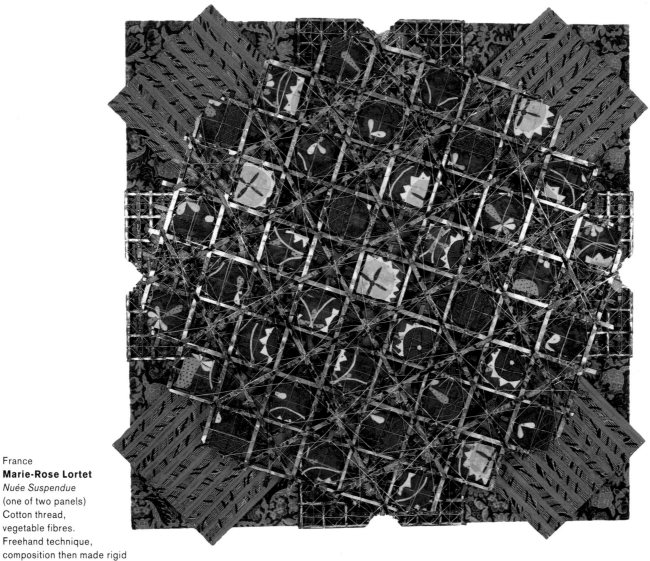

◀ UK
Michael Brennand-Wood
Slow Turning
Wall-hung construction,
painted wood,
interlaced fabric, metal,
wire, thread.
Moving central section
makes musical noises.
Winner of 1989 Kyoto Textile
Competition Fine Art Prize
165x165cm / 65x65 in

▶
USA
Jane Burch Cochran
*Ring Around the Roses,
Ring Around the Moon*
Wallpiece, appliqué, stitched,
painted, beads
172x196cm / 68x77 in

USA
Mary Bero
(Opposite, below)
Danny and Jane
Cotton and cotton floss,
embroidery techniques
8cm / 3½ in square

France
Marie-Rose Lortet
Nuée Suspendue
(one of two panels)
Cotton thread,
vegetable fibres.
Freehand technique,
composition then made rigid
90x110x30cm / 35x43x12 in

France
Marie-Rose Lortet
Masque Jaune
Wool, cotton, silk,
crochet/knitting lace
techniques
26x17cm / 10x7 in
▼

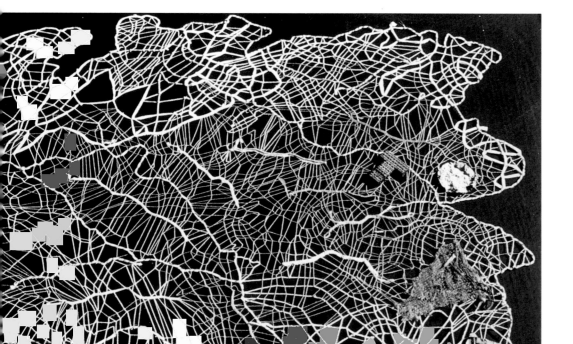

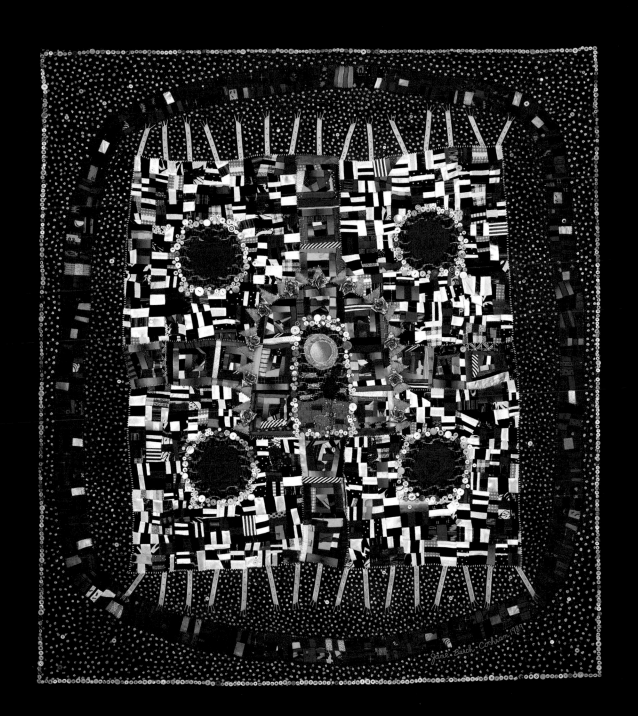

France
Odile Levigoureux
Yori Shita
Felt, straw, wood,
osier, woven wallhanging
109 x 109 cm / 43 x 43 in

USA
Joan Livingstone
Sirens
Industrial felt, epoxy resin,
stain
75 cm / 30 in each

Sweden
Kajsa Af Petersens
Seashore Fell (and detail)
Synthetic fibers and cotton,
tying technique on net
350 x 200 cm / 140 x 79 in

Finland
Maisa Tikkanen
Medallion (and detail)

Wool felt on a
pure silk undercover
250 x 200 cm / 98½ x 78½ in

■ The 1980s saw feltmaking revived as
a versatile, colourful aspect of textiles,
appearing in contemporary fashion and interiors.
Its elemental beauty as a substance
is strongest in compositions
which relate closely to nature.

New Zealand
Christina Hurihia
Wirihana
Woven flax *whariki* (floor mat).
Tainui/Ngati Rangiunuora
Maori tribes

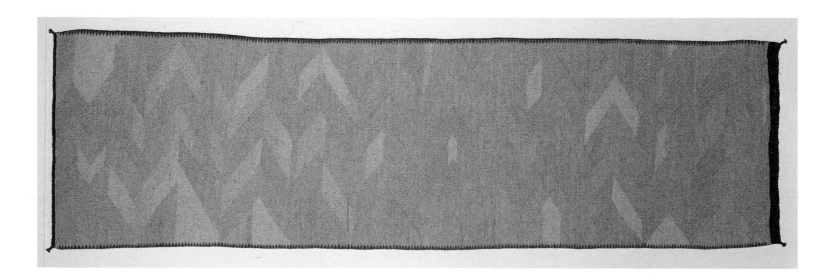

UK
Stella Benjamin
Yellow Runner
Hand vegetable-dyed,
handwoven runner.
Natural wool and
goat's-hair yarn
335 cm / 134 in long

■ While the tufting-gun has enabled rugmakers
to achieve deep-pile, Postmodern surface imagery quickly,
the time-consuming traditional hand techniques
of dyeing and weaving produce classic works.
Marinette Cueco's 'flooring' is part of
a strong conceptual base to
much French textile work.

◀ Denmark
Krestine Kjaerholm
Tommy
Plain-weave carpet
220 x 170 cm / 87 x 67½ in

France
Marinette Cueco
Making a' *jardin d'herbes
tressées*', part of conceptual
installation works

Colombia
Olga da Amaral
Lienzo Ceremonial 13
Gesso, gold leaf, acrylic paint
on cotton and linen,
mixed technique
200x38cm / 78x14 in

▶
Colombia
Olga da Amaral
Rios 4
Gesso, gold leaf,
acrylic paint on cotton
and linen, mixed technique
100x130cm / 39x51 in

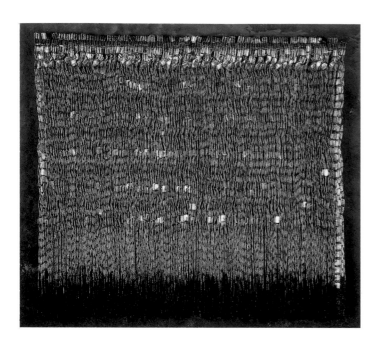

■ The huge, painstakingly constructed works
of Olga da Amaral and Helmut Hahn have
the presence of icons.

New Zealand
**Edward Poraumati
Maxwell**

Paki (rain cape) of
harakeke (flax) and twine,
handwoven without a loom.
Maori Te Arawa, Tuhoe,
Ngati Awa tribes
c.180cm / 60 in wide

74 TEXTILES

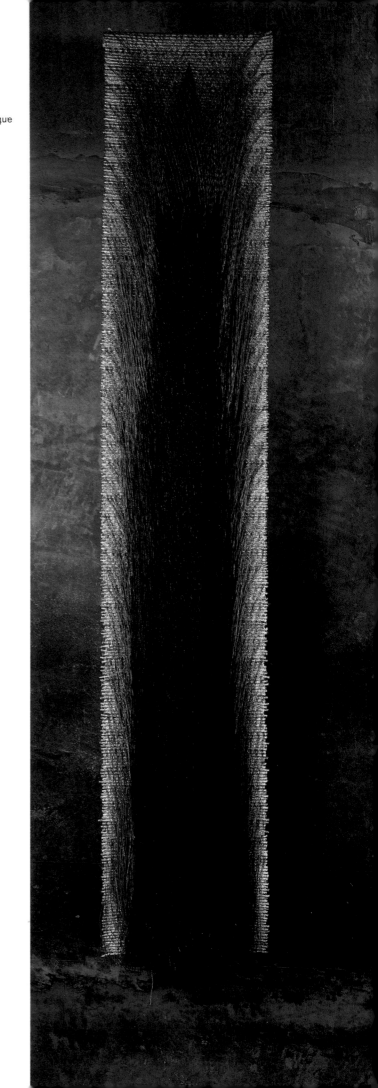

Norway
Ingunn Skogholt
Composition in Blue

Nylon, linen, wool,
cotton threads, hand-dyed
and woven using
Gobelin technique
140x310cm / 55x122 in

Germany
Helmut Hahn
Four Panels –
Metamorphosing Constellation

Appliquéd fabric
Each panel 200x100cm /
79x39½ in

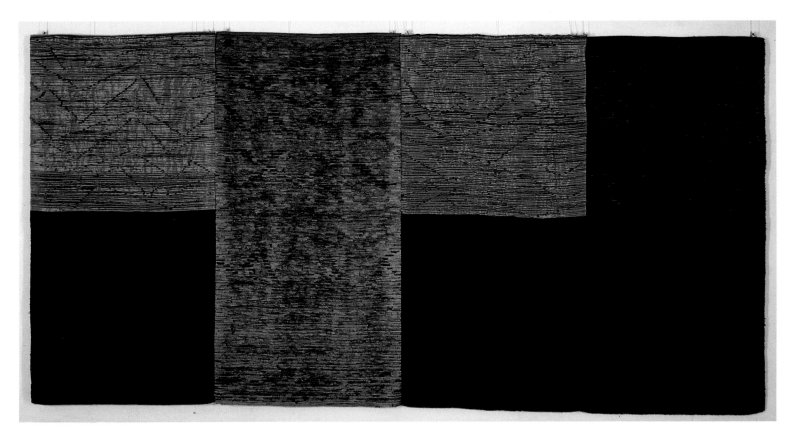

Sweden
**Elizabeth
Hasselberg-Olsson**
Sea-Landscape
Handwoven linen yarns
206x150cm/102x59in

■ Weaving techniques can fragment colour
and structure to dynamic effect, or serve
quite different aims:
Elizabeth Hasselberg-Olsson, a leading weaver
whose work hangs in the Swedish Parliament,
achieves an intensified gracefulness in
her characteristically enigmatic compositions
by self-imposed restriction in terms of techniques,
materials and colour.

Poland
**Anna
Wieckowska-Kowalska**
Landscape wallpiece (and
detail)
c.100cm/40in wide

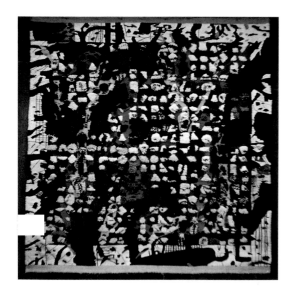

UK
Marta Rogoyska
Paper collage, design in
progress for large-scale
tapestry commission

Canada
Kaija Sanelma Harris
On the Way to Shangri-la
Mercerized cotton warp, wool
and silk weft, double weave,
design inlaid (version of Theo
Moorman's technique).
Weft-faced weave turned 90°
149.5 x 160 cm / 58½ x 63 in

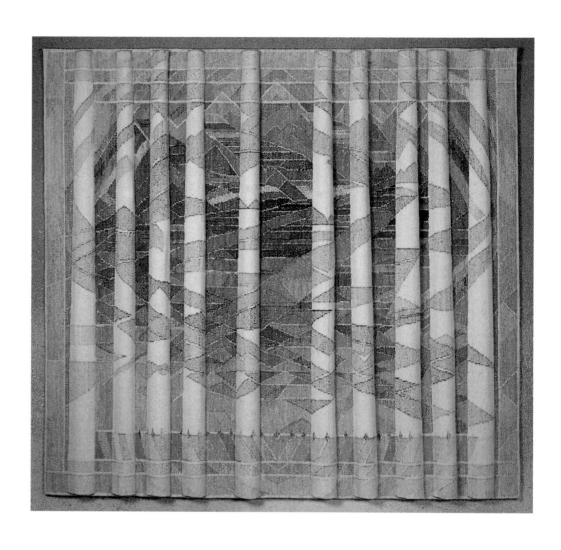

USA
Cynthia Shira
Highland Spring (detail)
Cotton, rayon, linen and
mixed fibers, painted warps
woven in integrated triple
weaves with supplementary
and sectional wefts
150 x 121 cm / 64 x 48½ in

Poland
Lekler Tymoteusz
Quotations
Rubber pressed in sponge
213cm / 84 in wide

Poland
Katarzyna Pazskowska
Kalu Rinpoche ('Dear is my
body, old is my motive, happy
is my spirit')
Handwoven wool and linen
tapestry
250x207cm / 100x83 in

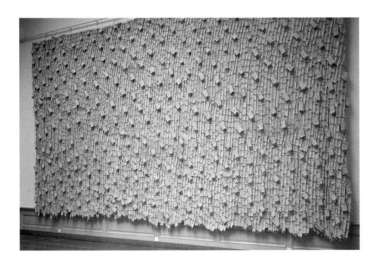

Germany
Ritzi Jacobi
La Première de Cette Série
Tapestry weaving
c.243cm / 96 in wide

Denmark
Naja Salto
Fragments
Gobelin tapestry weaving
100x140cm / 39x55 in

■ Established fine art methods
of collage, graffiti, photorealism
and montage are used to potent effect
by many leading textile artists,
notably Polish weavers and
the American Arturo Alonzo Sandoval.
The monumentality and
technical excellence of such works
as those by the distinguished Ritzi Jakobi,
have a lasting impact.

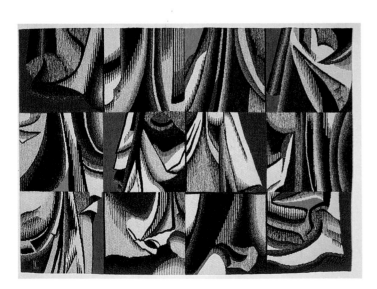

►
USA
Arturo Alonzo Sandoval
Lady Liberty/Babylon II
Base of Cibrachrome strips
and webbing under
acetate transparencies,
fabric, coloured threads,
paint and netting.
Machine-stitched and pieced
in several layers
218.5x152cm / 86x60 in

■ The sculptor's formal range,
of volume, mass, space and scale,
is articulated here
in animated works akin to waves, sails, torsos
and totems.

Japan
Shigeo Kubota
The Wavespace III
Sisal and *ramie*,
plain weave and sewn
170 x 220 cm / 67½ x 87 in

USA
Warren Seelig
Wings and wall suspensions,
nylon mesh, vinyl-coated
mesh, Tyvek (spun bonded
olefin fiber), articulated
stainless-steel framework

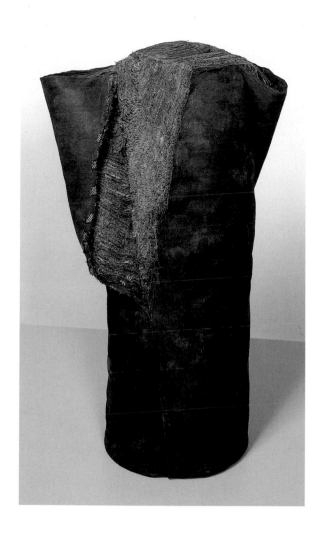

Holland
Sybil Heijnen
Colour-View
Cotton cloth
100x60x40cm /
38x23½x16in

Germany
Ingeborg Lorenz
Ort der Ruhe (A Quiet Place)
Cotton, nylon, iron
260x300x60cm / 104x120x24in

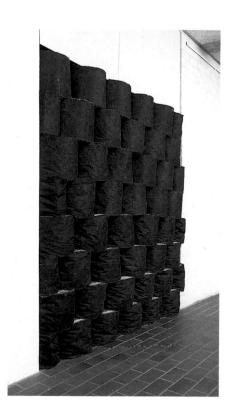

Holland
Sybil Heijnen
*The Two Sides of
the Same Coin*
(same piece front and back)
Cotton cloth
202x202x40cm / 86x86x14in

Japan
Naomi Kobayashi
Cosmic Ring
Hand-dyed cotton rope, own technique
c.360cm/144in wide

Japan
Kyoko Kumai
The Air-'90 G
Stainless-steel filaments installation, own technique

Japan
Yoichi Onagi
(Inset, far right)
Yellow Pyramid on the Wall
Canvas, sewn and painted
200x200x70cm/
79x79x27½in

■ The amibitious conceptions of Japanese textile artists, often complemented by inventive techniques, put them at the forefront of the contemporary textile scene.

Japan
Kyoko Kumai
(Inset, right)
Prayer
Stainless-steel filaments, own technique
200x300x300cm/
78x118x118in

JEWELRY AND METALWORK

Japan
Wahei Ikezawa
Neck of Man (and detail)
Fiber and metal necklace
50x30x15cm / 20x12x5 in

■ In 1973 Gijs Bakker, the pioneering Dutch jeweler and designer, wrapped wire around parts of the body; the imprint it left became 'invisible jewelry'. Here was (extreme) confirmation that the New Jewelry movement (the focus of these pages) prized idea above materials and form above technique.

■ Developments in jewelry over the past twenty-five years have been perhaps more popularly influential than those in any other craft. On the crest of the wave of Sixties libertarianism, affluence, new technology and materials (acrylics, titanium etc.) jewelers felt confident in abandoning the notion that one-off jewelry should be finely wrought, expensive and destined to confer status on the rich.

■ Jewelers evolved myriad new forms and methods of fixing and fastening. Some expanded the scale and form of their works to look more like clothing than jewelry, taking their inspiration from, for example, Oskar Schlemmer at the Bauhaus or tribal clothing and body decoration.

■ The aim was to challenge the *status quo*, the New Jewelry offering a manifesto for change that aligned the movement with a hoped-for social and economic democratization. But by the 1980s, the ingenuity, wit and invention of the pioneers' works had been copied and diluted to meet the mass demands of high-street costume jewelry.

■ The last five years have seen a shift of emphasis to exploring symbolic and narrative imagery and mixed-media materials, concentrating on personal expression rather than on purely formal invention. This trend has always been America's strong suit, first highlighted in the 1970s, notably by William Harper.

■ The *rapprochement* with traditional metalsmithing skills and techniques in jewelry has stimulated the whole area of metalwork. The diversity of form and surface treatment of both functional and sculptural work confirms the versatility and potential of an area which since the 1960s has been steadily loosening the stylistic yoke of traditionalist commissions.

Portugal
Paula Crespo
Necklace of anodized
aluminium tubes and
stainless-steel mesh
30x55x12cm /
12x21½x4½ in

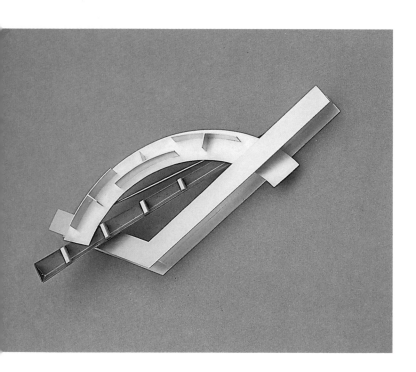

Austria
Fritz Maierhofer
Gold and silver oxide,
constructed brooch
5.5x15cm / 2x6 in

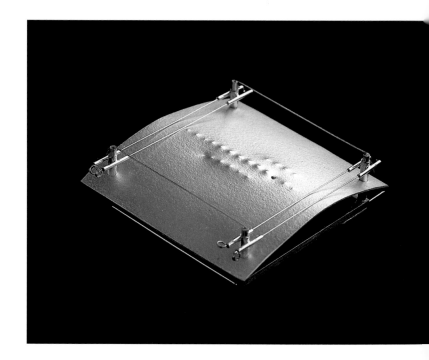

Norway
Sigurd Bronger
Impressed sheet silver, steel,
paint and wire brooch
1.2x0.35x0.35x0.35cm /
½x⅛x⅛x⅛ in

■ Geometric, constructed works,
articulating the body and mixing traditional
and new materials and techniques,
typify an early and enduring theme of the New Jewelry.

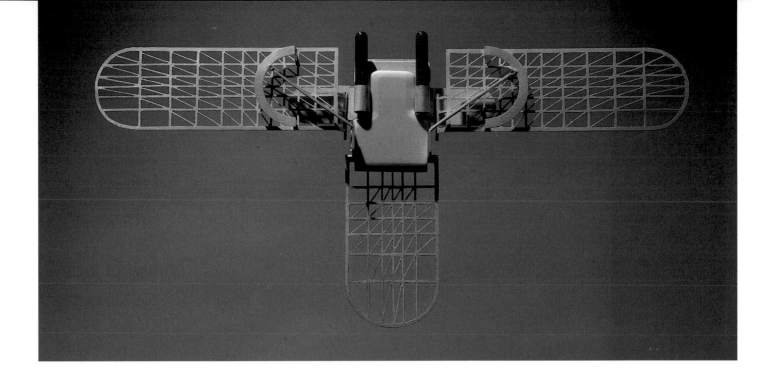

Czechoslovakia
Anton Cepka
Silver, plexiglass,
cut brooch
6.5cm / 2½ in

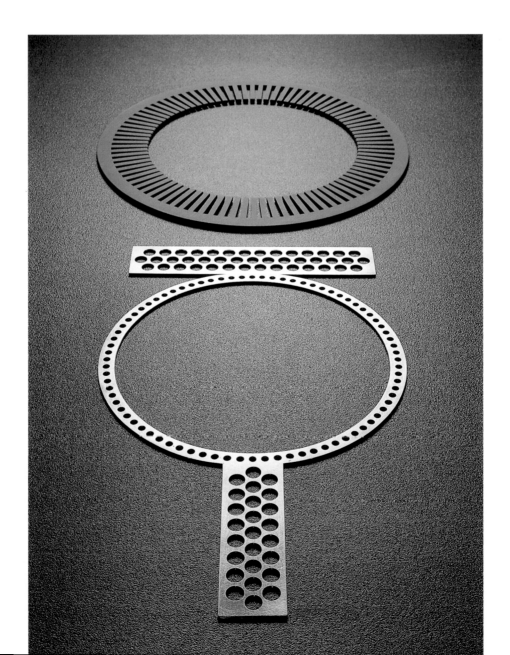

UK
David Watkins
Gilded brass, Colorcore,
laser-cut, machined,
hand-finished neckpiece
38x38x0.2cm / 15x15x¹⁄₁₂ in

■ Precious-metal jewelry
in a contemporary idiom
now thrives among
younger as well as older
generations.
'Multiple choice' ring sets
are the renowned Ramshaw's
refined signature tune.
Jünger and Fisch are
masterful, influential metalsmiths
and teachers.
Vigeland and Falkena
brilliantly exploit the potential
of constructed bracelets.

Portugal
Tereza Seabra
Brooch, bronze, 24-carat
gold and opals. Fabricated,
patinated, gold inserted and
stones set
8x8x1cm / 3x3x¼ in

Holland
Sita Falkena
(Inset, left)
Cocoon
Anodized aluminium, stainless
steel
10x27cm / 4x10½ in

Norway
Tone Vigeland
(Inset, far left)
Bracelet, steel pieces
connected to silver mesh,
oxidized, flexible
11x9cm / 4¼x3½ in

Germany
Hermann Jünger
Pure gold on tombak brooch
5.5x5.5cm / 2x2 in

◄ UK
Wendy Ramshaw
*Black and Onyx Rings For
Head of a Woman*
Turned brass stand, gold with
black enamel and onyx rings
17x4cm / 7x1½ in

USA
Arline Fisch
Square Spirit Figure
Brooch/pendant. Braided and
loom-woven gold, oxidized
sterling, black onyx dangles
14x9cm / 5½x3½ in

Australia
Susan Cohn
Hearing Aid
Anodized and dyed
aluminium, gold earpiece.
Diamond Valley Art
Collection/Award 1990
Limited edition of five
22x5cm / 43¼x2 in

Holland
Gijs Bakker
Adam
Laminated photograph, gilded
metal neckpiece

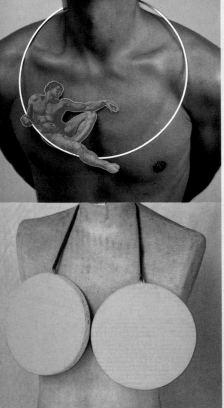

Canada
Kai Chan
Two Yellows
Corrugated cardboard,
paint, string, glue
84x19x1.6cm / 33x7½x½ in

France
Gilles Jonemann
Papier-mâché bracelet
12.7 cm / 5 in

■ These works epitomize
key tenets of the New Jewelry,
practised by pioneers
(Bakker, Künzli)
and young graduates (Wong) alike:
the use of non-precious materials;
allusions to things known in
another context;
witty/ironical presentation;
positive participation on
the part of the wearer.

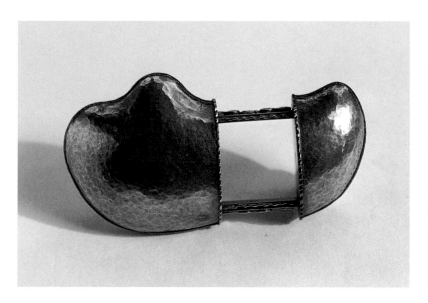

UK
Maria Ka Pick Wong
Pebble Ring
Closes into pebble shape,
shapes hand-raised, soldered
together, silver, brass and
copper 4x5x2cm / 1½ x 2 x¾ in

Germany
Otto Künzli
Houses
Brooch, Uriol (artificial
wood), pure pigments;
brooch, gold. Series of seven
7.3x6, 3x2.5cm / 3x2¼,
1¼ x¾ in

USA
Marjorie Schick
Collar
Painted wood
63.5x53.3x24.6cm/
25x21x9¼in

Norway
Liv Blåvarp
Flexible neckpiece, painted
wooden sections on elastic
band
25cm/10in wide

▲
Switzerland
Verena Sieber-Fuchs
(Inset, above)
#26
Bottle-cap necklace
22cm/9in wide

UK
Peter Chang
Bracelet, carved styrofoam
core, laminated with plastic
shapes, some with gold leaf
5.5 x 16.5 cm / 2 x 6½ in

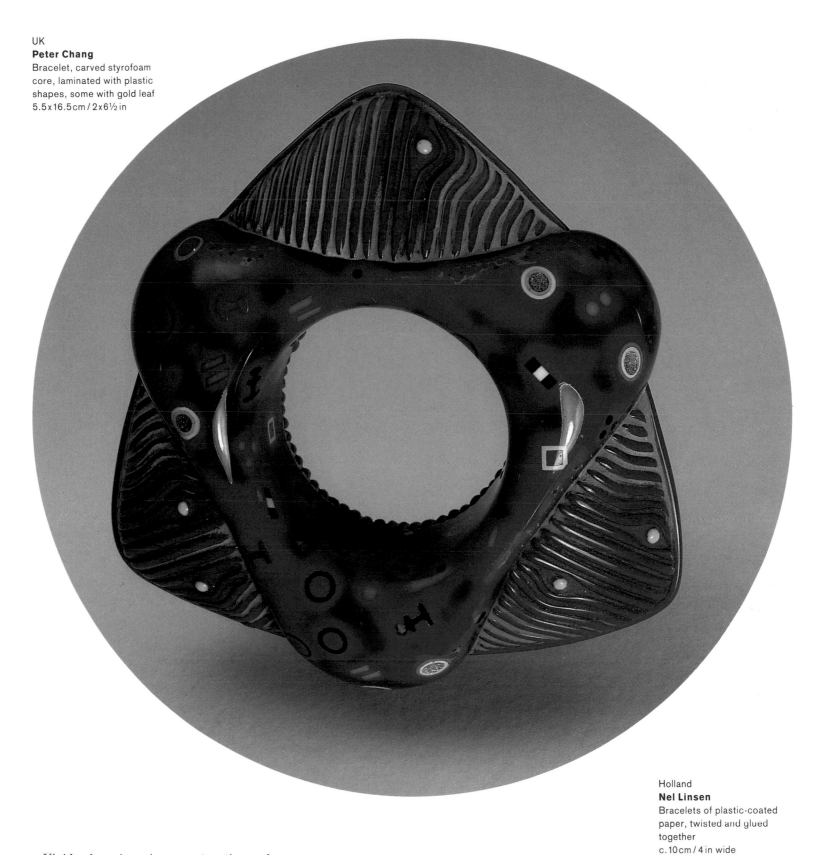

Holland
Nel Linsen
Bracelets of plastic-coated
paper, twisted and glued
together
c. 10 cm / 4 in wide

■ Vivid colour, ingenious construction and
non-precious materials are common denominators
of these works and much contemporary jewelry.
Marjorie Schick and comparative newcomer Peter Chang
are part of a movement of makers whose jewelry
can function as sculpture when not worn.

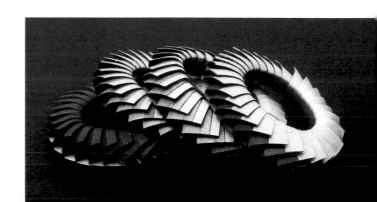

UK
Judy McCaig
On a Sandy Plateau, Zebu, Atlantis, Nymph
Silver, golds, copper, brass, onlayed, inlayed, enamelled brooches
3x4.5 (one), 3.5x5.5 (rest) cm / 1x2, 1¼x2⅛ in

Korea
Dong-Lin Kim
(Above)
Brass, copper, gold foil, sterling. Korean *Cumbou* (like doublée) technique
5.7x6x30cm / 2¼x2¼x12 in

USA
Bruce Metcalf
(Top left)
Brooch, sterling, 22-carat gold, photo-etched and constructed
11.4x3.8x1.3cm / 4½x1½x½ in

◄ Japan
Sunao Sera
Brooches of silver, brass, lead, copper, plastic, silk thread and old *kanzashi*
16x18cm / 6¼x7 in

Japan
Morio Funakushi
(Opposite, inset far left)
Glove for their child
Egyptian cotton, pure gold, rice husks, wood
17.5cm / 7 in wide

Germany
Wilhelm Mattar
Brooch, mother-of-pearl with gilded brass
6x14x3.5cm / 2¼x5½x1¼ in

Holland
Lam de Wolf
Textile and metal shoulder brooch

■ Personal mythologies, surrealism and elements of *art brut* are common ground for these prominent jewelers.

JEWELRY AND METALWORK 95

■ The latest trends
include narrative pieces and a
return to refined, decorative jewelry,
but this time with a witty twist.

Germany
Daniel Krüger
Tumbled chrysoprase
fragments shaped and drilled,
rubies, opals and gold
3.5x5cm/1¼x2in

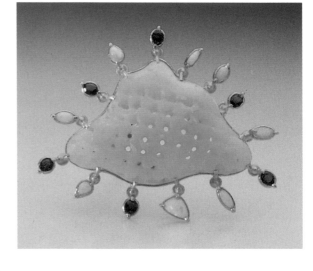

USA
Judy Onofrio
Get Along Little Doggie
Mixed-media brooch
c.7.6cm/3in

UK
Mike Abbott
Hang Luce!
Embossed brass brooch,
hand-pieced and soldered,
patinated and painted
8x6x1.5cm/3x2¼x½in

Spain
Roman Puig Cuyas
Sol (Medusa)
Painted metal brooch
10 cm / 4 in wide

Spain
Silvia Walz
Windmill
Oxidized alpaca and paper
7 x 10 cm / 2¾ x 4 in

Austria
Anna Heindl
Garden Brooch
Silver and coral roses
4 cm / 1½ in wide

Germany
Peter Verburg
Handmade silver tableware
(both pictures)
Jug c. 25 cm / 10 in

■ Handmade tableware flourishes,
with German craftsmanship to the fore.

Germany
Ulla Mayer
Handmade silver teapots
c. 13 cm / 5 in

USA
Chunghi Choo
(Far left)
Handmade teapot,
electroformed copper,
silverplated, wood,
alkyl-enamel and enamel paint
44.5x15.2x2.5cm/
17½x6x10in

Germany
Werner Bünck
Hand-forged silver and
ambuino wood teapot
29x12cm/11¼x4¾in

Sweden
Wolfgang Gessl
Handmade coffee-set with
pot, milk-jug and sugar-bowl,
sterling silver, soldered and
planished, pot-handle in ash
30x7.7, 17.6x5.5, 7.5x9.1cm/
12x3, 7x2, 3x3½in

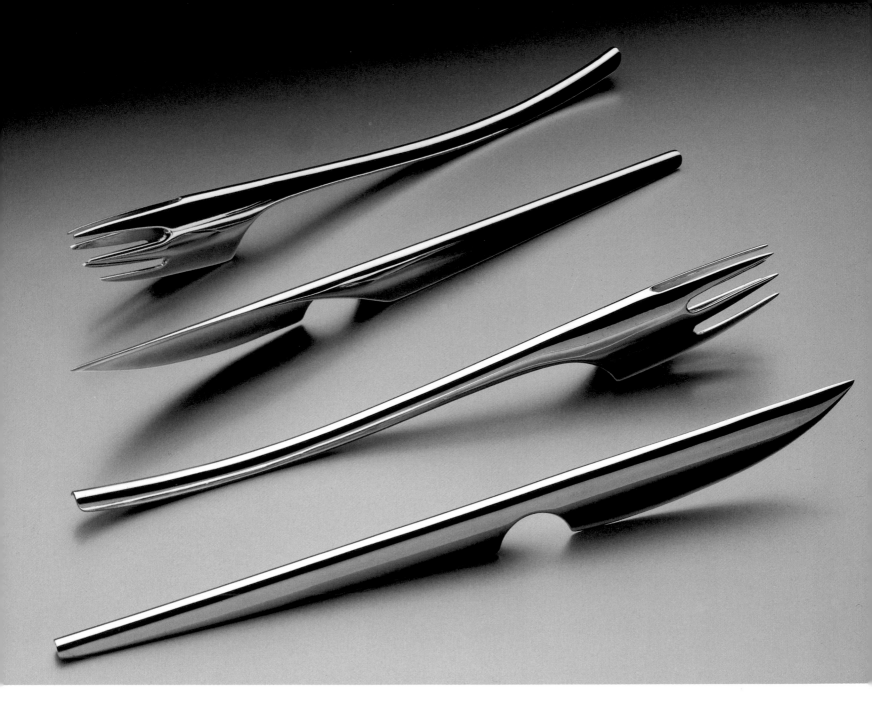

Italy
Lino Sabattini
Hand-forged spaghetti forks
and knives, silverplated brass
cutlery. Limited production
20.5 cm / 8 in long (fork)

USA
Phillip Baldwin
Kitchen Pain
Blades: laminated steel,
handles: rosewood, *mokume*
ferrules
30.5 x 5 x 2, 20.3 x 2.5 x 1.2 cm /
12 x 2 x ¾, 8 x 1 x ½ in

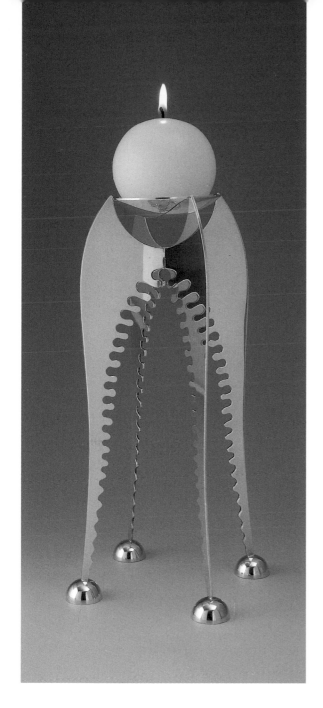

■ Fresh shapes for tableware include work by Sabattini, the enduring Italian master, and Robert Foster, part of a vigorous current metalwork movement in Australia (including Frank Bauer, Ragnar Hansen, Mark Edgoose, Andrew Mathers, Johannes Kuehnen).

Italy
Guido Niest
Handmade silverplated brass alloy candle-holder. Limited numbered series
32 cm / 13 in

Australia
Robert Foster
Raised and welded stainless-steel coffee pot; raised anodized aluminium, rubber
35 x 10 x 35 cm / 13¾ x 4 x 13¾ in

Germany
Rudolf Bott
Rock-crystal spoon
28 cm / 11 in long

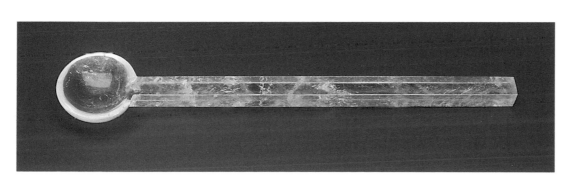

UK
Mike Savage
Dish; cut, folded, hammered
and welded sheet copper.
Tool marks left
20 x 45 x 60 cm /
8 x 18 x 24 in long

USA
Robin Quigley
Stacked Pyramidal Vessels
Patinated bronze
9 x 22.8 cm / 3½ x 9 in

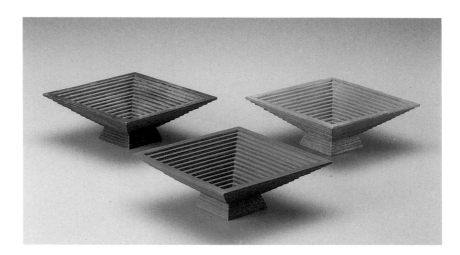

Germany
Peter Schmitz
Welded and forged steel
bowls
37, 32 cm / 10½, 12½ in wide

■ Varied techniques and
textural metalwork forms
range here from
the purist monumentality of Tore Svensson
to the complex metaphors of Helen Shirk,
both renowned metalsmiths.

USA
June Schwarcz
Copper and vitreous enamel
vessel, electroplated,
plique-à-jour
17 x 15.2 cm / 6¾ x 6 in

USA
Helen Shirk
Margin for Change
Copper, fabricated, riveted,
patinated, spray-etched,
soldered
17.8x61x61cm / 7x24x24 in

Sweden   Chased steel and gilt bowl,
Tore Svensson   burned with linseed oil
                15x32cm / 6x12½ in

UK
Michael Rowe
Conditions for Ornament No.7
Brass and copper with tinned
finish
43x28x25cm/17x11x10in

Holland
Ruudt Peters
Hephaistos
Constructed vessel, steel and
stone
26x25x25cm/10¼x10x10in

Czechoslovakia
Jiři Pelcl
Isktia
Metal and pebble fruit bowl
45cm/18in long

■ Michael Rowe is among
the world's most important contemporary metalsmiths,
influential as maker, teacher and researcher
(he is co-author of the seminal
The Colouring, Bronzing and Patination of Metals).
His containers are a yardstick for
conceptual thinking about the nature and purpose
of decorative art today.
The brooding pieces by Pelcl and Peters
are a foil for the traditional piece
by Kakutani, aged 87 and
a Living National Treasure in Japan.

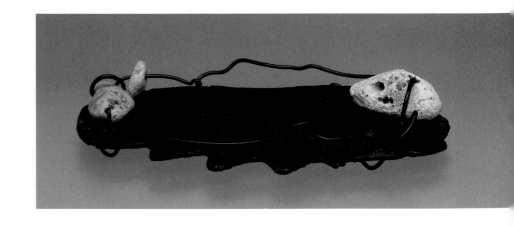

Japan
Ikkei Kakutani
Kettle of Japanese pig iron
with phoenix ears for
handle-rings
27.3 x 18.3 cm / 10¾ x 7¼ in

Germany
Christian Rudolph
Metal flask, patinated
c.12.5cm / 5 in wide

UK
Gordon Burnett
Three Phase Clock
Oxidized copper and
aluminium with three
movements. Small and large
perspex discs rotate at the
speed of minutes and hours
respectively
c.90cm / 36 in wide

■ Goudji, a Georgian
working in Paris,
is perhaps the most inspired by
traditional goldsmithing here,
but all these works
demonstrate a delight in
ornamented function.

Germany
Erhard Hössle
Wind-wheel for the tower of
the old town hall, Marienplatz,
Munich
200x110cm / 80x44 in overall

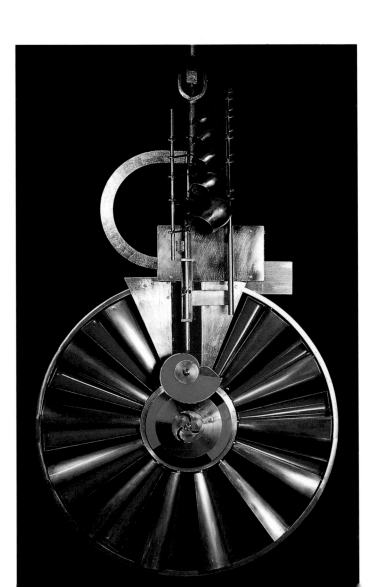

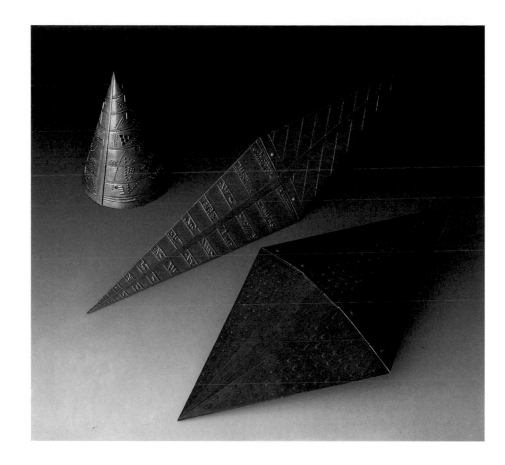

Germany
Hans-Joachim Härtel
Boxes, stamped, raised and
folded, nickel, silver, black
oxidized brass
Largest 55 cm / 21½ long

France
Goudji
Dish, animal theme in vermeil,
mother-of-pearl and sodalite
21 x 46 cm / 8½ x 18¼ in

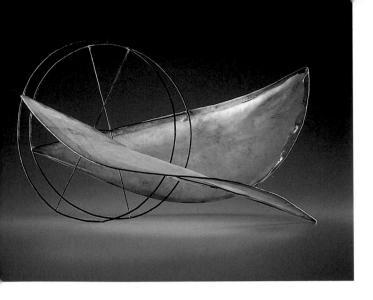

Holland
Iene Ambar
The Immigrant
Wall object, tinplated, paint
and iron wire
51.5x50cm / 20¼x20in

■ As in other craft disciplines,
the human condition
provides an impulse for
atmospheric works.
Rouré, Illsley and Jensdóttir
also work on a large scale
and in other media;
Ambar's pieces notate
her experiences as
a Cambodian in exile.

Iceland·
Hansína Jensdóttir
House
Handmade iron
52x31cm / 19x12in

►
USA
Robin Kraft
(Opposite, inset)
Cache
Constructed copper, carved
and painted wood
9x15.2cm / 3½x6in

France
Roland Rouré
Metal portrait
c.38cm / 15in

UK
Pierre Degen
Beach Collection Chariot
Found materials: iron, wire,
wood, rope, plastic, shell,
feather. Bent and constructed
82x63x52cm /
32¼x24¾x20½in

►
UK
Bryan Illsley
Bust of a Woman
Forged iron
60cm / 24in high

■ Clever product designers are giving glassware a high profile. Memphis glass in the 1980s and recent work for glass factories by maverick designers such as Bořek Šípek set the standard for innovative tableware.

■ Glass designed and made by individuals in their own studios is a comparatively self-contained area. Glass technology requires space and money, so the commitment cannot be ephemeral.

■ Although glass factories such as Orrefors and Kosta Boda in Sweden, Daum in France, Vistosi in Italy, have always involved artists and designers, the development of the glass art movement since the 1960s rests on the initiatives and works of individual designer-makers.

■ The movement was sparked off in 1962 in the United States at a workshop with Harvey Littleton and at a meeting at the University of Wisconsin. The discussion focused on the possibility of working glass in an individual studio away from an industrial context and on forming a way of melting glass in a furnace small enough to achieve this aim. By the mid-1970s, a hundred glass courses flourished in American universities and glass was established as an artistic medium for individuals.

■ The first wave of glass artists revelled in the seductiveness of the material itself. But since then, glass artists have expounded personal ideas and concepts, with material and techniques in a subordinate role. As Dan Klein notes (*Glass: A Contemporary Art*), 'When the success of a piece is reliant on the material alone, it will forever remain suspect on a conceptual level.'

■ Besides the blowing of hot glass, other techniques such as slumping, cutting, casting and pâte de verre are now widely used. Many treat, even disguise the material, to emphasize conceptual concerns; others mix media, often combining glass with metal.

■ Installation and large-scale sculptural works are commanding increasing attention, linking glass works to the wider art world and to architecture. The fashion for dramatic glass screens, furniture and lighting in interiors has further encouraged these developments.

■ The glass art world has become international, with specialist galleries, collections, organizations, art-school courses, magazines, exhibitions and prizes. The Czechs and the Americans still dominate activity, together with the Scandinavians, British and Germans, but the spotlight currently falls on France and Japan.

111

Germany
Albrecht Greiner-Mai
Filigrau (and detail)
Lampworked blown glass
15 cm / 6 in

Holland
Bert Frijns
Staple Bowls
Handblown glass
36x51cm / 14x21 in

UK
**Steven Newell and
Simon Moore**
Individually handblown,
batch-production tableware
Tallest 41cm / 16 in
▼

Japan
Yoshihiko Takahashi
Untitled
Blown glass, sandblasted
21 x 26 x 11 cm / 8 x 10 x 4 in

■ Colour is often
the most immediately
seductive aspect
of glass objects, but
these works demonstrate
the beauty of conceptual,
functional and textural glass
in monochrome.

UK
Brian Blanthorn
Laminated Dish
Fused sheet glass with oxides
and chemicals applied
between layers.
Ground and slumped
45.7 cm / 18 in long

Holland
Floris Meydam
Untitled
Blown glass, batch
production
15x23cm / 6x9in

Japan
Yumiko Noda
Shower of Flowers
Glass, blown, cut,
sandblasted, slumped and
fused
4.5x48x39.5cm /
1½x19x15½in

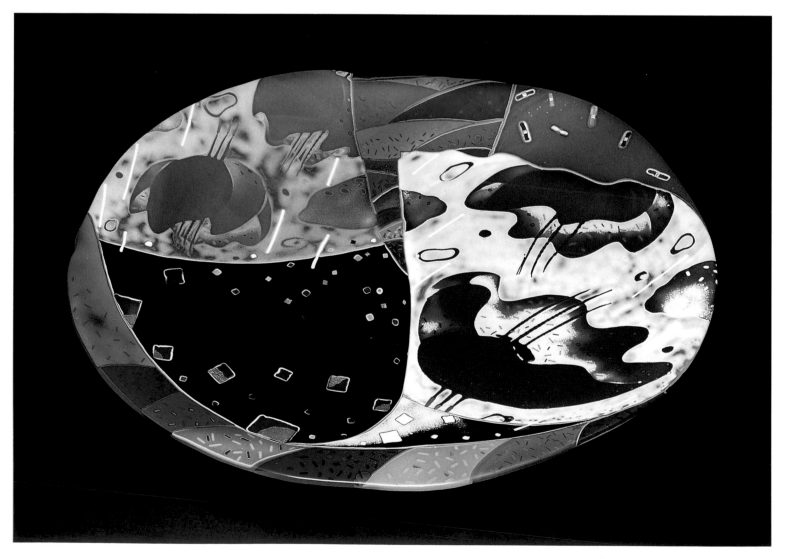

Germany
Günter Knye
Untitled
Lampblown glass
7 x 17 cm / 2½ x 6½ in

■ Günter Knye,
with Albrecht Greiner-Mai
(p.110),
is one of
the foremost exponents
of the eastern German
tradition of lampworking,
which produces
the characteristic
feather-swirl lines.
Other varied possibilities
for formal and surface
patterning in glass
include the
fashionably enigmatic
pâte de verre.

USA
Karla Trinkley
Blue Bowl
Pâte de verre
21.6 x 26.6 x 26.6 cm /
9 x 10½ x 10½ in

USA
Sonja Blomdahl
Cherry/Violet
Handblown, two or three
bubbles joined while hot then
blown out, shaped and
finished
20.3x36.8cm / 8x14½in

■ Fusing and slumping
techniques,
as well as blowing,
produce dynamic
functional pieces
in the hands of
top practitioners.
Klaus Moje,
teaching at Canberra,
is influential
in the growing Australian
glass movement.

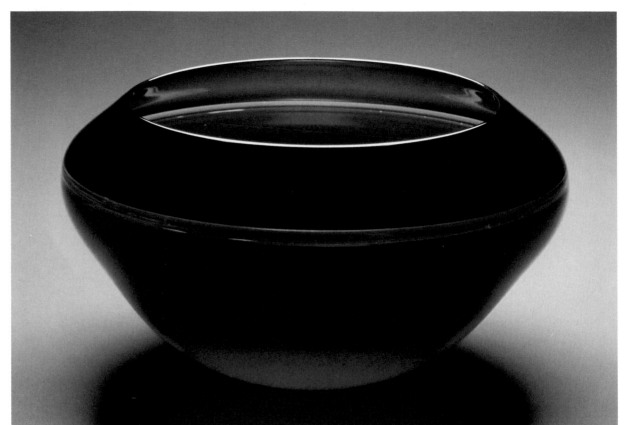

Australia
Klaus Moje
Fused, slumped, ground and
polished dish
7x53cm / 2½x20¾in

France
Alain Begou
Blown glass vase
25.4cm / 10in

Denmark
Tchai Munch
Andamooka
Glass, fused and slumped
8 x 43 x 72.5 cm / 3 x 17 x 28½ in

USA
Toots Zynsky
Tierra del Fuego
Fused glass rods
15.2 x 28.5 x 25.4 cm /
6 x 11½ x 10 in

Germany
Sibylle Peretti
(Near right)
Untitled
Glass and wire, mould-blown,
sawn, enamelled, engraved
20x10cm / 7¾x4 in

Australia
Jan Blum
(Far right)
Golden Rain
Blown glass with lampworked
and kiln-formed enamel,
applications and copper
strips
71x45.7cm / 28x18 in

France
Marie Ducate
(Near right)
Untitled
Blown glass
34cm / 13½ in

USA
Richard Meitner
(Far right)
*Irresistible Forces and
Immovable Objects:
Momentum*
Glass and cast aluminium
55x50x17cm / 21½x19½x6½ in

■ Richard Meitner,
an American working
in Holland,
is well-known for
his ironical
conceptual work, while
a younger generation
of glass artists
are exploring narrative,
metaphor, mixed media
and decoration in
vessel forms.

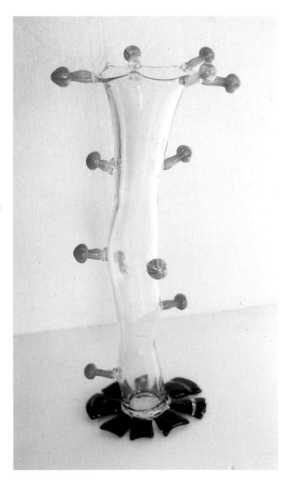

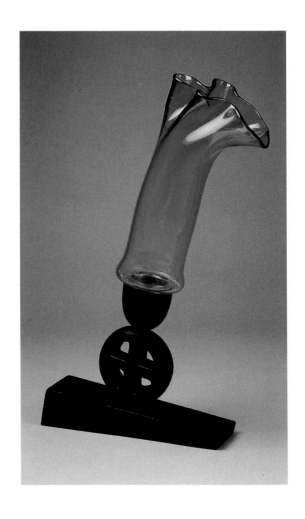

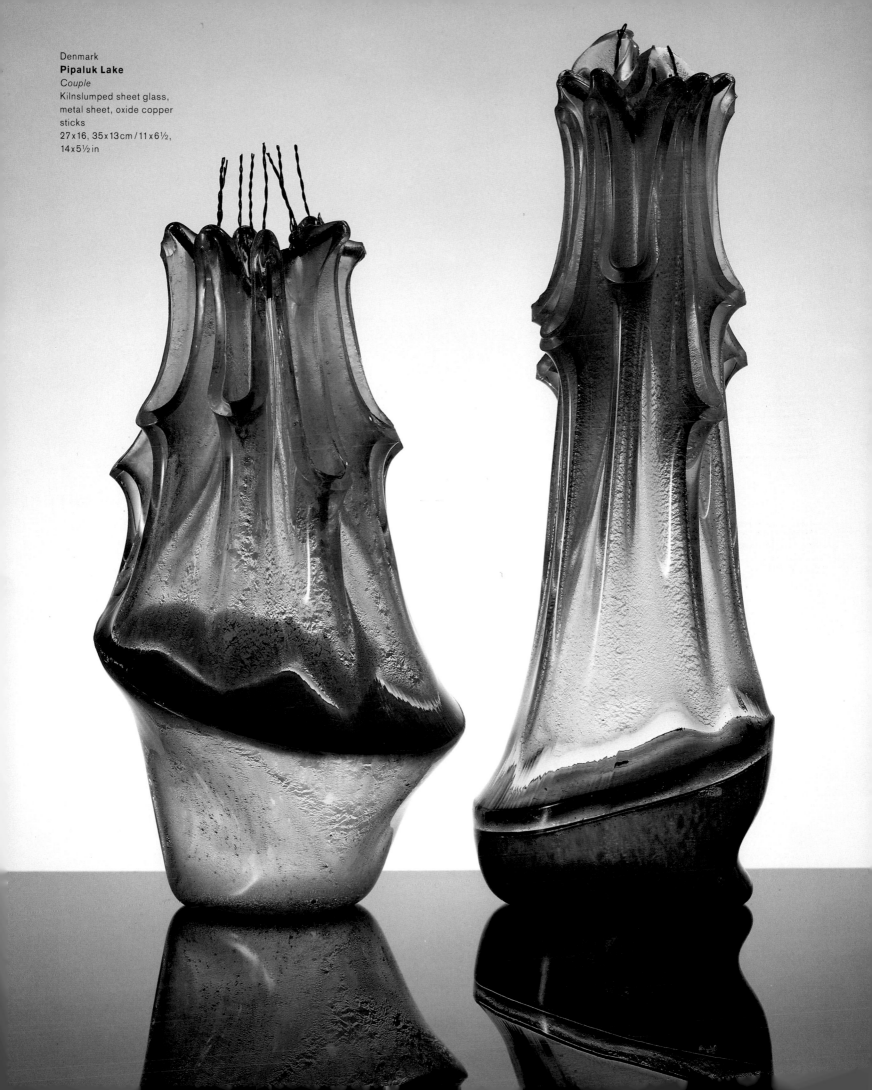

Denmark
Pipaluk Lake
Couple
Kilnslumped sheet glass,
metal sheet, oxide copper
sticks
27 x 16, 35 x 13 cm / 11 x 6½,
14 x 5½ in

■ Kyohei Fujita is a revered Japanese glass artist
with a characteristic style.
Glass is blown in the mould,
colour and gold or silver foil is melted in,
giving his boxes an effect akin to
Japanese lacquerwork.
As in the work of the distinguished Iwata and Leperlier,
past aesthetic styles are now frequently reinterpreted.

Japan
Kyohei Fujita
Red and White Plum
Blossoms
17.5 x 24 x 24 cm / 3 x 9½ x 9½ in

France
Antoine Leperlier
Evidence de la Pierre
Pâte de verre and bronze
28 x 21 x 21 cm / 11 x 8 x 8 in

Japan
Hisatoshi Iwata
Kokuyoko
Blown glass
33 x 29 cm / 13 x 11½ in

Czechoslovakia
Frantisek Vizner
Cut-glass bowl, sandblasted
28 cm / 11 in wide

■ The works of Harvey Littleton and of Frantisek Vizner, a leader in the Czech glass scene, owe their striking presence to the incisive formal treatment of the material.

A younger generation, exemplified by Antoine Leperlier's brother and Yan Zoritchak, inflect such consistent geometry with metaphorical elements.

France
Etienne Leperlier
Coupe Flèchée
Pâte de verre
18.5 x 44 cm / 7 x 17 in

France
Yan Zoritchak
L'Oiseau Lyre
Fused optical glass, pâte de verre, enamels, cut, polished and assembled
59.5 x 38.5 cm / 23½ x 15 in

Japan
Naito Yokoyama
Blown and assembled vases
22.86, 15.2cm / 9, 6 in

▶
USA
Peter Shire
Untitled
Glass made at Vistosi
in a limited edition
83.8x45.7x20.3cm /
33x18x8 in

■ An anthropomorphic,
mutant air pervades
these works.
Chihuly,
Littleton's talented pupil
and lynchpin of
the famous Pilchuck School
at its start in 1971,
has been a beacon
in the American
glass scene since
the mid-1970s.

USA
Dan Dailey
Bug Man
Blown and applied glass,
enamel paint
50.8x28.5x28.5cm /
20x11½x11½ in

Japan
Makoto Ito
Man and Woman
Semi-crystal, hot work,
glued
40x12x12cm /
15½x4½x4½in

USA
Dale Chihuly
*Cobalt Blue and Gold Venetian
No.454*
Blown glass with gold leaf
70x35x30cm / 28x14x12in

125

UK
David Taylor
Handblown scent bottle, 24%
lead crystal, carved,
sandblasted and polished
17x27cm / 6½x10½ in

Wit, surprise
and functional ambiguity
are common ground here.

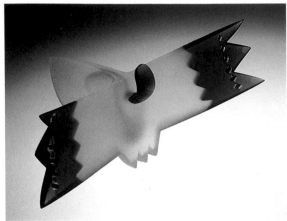

David Taylor is
a founder member
of The Glasshouse,
the UK's
longest-established
studio.

Sweden
Ulla Forsell
Tulip Tree
Blown cased glass, fused
tulip
40cm / 19½ in

USA
Susie Krasnican
Red Wine with Bowl of Fruit
Found objects and plate
glass, fired enamels
33.7x7.6, 19x27.9cm / 13x3,
7½x11 in

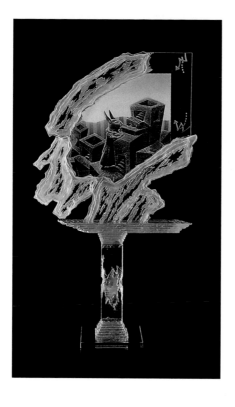

Japan
Kazumi Ikemoto
Scene 1
Flat glass, painted (high
temperature-enamelled),
sandblasted and bonded
70x40x15cm / 27½x15½x6in

■ Pictorial narratives
and emotional states
explored in works by
Ikemoto and Zuber
typify these
increasingly evident themes
in contemporary glass.

France
Czeslaw Zuber
Cut and coloured glass
46x63x24cm / 18x24x9½in

Czechoslovakia
Dana Zámecnikova
(Below)
Shout
Flat glass pieces, etched and
assembled
162 cm / 63 in

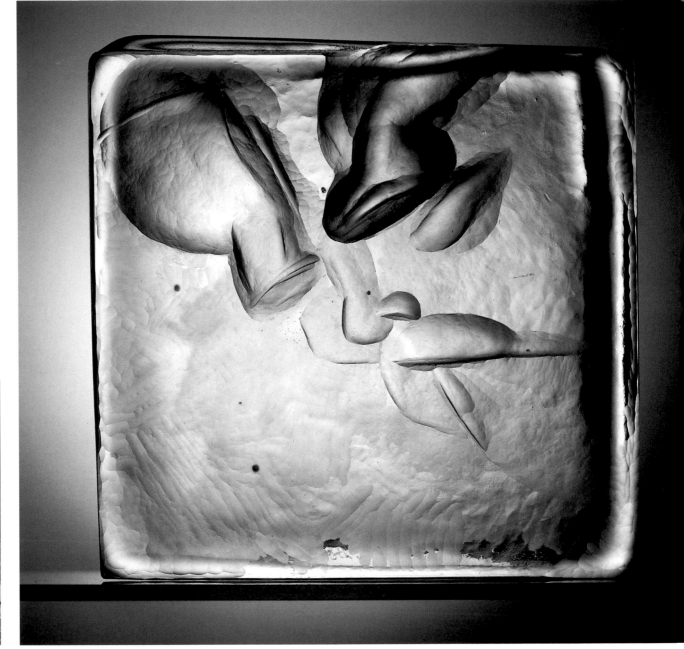

Czechoslovakia
Jiří Harcuba
Dostoevsky
Glass block, deeply
intaglio-cut, some areas
roughly and irregularly cut,
also worked on back
20 x 20 x 4 cm / 8 x 8 x 1½ in

Italy
Paolo Martinuzzi
Untitled
Scratch-engraved glass
48 cm / 19 in

■ The commanding expressiveness of
the great Czech glass artists has been
a yardstick of achievement over three decades.
Libenský, who works with his wife Brychtová, is perhaps
the most respected glass artist in the world,
both for his work and his teaching.
Martinuzzi is a key figurative engraver;
the versatile Lechner executes
both meditative works and large
architectural commissions.

Czechoslovakia
**Stanislav Libenský/
Jaroslava Brychtová**
Silhouettes of the Town III
Glass, cast in the mould,
some parts cut and polished
52x75cm / 20½x29½ in

Germany
Florian Lechner
The Seer
Kiln-formed, flat glass
76x86x90cm /
29½x34x35½ in

USA
William Carlson
Contrapuntal
Cast and laminated glass,
granite
54.6x50.8x17.7cm/
21½x20x7in

■ Geometric abstraction and light
filtering through prismatic laminations
are enduring formal themes in glass, outstanding
amongst the Czechs and, latterly,
the Japanese.

Czechoslovakia
Pavel Hlava
Lightning
Coloured glass with clear
glass thread, cut, glued and
cut again
44x57cm/17x22½in

Japan
Shimpei Sato
Future Sound Machine
Plate glass and glass rods,
laminated, cut, cracked,
ground and sandblasted
45 x 80 x 20 cm / 18 x 31½ x 8 in

Japan
Toshio Iezumi
Divided Mass
Plate glass, laminated
and polished
20 x 50 x 46 cm /
8 x 19½ x 18 in

■ Glass reveals its paradoxes – vulnerable but strong,
delicate yet massive, abstract yet allusive – in symbolic works.
Vallien, a world-famous glass artist
as well as teacher and designer,
has perfected sandcasting
to suit his ideas about existence,
freedom and survival
(after the final blast,
when everything else has gone,
glass fragments will remain).

Japan
Shimpei Sato
Wind Facts
Plate glass and glass rods,
cut, painted, cracked,
laminated, ground and
sandblasted
200x60x40cm /
79x23½x15½in

Sweden
Bertil Vallien
Pendulums
Sandcast crystal with off
hand inclusions, parts cut and
polished
250x300x200cm /
98½x118x79in

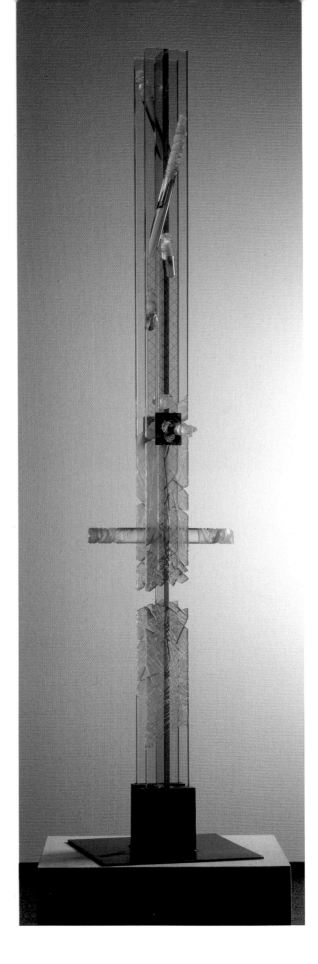

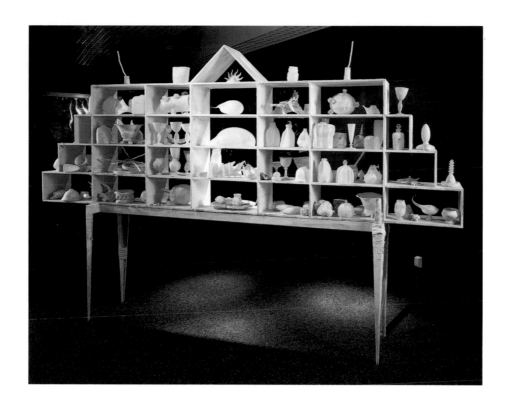

Japan
Yoshihiko Takahashi
Mind-box
Glass, mixed media.
Blown glass in wooden box,
painted with acrylic, recorded
sound of water and noises
210x300x35cm /
82½x118x13½ in

Japan
Osamu Noda
Sea Garden
Glass, stainless steel, stone,
light fitment.
Mould-blown, glued
95x200x300cm /
37½x79x118 in

Germany
Ludwig Schaffrath
Window, Wiesbaden
Town Hall
Stained and leaded glass
420 x 150 cm / 165½ x 59 in

■ Germany has been in the vanguard
of architectural glass for two generations.
The past decade has seen
a notable increase in
architectural glass commissions worldwide
and in the range of styles
and imagery.

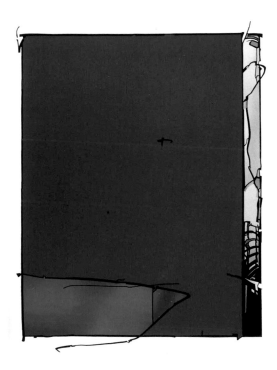

Germany
Johannes Schreiter
Blown glass, plexiglass, lead,
traditional stained-glass
techniques
200 x 160 cm / 79 x 63 in

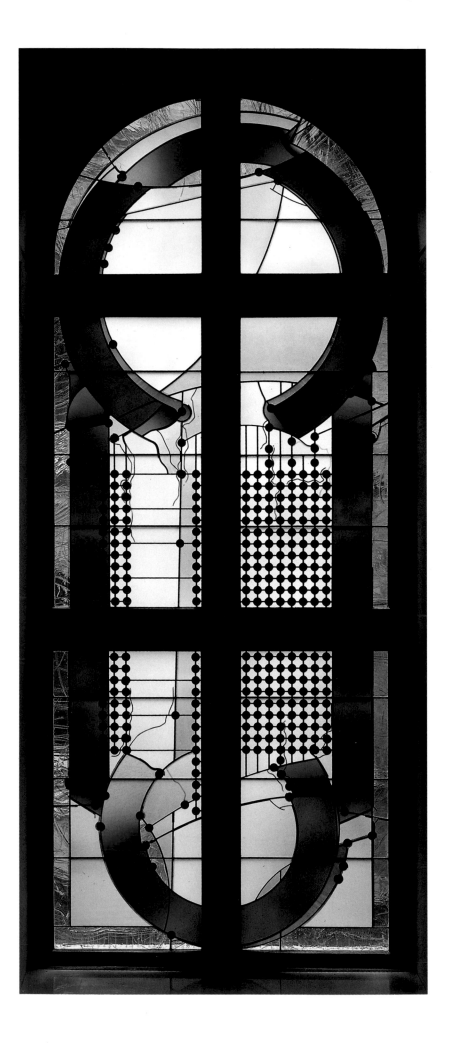

UK
Brian Clarke
Roof, Queen Victoria Street
Arcade, Leeds
Stained glass, assembled in
panels
752.4 square metres / 900
square yards

UK
Deborah Thomas
Blue Rose Chandelier
Broken blue glass,
hand-threaded with wire and
attached to steel armature
102 x 100 x 100 cm /
40 x 39½ x 39½ in

Japan
Toshio Iezumi
Light and Water
Plate glass, laminated and
polished, steel fountain
340 x 40 x 40 cm /
134 x 15½ x 15½ in

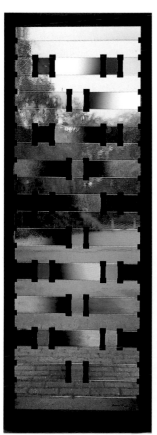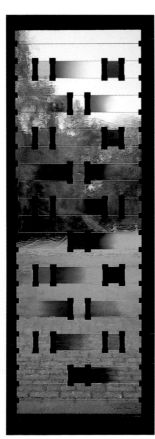

Germany
Jochem Poensgen
Between the Lines I and
Between the Lines II
Handblown antique glass
(acid-etched),
individual pieces held
together by lead
'corners' (incomplete
leading)
188.5 x 61 cm /
74 x 24 in each

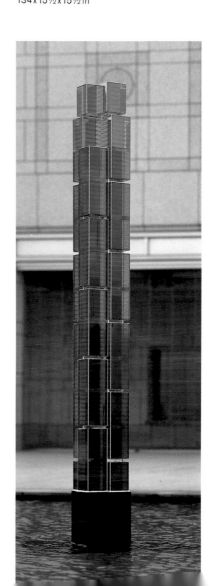

BASKETS AND WOOD

Throughout its long history, the basket has been so bound up with utilitarian needs that its entry in the 1950s into the Western art world appeared surprising. The American fiber artist Ed Rossbach revolutionized the basket's status in the West, exploring form, materials, techniques and colour to redefine the object.

This dramatic new focus on the craft must be put in the context of ethnic and vernacular traditions, from the Navajos to the Maoris, the Africans to the French. The Japanese, especially, had long ago brought basketmaking to a sophisticated sculptural level with expressive forms denoting seasonal and elemental cycles. It is perhaps the proliferation of baskets from Taiwan, the Philippines and China which gives basketmaking a misleading gloss of uniformity.

Raw materials such as willow, bark, flax and bamboo, together with techniques such as wrapping, coiling, stitching and weaving, unite baskets with nature's lively, tactile qualities. Alongside this, the use of found, recycled and synthetic materials and an increasing exploration of decoration, form, narrative and scale, continue to add new dimensions to the craft.

Polished, cut, lacquered or laminated works in solid wood offer stark contrasts to baskets, in their use of light, space, mass, volume, surface and imagery. The obvious love of the material in works on these pages is balanced by a formal and conceptual control and a wish to put the material at the service of narrative and figurative ideas, sometimes on a monumental scale.

USA
Karyl Sisson
Just Ripe (and detail)
Vessel, dyed miniature
wooden clothes-pegs, twined
with wire
Edition of 3
23x30.5x33cm / 9x12x13 in

Finland
Markku Kosonen
Willow and rosewood basket
30 x 30 x 35 / 11¾ x 11¾ x 13¾ in

USA
Dona Look
No. 898
White birch bark, silk thread,
sewn and partially wrapped
31 x 35 x 35 cm /
12¼ x 13¾ x 13¾ in

Japan
Shokansai Iizuka
Mount Fuji
Handwoven basket with
frosted bamboo sprits and
cracking ice motif
22 x 46 x 25 cm / 8½ x 18 x 10 in

New Zealand
**Daisy Cameron,
Maori Te Ati Haunui a
Paparangi tribe**
Kete Whakairo
Handwoven *kiekie* (flax) bag

USA
Lillian Elliott
Celebration
Palm bark, plastic tubing
43 x 53.3 x 10.8 cm /
17 x 21 x 4¼ in

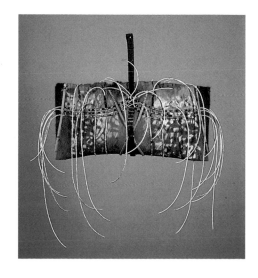

■ The fertile, lively, tactile qualities
of nature's raw materials are here pointed up
by sympathetic techniques.
The 72-year-old Iizuka's charged form,
admixing control and spontaneity, uses
one of Japan's 600 types of bamboo.

◀ Japan
Shokosai Hayakawa
Flower Basket
Handwoven with linear
rhombus design
20x33cm / 7¾x13in

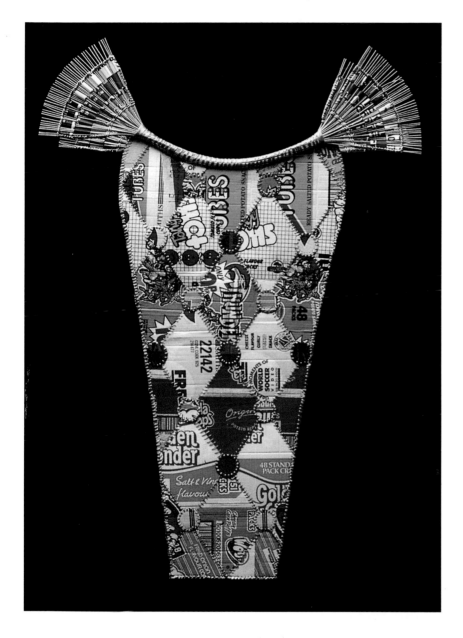

USA
Karyl Sisson
Faux Pot with Lid
Coiled tape-measures,
interior coated with fabric
stiffener
21.6x8.3cm / 8½x3¼in

◀ UK
Lois Walpole
Linen Basket (and detail)
'Crisps' boxes, cane and
synthetic raffia.
Patchwork diamonds stitched
together, bound cane rim
splayed and woven at ends
145x105x27cm /
57x41x10½in

■ A contrast of
traditional and unexpected
materials for baskets
from renowned craftspeople.
Karyl Sisson
(see also pp.136–7)
explores 'the physical
and metaphysical possibilities
that result when materials,
structure and form interact'.
This piece, using
twenty-five metres of
tape measures,
is coiled then raised,
like a thrown pot.

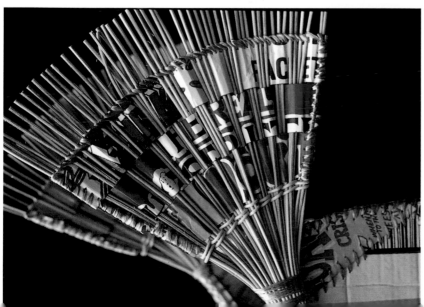

USA
Kay Sekimachi
Patched Pot XVI
Japanese handmade papers
and handwoven dyed linen,
laminated in layers
28x35.5cm/11x14in

USA
John McQueen
Basket of spruce bark
43cm/17in

USA
Ferne Jacobs
Heart Dance
Waxed linen thread, twined
29 x 28 x 20 cm / 11½ x 11 x 8 in

■ Leading basketmakers
keep America at the forefront of
invention in terms of form,
construction, surface treatment
and metaphorical content.

USA
Jane Sauer
*Summer Days/Red and Yellow
Cliffs*
Waxed linen thread and paint
132 x 29 x 25 cm /
52 x 11½ x 9¾ in

◀ USA
Platt Monfort
Geodesic Airolite (inset)
Wood framework boat,
braced with Kevlar roving,
covered with heat-shrunk
Dacron. Batch production; kit
available
35.5x76cmx226cm/
14x30x89in

■ Sekijima breaks
the mould of basketmaking
in Japan.
Monfort's boat echoes basket forms.

The apparently random structure
and texture of Elliott's piece is
a deceptively 'primitive' work
with a controlled technique.

◀ Japan
Hisako Sekijima
Untitled
Cedar bark, plaited and
interlocked
23x29x29cm/9x11½x11½in

USA
Lillian Elliott
Column
Pandanus, rattan, acrylic
paints
61x58.5x51cm/24x23x20in

Japan
Showasai Ono
Mulberry wood with inlaid
linear design
21.3x12x15cm / 8¼x4¾x6 in

UK
David Pye
Detail of turned and carved
walnut dish
53x21cm / 21x8¼ in

UK
David Pye
(Inset)
Turned and carved dish
32x12½cm / 12½x5 in

Japan
Zuishin Nakadai
Lobed box of paulownia wood
43x36.5x11cm /
17x14¼x4¼ in

■ The complete integration
of masterful form and technique,
exuding an intellectual and spiritual clarity,
is exemplified by
two 89-year-old
Living National Treasures in Japan
and by 77-year-old David Pye,
Britain's most distinguished
woodcarver and turner.

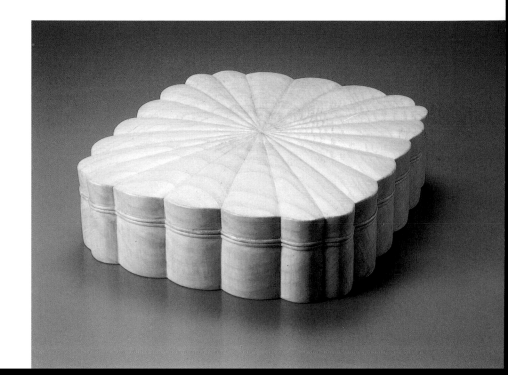

USA
Ron Kent
(Right)
Spalted translucent wood
bowl, lathe-turned pine,
multiple oil saturation and
hand-oil-sanding finish
35.5x50.8cm/14x20in

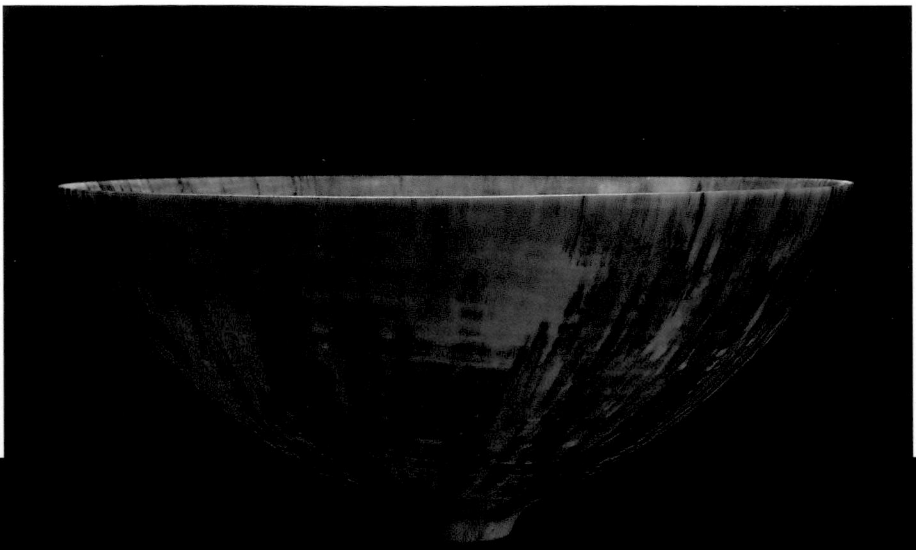

USA
Mark Lindquist
Unsung Bowl Ascending No.7
Turned maple burl
31x39.5cm/12¼x15½in

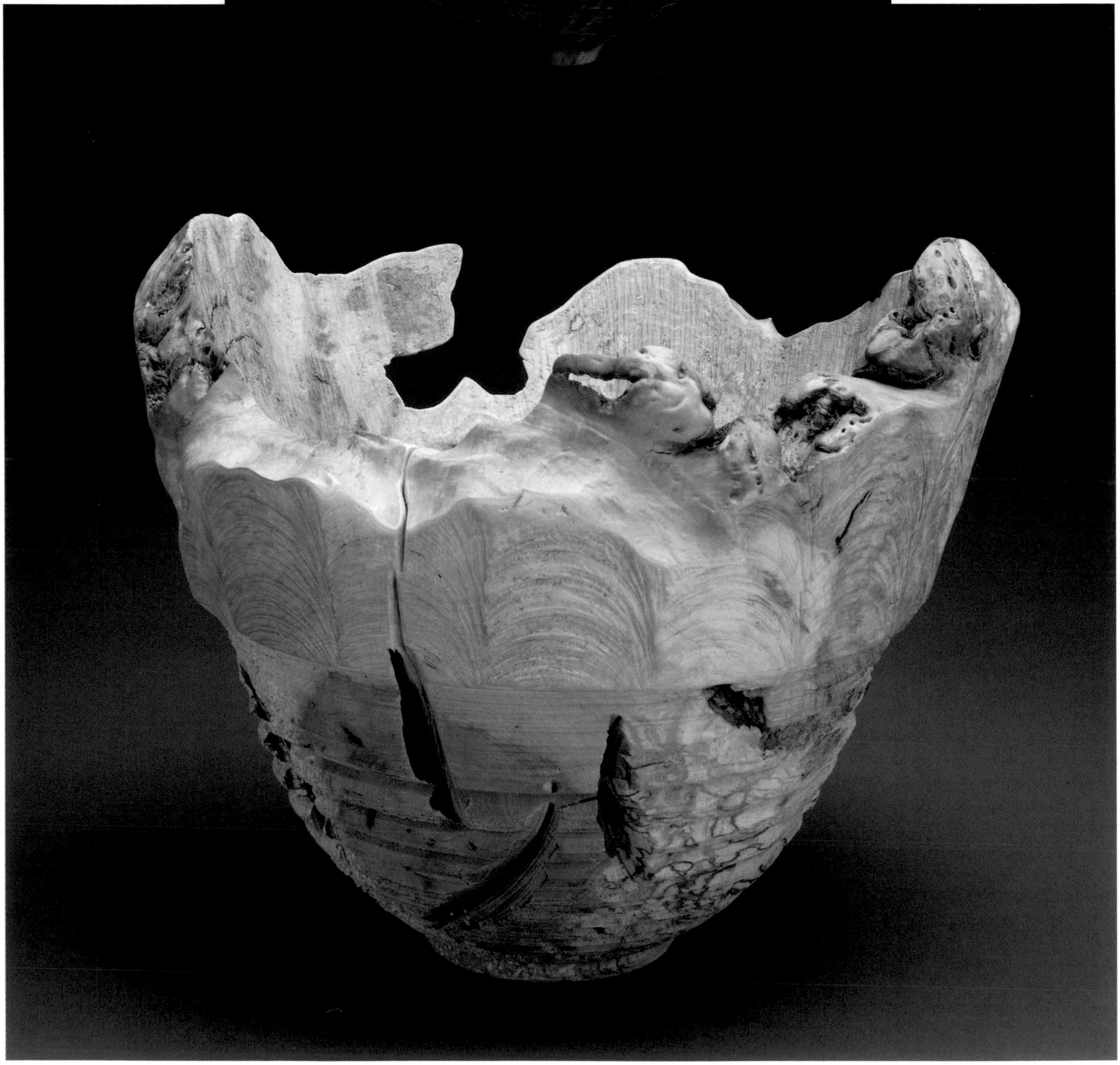

UK
Jim Partridge
Turned bowls, blackened,
stained oak
37.5, 32.5 cm /
14¾, 12¾ in wide

■ The formal and
surface treatments by
four outstanding
individualistic woodturners
contrast the exploitation
of the raw material
with its disguise
(by blowtorch or stain)
to achieve conceptual
ends.

Holland
Maria van Kesteren
Concealed Volume
Turned elm, sprayed with
ivory colour
14 cm / 5½ in

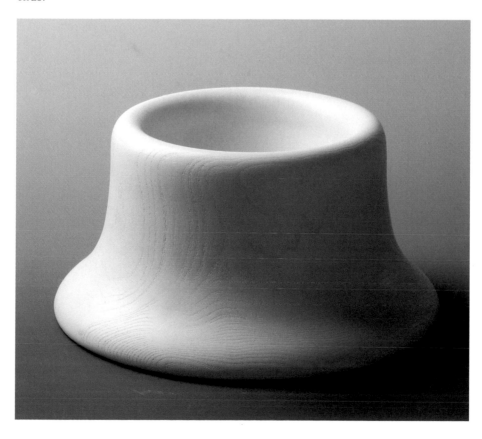

UK
**Peter Chatwin and
Pamela Martin**
Spliced Bowl I
Dyed and laminated sycamore
veneer, constructed and
surface-ground
45 cm / 17¾ in long

Norway
Odrun Molnar-Chiodera
Reliquary
Carved and oil-painted birch
with patinated copper,
drawers gold-plated
30x50x20 cm / 11¾ x 19¾ x 8 in

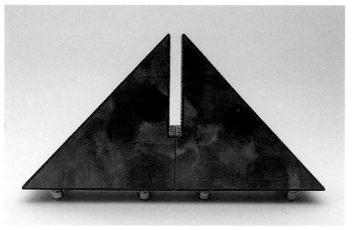

Germany
Pini Brokmann
Roller (closed and open)
Varnished card box.
Limited edition
22.5 x 10 x 41 cm / 8¾ x 4 x 16 in

Finland
Markku Kosonen
Disketti
Birch box
12 x 12 x 30 cm / 4¾ x 4¾ x 11¾ in

■ Colour, pattern and symbolism
are combined with unusual forms
in boxes that have
the aspect of
small-scale architecture,
exploring interior and
exterior space.

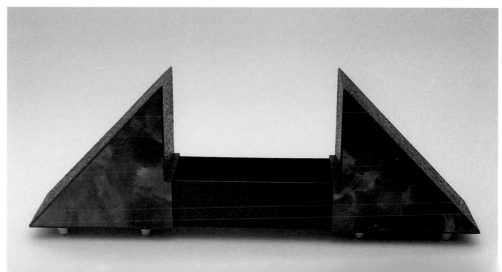

■ Lacquerware is regarded as the highest-quality tableware in Japan.

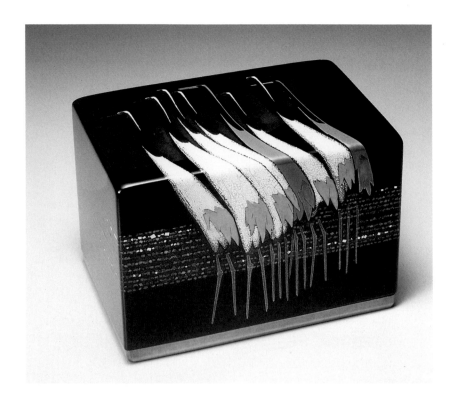

Japan
Kōdō Otomaru
Monstera
Vessel for cake with lacquer carving
15.5 x 15.5 cm / 6 x 6 in

The sap of the lacquer tree yields the best adhesive and paint to achieve the refined lustre after layers and layers are burnished.

Japan
Naoji Terai
Cranes

Makie decoration
21.4 x 14.4 x 15.7 cm
/ 8¼ x 5¾ x 6 in

Japan
Kado Isaburo
Lacquered wood tray,
Victoria and Albert Museum
Collection
60 cm / 23½ in long

The response to nature's inspiration
is also reflected
in the work of Guy Taplin,
one of the world's most celebrated
birdcarvers.

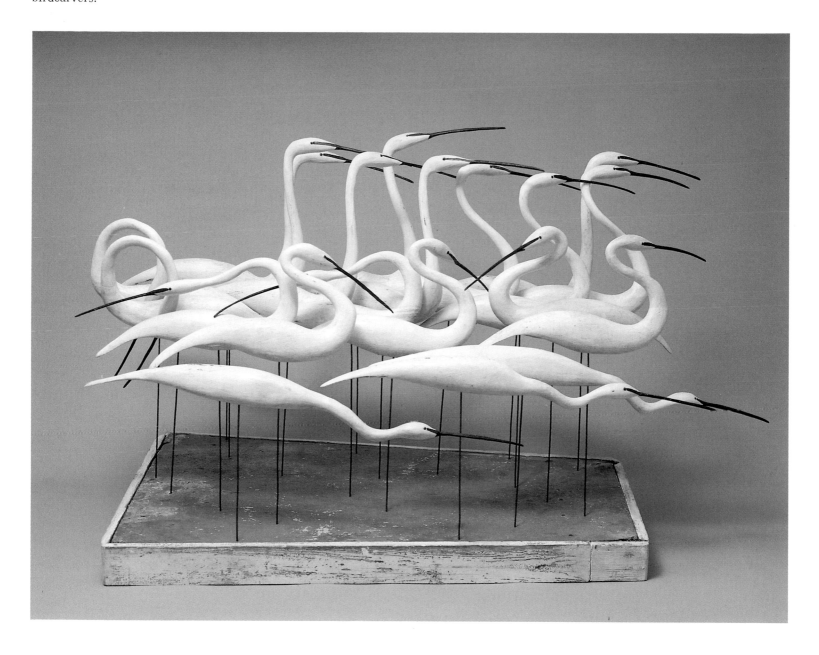

UK
Guy Taplin
Group of Twenty Egrets
Carved wood, paint, wax,
driftwood
60.9 x 76.2 x 76.2 cm /
24 x 30 x 30 in

UK
José Luis Romanillos
La Bujarrabal No.695
Concert guitar (head, rosette
and bridge), cedar veneered
with rosewood. Soundboard
of Swiss spruce, yew, ebony,
maple, holly and laburnum
inlays

■ The exquisite execution of things
to meet specific needs
is a fundamental part of craft activity
round the world.
The tradition of musical instrument-making
is balanced by the innovative works
of an international network of craftspeople.

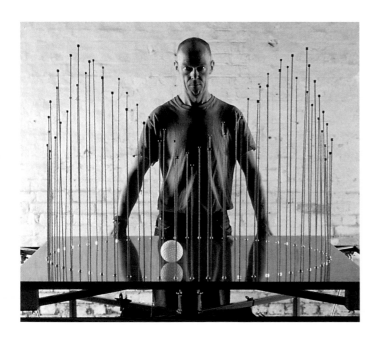

UK
David Sawyer
Pinball Composer
Mixed media, musical
instrument

Germany
Jack Mankiewicz
Handturned pens, wood and
gold. Pens made to order in
two styles, large range of
exotic woods, ink or
cartridge, five types of nib

UK
Desmond Ryan
Portable easel/watercolour box
African and Andamaw padauk
and brass, legs fold
10x30x40cm / 4x12x16in
(closed)

Portugal
Teresa Segurado
Nona Lança (and detail)
Moulded, wood-fired ceramic,
palm-tree bark, hand-plaited
and dyed palm-tree thread,
wood, hemp, raffia, seeds
159x19x11cm /
62½x7½x4¼in

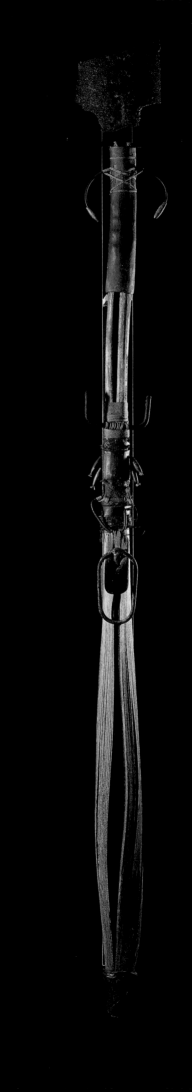

USA
Mark Lindquist
Unmet Friend 1
Turned walnut, maple and ash
183 x 38 cm / 72 x 15 in

■ Monumental totemic works
and Hosaluk's primitivist/futurist piece
exemplify a widespread theme
in contemporary woodwork.

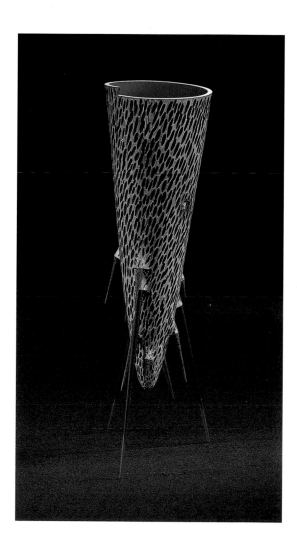

Canada
Michael Hosaluk
*Future Species: One-eyed
Jack*
Elm, maple, casein and
amber, turned, carved,
painted and constructed
35.5 cm / 14 in

Czechoslovakia
Irena Marečková
Marionettes
Textile, wood, metal, bones
(opposite) and leather (above)
for Theatre Minor, Prague.
Puppet-making techniques
111 x 57 cm / 43¾ x 22½ in
tallest

UK
Eleanor Glover
Bird Box
Carved wood, acrylic paint
33 cm / 13 in long

UK
Jan Zalud
The Kwakiutl Principle
Lime, various woods, ply
cogs, wire. Automaton, last of
a series
30 x 25 x 25 cm / 11¾ x 9¾ x 9¾ in

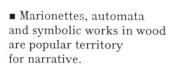

■ Marionettes, automata
and symbolic works in wood
are popular territory
for narrative.

LETTERING AND BOOKS

■ Bookbinding and book art, artists' books, calligraphy and lettering, are all devoted to the experience of literature, the process of reading and the visual power of language. In this century, French bookbinders have been leaders in the field; Jean de Gonet is today. But since the 1970s, bookbinding as an art form has developed rapidly in many countries, with Czechoslovakia, Britain and the United States to the fore.

■ Although by the 1920s the idea of artists' books had been explored, they have flourished since the 1960s. In that decade, an impetus was supplied by the wish to 'dematerialize' art, to remove art from static grand statements in galleries and museums. In aiming to democratize and disseminate ideas widely, use has been made of new technology and communications media. Repeatable works using typography, xerox, photographic litho and computer-printing techniques and 'deconstructed' forms have proliferated, with both content and form created by the artist.

■ Calligraphers, too, compose as well as deconstruct language, in a musical way (outstandingly in Islamic works), so that often it is the shapes which lead one to analyse the language and meaning of the piece. The gestural aspect of contemporary calligraphy, so eloquent in Japanese examples, has the potential for dynamic effects, in the manner of Abstract Expressionist painters. But the tradition of freehand drawn and painted classic lettering remains important. The craft of lettercutting is at present predominantly reliant on commissions for its survival, but unique art pieces of cut letter forms are attracting connoisseurs and collectors. Some lettercutters are also experimenting with new lettering forms, techniques and materials for architectural contexts. In this area, there are signs of a sympathetic response to innovation.

Spain
Santiago Brugalla
Poemes de Mao Tse Toung,
illustrated by Salvador Dali
(and detail)
Binding techniques
38x28cm/15x11in

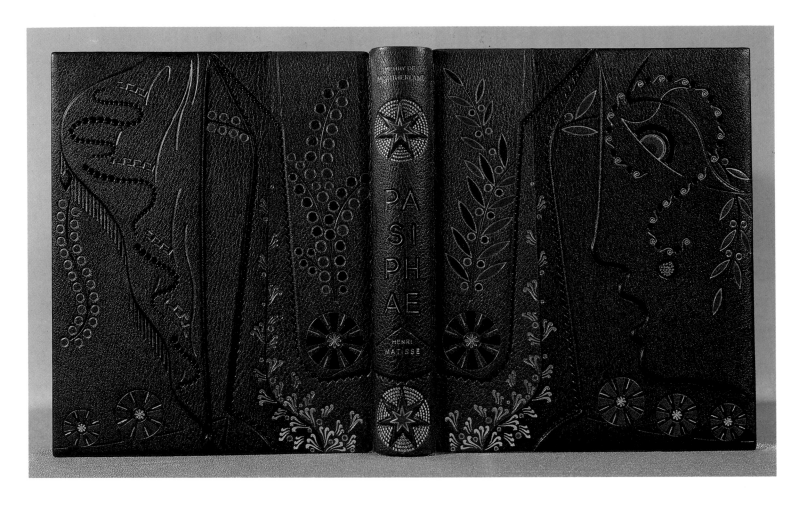

Spain
Santiago Brugalla
Pasiphae by Henri de
Montherlant, illustrated by
Henri Matisse
Binding techniques
33 x 27 cm / 13 x 10½ in

■ The spectacular tooling
and relief compositions of
Brugalla (see p.160-61)
are balanced
by the varied constructional
techniques and surfaces
of other leading binders.

Belgium
Jacqueline Liekens
Ode Inachevée à la Boue
by Francis Ponge
Portfolio binding in brown
morocco and rust calf, leather
inlay, handpainted Kromekote
endpapers
18.5 x 11 cm / 7¼ x 4¼ in

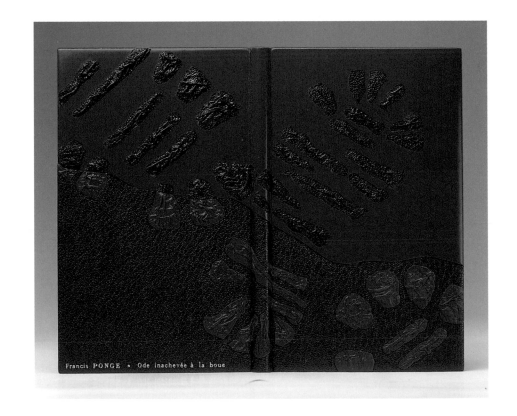

USA
Timothy Ely
Movement and Path
Full goatskin binding, tooled
in aluminium, copper and
gold, embossed, scraped,
dyed. Arches buff paper with
ink, watercolour, graphite and
acrylic applied. Victoria and
Albert Museum Collection
25 x 14.5 cm / 10 x 6 in

UK
Trevor Jones
*The Addresses of Her Majesty
Queen Elizabeth II on the
Occasion of her Silver Jubilee*
Archival calfskin binding with
leather dyes, stencil and
resist applied, coloured
tooling and gold
6.8 x 4.5 cm / 2¾ x 1¾ in

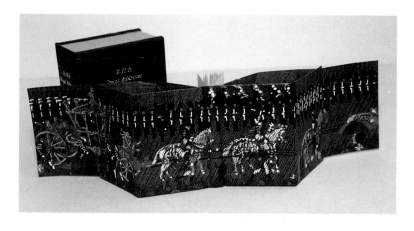

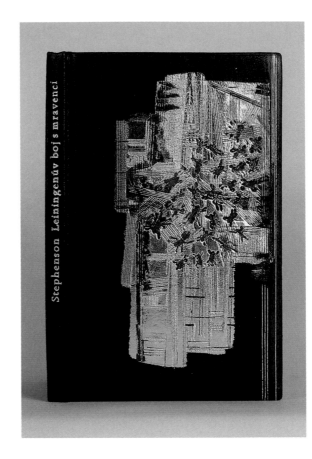

■ Hodny, with binders
such as Kocman and Hadlač,
is leading the impressive
Czech bookwork movement.
The Belgians remain dominant
within a traditional idiom,
combining superb technique
and emphatic articulation
of space in their
compositions.

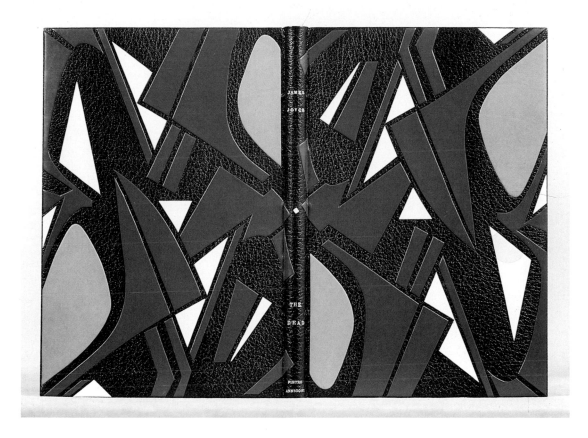

Belgium
Christine Leonard
Le Paysan de Paris by Louis
Aragon
Portfolio binding, lizardskin
and snakeskins
19 x 11.5 x 2.2 cm / 7½ x 4½ x 1 in

Belgium
Liliane Gerard
Morocco leather binding

USA
Daniel E. Kelm
A Dog Story, illustrated by
Nicolette Jelan
Leather and paper coated
with acrylic and starch
mixture, photocopy transfer
images on decorated paper
35 cm / 13¾ in

USA
Jan Sobota
Heir of the Devil by Honoré de
Balzac (closed and open)
Box: board, calfskin, marbled
paper. Book: blue calfskin
with applied relief in dark-blue
calf
36.5 x 33 x 3 cm / 14¼ x 13 x 1¼ in

■ These renowned bookbinders
treat the binding as
an art object, mixing media
and techniques and moving
confidently between two
and three dimensions,
the works resonant
with imagery.

France
Daniel Knoderer
Mixed-media binding, own
techniques

UK
Philip Smith
Moby Dick III
Bookedges and endpapers
hand-painted with acrylics,
modelled relief forms; book
printed on handmade paper.
One-off, but limited edition
printed
42x30x9.5cm/16½x12x3¾in

Germany
Axel Heibel
Book object – D
Sixty-four pages
31.4 x 32.8 cm / 12¼ x 13 in

Germany
Robert Schwarz
Pindar, Pythische Ode 1 & 2
by Friedrich Hölderlin

Lithography, printing and
collage, set, printed and
bound by hand. Limited
edition
32 x 21 x 2 cm / 12½ x 8¼ x ¾ in

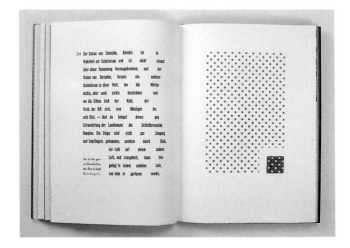

USA
Daniel E. Kelm
Earth II (detail)
Paper coated with acrylic and
corn-starch paste, photocopy
transfer technique
9 x 30.5 x 30.5 cm /
3½ x 12 x 12 in

USA
Keith A. Smith
Book 151
Photographs, machine-quilted
in block patterns onto paper,
interlaced leather-strap cover
21 x 21 x 2.5 cm / 8¼ x 8¼ x 1 in

■ Not just the binding but the whole book
is here the subject of outstanding practitioners.
Nishimura's kiln-fired book is in the idiom of
Anselm Kiefer's lead bookworks, thought-provoking
on the place and value of literature in society.

Japan
Yohei Nishimura
The Black Fine Art Book
Paperback
8.5 x 18 x 10 cm / 3½ x 7½ x 4 in

UK
Ken Campbell
Tilt: the Black-Flagged Streets
Letterpress
30x24cm / 12x9in (irregular
rectangle)

UK
Ken Campbell
A Knife Romance
Letterpress etching, blind
embossing
50x85cm / 20x34in (open)

USA
Walter Hamady
Neopostmodrinism or Dieser Rasen ist kein Hundeklo or Gabberjabb Number 6, illustrated by Walter Hamady 118 pages, surfaces all printed, perforated, drawn, cut, die-cut, rubberstamped, collaged, taped, debossed, grommeted, ponce-wheeled, signed, notarized, numbered, notched, torn and bitten by the author.
There are 18 typefaces printed in 88 colours on/into variegated Shadwell papers handmade in the barn. Six signatures sewn to six cords by Marta Gomez and forwarded in many steps and procedures by Kent Kasuboske into former Tax-Roll-Records-Marbled-Covers retrieved from the State Historical Society's dumpster. The edition is 125 copies numbered five times and signed seven times by all involved including the printer's mother
18 x 24 x 2 cm / 7 x 9½ x ⅞ in

■ Ken Campbell and Walter Hamady are twin peaks in the book art world, pursuing different ends.
Hamady, a 'visual groundbreaker', has for years established ground rules for construction, layout and typography combined with entertaining content.
Campbell, a politicized romantic, achieves a discrete spirituality in more narrative and literary works. These are a synthesis of quotation, his own poetry and visually rich surfaces achieved through a variety of traditional techniques, which include blockprinting, embossing and metallic dusting.

UK
Ann Hechle
In the Beginning
Vellum panel with raised and
burnished gold leaf,
powdered gold, watercolour
and stock-ink applied
71 x 89 cm / 28 x 35 in

France
Jean Larcher
La Cuisine des Terroirs (detail)
Ingres d'Arches paper, Indian
ink applied with Speedball
pen. Book-jacket commission
24 x 24 cm / 9½ x 9½ in

■ Calligraphers can use virtually any tools and any surface to integrate form and content – words as mass, line and volume. Clayton has also experimented with computers and laser printers.

USA
Marsha Brady
The Starlight Night
Gerard Manley Hopkins poem on Canson *mi-teintes* paper, gouache, Speedball with B6 nib. Reproduced as a limited edition
37 x 45 cm / 14½ x 17¾ in (w x l)

UK
Ewan Clayton
Spring's Fire Birds (and detail)
Watercolour paper, acrylics and pastels
46 x 69 cm / 18 x 27 in

■ The choice of letter forms, materials and use of space puts across the calligrapher's response to words.

Germany
Werner Schneider
The Passage of Time
Roma handmade paper,
watercolour applied
62 x 49 cm / 24½ x 19¼ in

KURT WEIDEMANN
THE PASSAGE
OF TIME
LEAVES
BEHIND
BUT ONE
STANDARD-
QUALITY

Czechoslovakia
Jovica Veljovič
Jenino Dedino
Watercolour, wooden stick
and art masking fluid
22 x 11 cm / 8¾ x 4¼ in

Ireland
Denis Brown
*Oliver Kearney Presentation
Address*
Paper with Japanese
stick-ink, gouache, powder
gold and gold leaf burnished
on gesso support
107 x 37 cm / 42 x 15 in

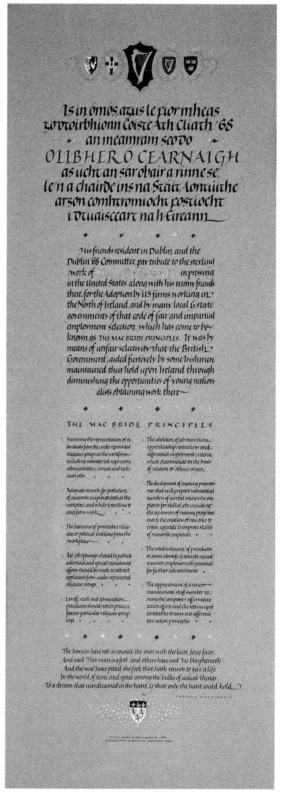

■ Four of the world's outstanding lettercutters,
including brothers who work separately,
illustrate the rhythmic power
and timelessness of words cut in
the earth's densest materials.

Belgium
Kristoffel Boudens
Tulius
Carved with wood-carving
chisel in freshly cast plaster
18 x 42 x 3 cm / 7 x 16½ x 1¼ in

France
Jean-Claude Lamborot
La Mort
Cut in stone

■ Logical, economical, comfortable . . . these are not adjectives which spring to mind in the observation of current furniture. Sensationalism and revisionism are dominant trends: Modernism – Art Deco – Memphis – Postmodernism – Postholocaust – Postindustrial. Postholocaust metalbashers have stayed the course, refining their techniques and forms. However, found materials are less in evidence now and there is a move towards a pared-down aesthetic.

■ Revisionism lurks in every corner of a room. A trawl through Art Deco and the Fifties, in particular, reaps ocean-liner craftsmanship and materials such as leather and hardwood veneers. Modernism remains a tap-root, enabling practitioners to continue exploring the essence of functional, constructed pieces.

■ After hi-tech comes low-tech. In a decade with an environmental conscience and a consumerist hangover, the use of unexotic woods and basic techniques is particularly attractive. A whole range of naïf furniture is finding an audience.

■ One-off furniture-makers, unfettered by the exigencies of large-scale production, can offer the most personal interpretations of form and content. But there are also many craftspeople who confront issues of function and economy on the same terms as, say, Italian designers. A unique boardroom table can be commissioned from an individual craftsperson at the same price (or less) than a shop-bought piece. Custom-designed and -made architectural metalwork should also be far more widely commissioned. Furniture for outside, too.

■ The difficult task of combining designing, making, marketing and distributing is a great burden for a small business. Some decide to run their own gallery to show their work, while others work in association with excellent organizations such as VIA in Paris and Anthologie Quartett in Germany which seek out talented designs and put them into limited production.

■ Towards the *fin de siècle*, furniture production is mutating: furniture designers for industry and individual designer-makers are moving closer together in the production of limited edition pieces to meet the consumer demand for more individualistic furniture at an affordable price.

USA
Wendell Castle
On the Tip of My Tongue
(and detail)
Madrone, ebony, mahogany
cabinet
132x167x46cm/
52x66x18 in closed

■ Traditional craftsmanship and functional design solutions remain *leitmotivs* of contemporary furniture making.

USA
Sam Maloof
Fiddleback rocking-chair,
constructed of hard rock
maple and ebony
115 x 65 x 115 cm / 46 x 26 x 46 in

UK
Rod and Alison Wales
Chess Chairs
Shotblasted ash, steel and
riven slate.
Thirty-two piece 'chess set'
commissioned by Rosehaugh
Stanhope Developments for
an atrium at Broadgate,
London
270cm/106in max. height

UK
David Colwell
C3 Triflex Chairs
Steam-bent ash stacking
chair. Batch production
85x50x52cm/33½x20x20½in

France
François Bauchet
Birch plywood cabinet
182x73x40cm /
71½ x 28¾ x 15¾ in

Australia
D4 Design
Michael Scott Mitchell,
Stephen Roberts and
Bill MacMahon
(Far right)
Rockpool Pod
Mobile servery pod first
designed and made for the
Rockpool Restaurant,
Sydney.
Cast-iron base,
satin anodized aluminium,
pausander veneer.
Batch production
87.5x45cm / 34½ x 17¾ in

Germany
Andreas Eckhardt
Cupboard composed of
birch boxes on mobile,
multi-position steel frame
330x40x40cm /
130x15¾ x 15¾ in

Holland
Dick Roose
Screen, wood, cardboard,
paper tape, acrylic, paint and
paper, steel under-carriage
300x165cm / 118x65 in wide

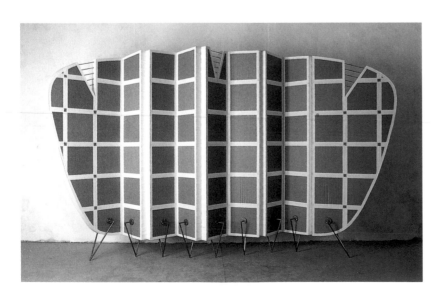

■ Late Modernism could be the term applied to these works: functional, constructed, true to materials, but with individualistic formal elements and detailing. All the countries represented here are producing interesting furniture ideas in the early 1990s. Clapés and D4 are internationally known

Spain
Jaime Tresserra Clapés
Butterfly (open and closed)

Varnished walnut and sycamore desk with nickel-plated detailing
84 x 144 cm / 33 x 56¾ in

Australia
Helmut Lueckenhausen
Daughters of Coercri
Mahogany, medium-density
fibreboard and
catalyzed enamels
76 x 180 x 105 cm /
30 x 71 x 41¼ in

USA
John Cederquist
Mexican Madness
Baltic birch plywood chest of
drawers, Sitka spruce,
Formica, epoxy
146.5 x 101.5 x 35.5 cm /
76 x 40 x 14 in

USA
Edward Zucca
Eighteenth Dynasty Television
Mahogany, ebony, poplar,
paper rush, gold leaf, paint.
Traditional joinery,
faux patinated, top piece
bronze-finished
129.5 x 86 x 107 cm /
51 x 34 x 42 in

184

USA
Edward Zucca
Mystery Robots Rip Off
the Rain Forest
Mahogany, maple and
poplar table.
Traditional joinery techniques,
painted
78.5x335x77.5cm/
31x132x30½

■ The Postmodernist idiom
continues to thrive, mixing materials,
colours, historical stylistic references,
ironical and narrative commentary.

USA
Garry Knox Bennett
Partner's Desk
Painted Colorcore,
aluminium, gold leaf
over wood
74x178x91cm/29x70x36in

■ Prominent makers recall
ocean-liner Art Deco,
emphasizing superb craftsmanship
and the sumptuous effects
of exotic wood veneers
and leather.
The sunburst detail
represents a trend towards
custom-made flooring
in interior design.

Holland
Dick Dankers
Chest of drawers, bird's-eye
maple veneer, traditional
cabinet-making techniques.
Winner of 1990 Dutch Classic
Design Prize

UK
John Makepeace
Eclipse II
Burr yew cabinet framed with
bog oak, holly interior
147x57x37cm
58x22½x14¾in (closed)

UK
Sinclair Till
Hand-cut linoleum floor
tile with sunburst, detail
of custom-designed
and laid floor
30x30cm/12x12in

USA
Wendell Castle
Triangle Buffet
Bird's-eye maple,
curly maple, maple
74x175x43cm / 29x69x17in
▼

Holland
Jan Siebers
Twenty-seven Point Five
Red leather and Oregon pine

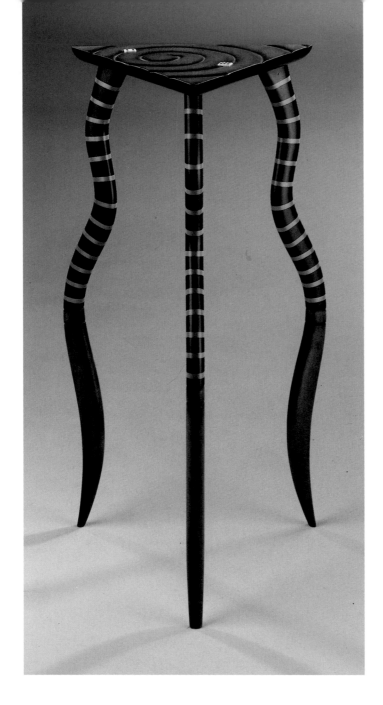

USA
Bob Trotman
Dancing Table (with Dice)
Cherry-wood table, traditional
joinery, lacquering, carving,
dice inlaid in top
65 x 33 x 33 cm / 25½ x 13 x 13 in

■ If these animated pieces
were human, they would dance.
Upholstered furniture
and interesting legs have
made a comeback.

Australia
**Christopher and Jennifer
Robertson**
Coil-sprung sofa in wandoo
and epoxy-coated steel,
upholstered in handwoven
wool doublecloth, Australian
National Gallery Collection,
Canberra
80 x 150 x 65 cm /
31½ x 60 x 25½ in

USA
Alex Locadia
Thomas's Promises
Fabric, glass, leather, metal
43 x 183 x 244 cm / 17 x 72 x 96 in

Holland
Bob Verheyden
Black and White
Chair, wool upholstery on
wood frame. Limited edition
85 x 45 x 40 cm /
33½ x 17¾ x 15¾ in

USA
Thomas Loeser
Chest Over Drawer
(and detail)
White oak, mahogany, paint
74x117x46cm / 29x46x18in

■ After hi-tech, low-tech.
Painted and carved 'country' furniture
(actually a sophisticated contemporary vernacular)
has a very wide appeal in a decade
which has replaced rampant consumerism
with ecological conscience.

USA
Bob Trotman
Chair with Leaves
Carved, bleached, dyed and
pigmented maple wood
79x58x53cm / 31x23x21in

UK
Howard Raybould
Bathroom cabinet, dowelling
and medium-density
fiberboard (MDF)
91cm / 36 in wide

France
Gérard Rigot
Armchair, carved and
painted wood
110x60x60cm /
43¼ x 23½ x 23½ in

France
Federica Matta
Seat
Polyester resin, moulded and
polyurethane-painted.
Limited edition
108x54x34cm /
42½ x 21¼ x 13¼ in

Finland
Sami Wirkkala
Treasure House
Whitewashed birch inlaid with
beech, black-coloured birch
inlaid with wenge. Made with
Reino Rutanen
46x32x30cm / 18x12½x12 in

■ Wooden furniture
with hidden secrets and subtle wit.
Richard Snyder invites us
to contemplate
'the strange and curious presents
from Kings, tsars and tribal chiefs
from the four corners of the earth
to a sultan encountered by Marco Polo
on his travels', his ideas
realized in carved and painted mahogany
and traditional techniques.

Germany
Dieter Zimmermann
Wood cupboard on wheels
180cm / 72 in

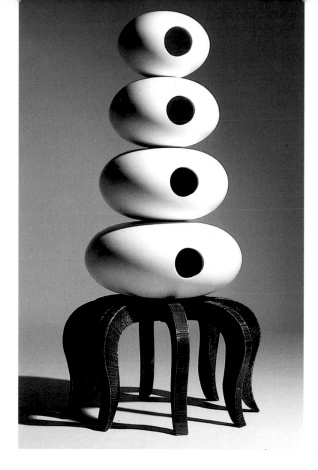

USA
Richard Snyder
Cabinet of the Ancient Squid
Lacquered wood
165x76cm / 65x30in

USA
Richard Snyder
Gift from the King of Nubia
Painted wood
200x125x30.5cm /
79x49x12in

USA
Richard Snyder
Cabinet of Four Wishes
Lacquered mahogany and
brass, Art Institute of
Chicago Collection
213x84x84cm / 84x33x33in

■ The cliché that the Germanic temperament is too serious is subverted here.
Stiletto Studios made a name with a supermarket-trolley chair;
Mülhaus and Leeser are versatile designers in various media;
Eisl is a consummate Modernist, integrating form, function, materials
and technique in inventive light constructions, furniture and
other objects.

Germany
Stiletto Studios
TV-Dinner
Television tube,
stainless-steel base,
light-bulb glass, top with
photo silk-screen etching.
Limited edition
52x45.5x56cm /
20½x18x22in

UK
Thomas Eisl
Aluminium, wood,
festoon bulbs
243cm / 96in

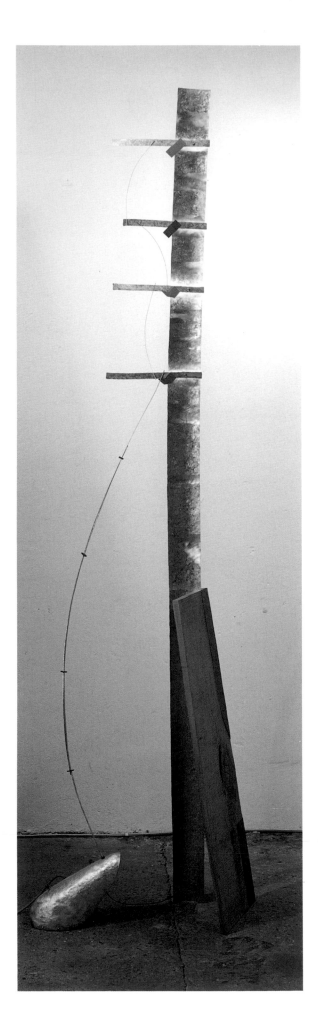

Germany
**Heike Mühlhaus
at Cocktail**
Ceramic mosaic and wood
mirror with light. Series of
ten, varied surface pattern
and lighting design
230x90cm/90x35in

Germany
Till Leeser
Bantu
Copper and stone lamp
200cm/79in high

Germany
Julia Lang and
Wolfgang Laubersheimer
Sheet-metal desk

■ Metal is still
a favoured material for
its constructional and surface
possibilities, but
here shedding
the stylistic excesses
of 'postholocaust'
works.

USA
Gloria Kisch
Waffled
Aluminium and glass table.
Chair, epoxy over steel and
rollers
74x152, 96.5x53x43cm/
29x60in, 38x21x17in

Australia
Bern Emmerichs
C'erà Una Volta
Steel and painted ceramic
mosaic chairs made with
Gerhard Emmerichs
91.5 cm / 36 in

UK
Tom Dixon
Crown chairs
Gilded metal. Limited edition
91.5 cm / 36 in

◀ France
Marco de Gueltzl
(Inset)
Table Ronde
Sandblasted glass and
brushed steel
75x130cm / 29½x51 in

◀ UK
André Dubreuil
Chest of drawers,
welded and beaten metal
107cm / 42 in wide

France
Peter Keene
*La Tour Eiffel, Hot Tea
and Television*
Television with twisted
metal 'sarcophagus' and
robotic tea-machine

UK
Ron Arad
A.Y.O.R.
Stainless-steel and
lead chair.
One-off but repeatable
92x49x55cm /
36¼x19¼x21½ in

Australia
Mark Douglass
*Fishtank Desk and
Low Voltage Light*
Bent and cast glass, steel and
stainless steel
71x230x110cm /
28x90½x43¼ in

■ Prominent names
in metal furniture
continue to offer
heightened drama
in their treatment
of form, surface
and allusion.

FURNITURE **199**

Australia
Gay Hawkes
Driftwood chair
c.164cm / 66in

USA
Forrest Myers
Cardinal Richelieu
Anodized aluminium
99x89x81cm / 39x35x32in

Czechoslovakia
Jiří Pelcl
Private Universe
Iron and fur chair
140 cm / 56 in

UK
Jon Mills
Castle Cupboard
Beaten metal, constructed
182 cm / 72 in high

Finland
Stefan Lindfors
Throne for Gorbachev
Bamboo. Spines can move
mechanically
c. 180 cm / 72 in

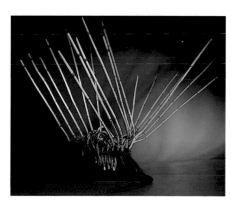

■ 'Primitivism',
in terms of forms
and use of materials,
is an international theme
deployed to powerful
metaphorical effect.
A Lindfors piece from 1988
helped establish him
as a key new talent
in Scandinavia.

Germany
Paul Zimmermann
Rusted-steel garden gate

Czechoslovakia
Alfred Habermann Jnr
Door with six relief-worked
copper panels for Novy
Rychnov church

◀ Switzerland
Walter Suter
'Bosco'
Hand-forged and welded,
varnished oven, brass details.
Made to order, several
designs available
140 cm / 55 in

■ Because of their training and traditions,
architectural metalworkers (here and overleaf) offer exceptional quality
which architects and interior designers are increasingly acknowledging.
As with stained glass, the Germans dominated this area
until a wider renaissance dawned a decade ago.

Japan
Takayoshi Komine
(Opposite inset, detail)
Rail of Dragon
Iron exterior stair-rail
c.750 cm / 300 in overall

Germany
Achim Kühn
Remembrance plaque (detail)
for the restored French
Church,
Platz der Akademie, Berlin
200 x 200 cm / 80 x 80 in
overall

USA
Albert Paley
Forged and fabricated,
monochromed steel
garden gate
183x122cm / 72x48 in

Germany
Hermann Gradinger
Forged-steel garden gate
120 x 166 cm / 47 x 65½ in

Germany
Manfred Bergmeister
Forged-steel gates (detail)
c. 240 cm / 98 in

■ The contrasting benches, one in fibreglass
commissioned in a batch of twenty-four for a garden festival,
the other manifestly unique and 'eccentric', typify
the spectrum of craft activity today.

►
UK
Richard La Trobe-Bateman
'Green' oak and
stainless-steel footbridge
10m/11yds long

UK
Floris van den Broecke
Outdoor bench reinforced
with handlaid glass,
polyester, on steel frame.
Batch production
78x101x122cm/
30½x40x48in

UK
Julienne Dolphin-Wilding
Eccentrics
Cotswold stone, granite,
Yorkshire stone, flag stone,
semi-dry stone
walling technique
150x150x250cm/
60x60x246in

Italy
Wolfgang Sattler
Prototype bird-box made
for inaugural Mus'ign project
(Anthologie Quartett/Design
Connections . . .)

Sattler's birdbox,
made in a limited edition
by Anthologie Quartett,
also indicates
the increasing crossovers
between design and craft,
a bridge (like that
between art and craft)
that is currently proving
its strength.

206 FURNITURE

►
UK
**Jim Partridge and
Liz Walmsley**
(Inset)
Oak Bridge 1, Ardtornish
Green oak, carved.
One of a series of bridges
and seats made for
the Ardtornish estate
50x200cm/20x79in

INFORMATION

BIOGRAPHIES AND INDEX OF CONTRIBUTORS

Entries in the Information Section have been specially researched for this book. Details correct at time of going to press.

Mike Abbott p.96
Born 1963, Ferraby, East Yorkshire, UK. Educated: Newcastle Polytechnic; Royal College of Art, London. Exhibitions: various, in Western Europe and Japan.

Yoh Akiyama p.50
Born 1953, Shimonoseki, Japan. Educated: Kyoto Municipal University of Art. Exhibitions: numerous, in Japan, the USA, Italy and Belgium. Solo exhibition at Gallery Koyanagi, Tokyo in 1989. Awards: include the Kazuo Yagi Prize for Contemporary Ceramics, 1988. Collections: Museum of Modern Art (Shiga) and other major museum collections in Japan and Italy. Galleries: Gallery Koyanagi, Tokyo.

Olga da Amaral p.74
Born 1932, Bogotá, Colombia. Educated: Colegio Mayor de Cundinamarca, Bogotá; Cranbrook Academy of Art, Bloomfield Hills MI, USA. Exhibitions: numerous, international. Solo exhibition at Allrich Gallery, Santa Fé NM in 1989. Collections: Museo de Arte Moderno (Bogotá), Metropolitan Museum of Art (New York) and other major museum collections in the USA and Western Europe. Galleries: Bellas Artes Gallery, Santa Fé and New York. Photographic credit: Diego Amaral/Zona.

Iene Ambar p.108
Born 1951, Jakarta, Indonesia. Educated: Koninklijke Akademie voor Kunst en Vormgeving, 's-Hertogenbosch; Gerrit Rietveld Akademie, Amsterdam. Exhibitions: various since 1982 in Western Europe, Canada and Australia. Solo exhibition at Artoteek Zuidoost, Amsterdam in 1989. Collections: Museum Boymans-van Beuningen (Rotterdam) and other major museum collections in Holland. Galleries: Galerie de Witte Voet, Amsterdam. Photographic credit: Tom Haartsen.

Ron Arad p.199
Born 1953, Tel Aviv, Israel. Educated: Jerusalem Academy of Art; Architectural Association School of Architecture, London. Founded One Off Ltd with Dennis Groves and Caroline Thorman in 1981. Exhibitions: various, solo in the UK, Germany, Italy and Spain. One Off exhibition in Spain in 1990. Commissions: include designs for the new Tel Aviv Opera House with C. Norton and S. McAdam. Collections: Vitra Design Museum (Weil am Rhein), etc. Galleries: One Off Ltd, London.

Arne Åse p.24
Born 1940, Gaular (Sunnfjord), Norway. Educated: Bergen School of Art and Design. Teaching: since 1987, Ceramics Professor, National Institute of Art and Design, Oslo. Exhibitions: various, international. Awards: most recently, Gold Medal, Munich, 1989. Collections: the Oslo, Bergen and Trondheim Museums of Applied Arts in Norway, the National Museum (Stockholm) and Rohsska Museum (Gothenburg) in Sweden and other major museum collections in Scandinavia and the UK.

Rushton Aust p.15
Born 1958, Kidlington, Oxfordshire, UK. Educated: Derby Lonsdale College of Higher Education; Royal College of Art, London. Exhibitions: since 1979, in the UK, Germany, the USA and Japan. Solo exhibition at Contemporary Applied Arts, London, in 1990. Collections: Crafts Council Collection (London). Galleries: Contemporary Applied Arts and Crafts Council Shop at the V&A, London. Photographic credit: John McCarthy.

Rudy Autio p.9
Born 1926, Butte MO, USA. Educated: Montana State University, Bozeman; Washington State University, Pullman. Exhibitions: numerous, in the USA, Western Europe and Scandinavia. Collections: American Craft Museum (New York), Brooklyn Museum (Brooklyn), Portland Art Museum, Toledo Art Museum and other major museum collections in the USA, Scandinavia and the UK. Galleries: Dorothy Weiss, CA and the Greenberg Gallery. Photographic credit: The Greenberg Gallery.

Ralph Bacerra p.29
Born 1938, Garden Grove CA, USA. Educated: Chouinard Art School, Los Angeles CA. Teaching: since 1983, at Otis Parsons School of Design. Exhibitions: various, mainly in the USA, also in Japan. Solo exhibition at Garth Clark Gallery, New York in 1990. Collections: American Craft Museum, Cooper-Hewitt Museum, Smithsonian Institution (New York), Renwick Gallery, Smithsonian Institution (Washington D.C), Everson Museum of Art (Syracuse), Los Angeles County Museum of Art (Los Angeles) and other major museum collections in the USA and Japan. Galleries: Garth Clark Gallery, New York and Los Angeles. Photographic credit: John White/Garth Clark Gallery.

Gijs Bakker p.90
Born 1942, Amersfoort, Holland. Educated: Instituut voor Kunstnijverheidsonderwijs (now Gerrit Rietveld Akademie), Amsterdam.

Teaching: since 1987, senior lecturer at the Akademie Industriële Vormgeving Eindhoven. Exhibitions: numerous since 1966 in Western and Eastern Europe and the USA. Solo exhibitions at Helen Drutt Gallery, USA, Galerie Ra, Amsterdam and Centraal Museum, Utrecht in 1989. Collections: Stedelijk Museum (Amsterdam), Haags Gemeentemuseum (The Hague), Museum Boymans-Van Beuningen (Rotterdam) and other major international museum collections. Galleries: Galerie Ra, Amsterdam and Helen Drutt Gallery, Philadelphia. Photographic credit: Ton Werkhoven.

Gordon Baldwin p.38
Born 1932, Lincoln, UK. Educated: Lincoln School of Art; Central School of Art and Design, London. Teaching: Central School of Art and Design, London; Eton College. Exhibitions: numerous, international. Solo exhibitions at Hetjens Museum, Düsseldorf and Galerie Bowig, Hanover in 1990. Collections: Victoria and Albert Museum, Crafts Council Collection (London), Cleveland Crafts Centre (Middlesbrough), Ulster Museum (Belfast) and other major museum collections in Western Europe, Australia, the USA and Scandinavia. Galleries: Contemporary Applied Arts, London and Galerie Bowig, Hanover. Photographic credit: David Cripps.

Phillip Baldwin p.100
Born 1953, USA. Educated: Southern Illinois University, Carbondale IL. Exhibitions: various since 1976, mainly in the USA, also in the UK and Eastern Europe. Commissions: the American Craft Council 'Gold Medal' in 1987. Photographic credit: Wayne Goldsmith.

James W. Bassler p.55
Born 1933, Santa Monica CA, USA. Educated: University of California, Los Angeles CA. Teaching: since 1982, University of California, Los Angeles CA. Exhibitions: various, in the USA. Galleries: Brendan Walter Gallery, Santa Monica CA. Photographic credit: Tim Colohan.

François Bauchet p.182
Born 1948. Educated: École des Beaux Arts de Saint-Étienne. Exhibitions: various, including the VIA (Valorisation de l'Innovation dans l'Ameublement) at the Musée des Arts Décoratifs, Paris in 1990. Commissions: include designs for the reception area of the Musée d'Art et d'Industrie de Saint-Étienne and furnishings for the Abbaye de Léoncet in the Drôme. Galleries: Galerie Néotu, Paris.

Pierre Bayle p.34
Born 1945, France. Educated: CET, Castelnaudry, France. Exhibitions:

numerous, mainly in France, also in Western Europe and Japan. Solo exhibition at Galerie D.M. Sarver, Paris in 1990. Awards: most recently the Prix d'Achat, Faenza, 1987. Collections: Musée des Arts Décoratifs (Paris), Musée National de Céramique (Sèvres) and other major museum collections in western Europe and Australia. Galleries: Galerie D.M. Sarver, Paris and Galerie La Main, Brussels.

Alain Begou p.116
Born 1941, Crest, Drôme, France. Educated: apprenticeships at Verrerie de Biot and Verrerie d'Allex, Drôme. Exhibitions: various, in Western Europe, the USA, Japan and Korea. Solo exhibition at Galerie Place des Arts, Montpellier in 1990. Collections: Musée des Arts Décoratifs (Paris), Musée des Arts Décoratifs (Bordeaux), Musée de Sèvres, Musée du Verre (Sars-Poteries) and other major museum collections in France and the USA. Galleries: include Galerie Place des Arts, Montpellier, Galerie Nadir, Annecy, Galerie Epona, Galerie d'Amon, Paris, Galerie Momiron, Biot.

Micheline de Bellefroid p.165
Born 1927, Balen-Wezel, Mol, Belgium. Educated: École Nationale Supérieure d'Architecture et des Arts Visuels, La Cambre, Belgium. Teaching: from 1966, professor at the École Nationale Supérieure d'Architecture et des Arts Visuels. Exhibitions: numerous exhibitions in Western Europe, Denmark and the USA. Collections: Musée de Mariemont, Bibliothèque Royale (Brussels) and other major museum and library collections in Western Europe. Photographic credit: Faider.

Stella Benjamin p.73
Born 1933, Sidcup, Kent, UK. Educated: worked with Bryan Illsley (see below) and the jeweler, painter and weaver, Breon O'Casey, at St Ives, Cornwall. Exhibitions: since 1978, mainly in the UK, also in Japan. Solo exhibition at Contemporary Applied Arts, London in 1990. Collections: Holburne of Menstrie Museum, Bath. Galleries: Contemporary Applied Arts, London. Photographic credit: David Cripps.

Garry Knox Bennett p.185
Born 1934, Alameda CA, USA. Educated: California College of Arts and Crafts, Oakland CA. Exhibitions: numerous, in the USA only. Solo exhibitions at Franklin Parrasch Gallery, New York and Hand and the Spirit Gallery, Seattle, etc. in the USA in 1990. Collections: Renwick Gallery, Smithsonian Institution (Washington D.C.), San Francisco Museum of Modern Art (San Francisco), Museum

of Fine Arts (Boston) and other major museum collections in the USA. Galleries: Franklin Parrasch Gallery, New York and Snyderman Gallery, Philadelphia. Photographic credit: Greg Benson.

Manfred Bergmeister p.205
Born 1927, Ebersberg near Munich, Germany. Educated: Meisterschule für Kunstschmiede, Munich. Exhibitions: various, in Western Europe and North America. Participant in numerous international conferences and symposia. Many major commissions.

Mary Bero p.69
Born 1949, Two Rivers W1, USA. Educated: Stout State University, Menomonie WI. Exhibitions: various, mainly in the USA.

Jilli Blackwood p.57
Born 1965, Glasgow, UK. Educated: Glasgow School of Art. Teaching: Glasgow School of Art (1988); Scottish College of Textiles, Galashiels (1989). Exhibitions: various, mainly in the UK, also in Holland and Germany. Collections: Aberdeen Art Gallery and Glasgow Museum and Art Gallery, Scotland. Galleries: Crafts Council Shop at the V&A, London. Photographic credit: Patrick Shanahan.

Brian Blanthorn p.113
Born 1957, Manchester, UK. Educated: Rochdale College of Art, Stourbridge; Royal College of Art, London. Exhibitions: numerous, international. Awards: include a Corning Glass Prize, 1983. Collections: Victoria and Albert Museum (London), Broadfield House Glass Museum (West Midlands), Ulster Museum (Belfast) and other major museum collections in the UK, Germany and the USA. Galleries: Crafts Council Shop at the V&A, Wilson and Gough, London and Galerie d'Amon, Paris. Photographic credit: Masaaki Sekiya.

Liv Blavårp p.92
Born 1956. Educated: National Institute of Art and Design, Oslo, Norway; Royal College of Art, London. Exhibitions: since 1982, international. Collections: Kunstindustrimuseet (Oslo, Bergen, Trondheim and Gothenburg) and other major museum collections in Scandinavia. Galleries: Kunstnerforbundet, Oslo and V&V, Vienna. Photographic credit: Roger Fredrics.

Sonja Blomdahl p.116
Born 1952, Waltham MA, USA. Educated: Massachusetts College of Art, Boston MA; Glass School, Orrefors, Sweden. Exhibitions: various, international. Solo exhibitions at Vespermann Gallery, Atlanta GA and Sarah Squeri Gallery, Cincinnati OH in

1990. Collections: Corning Museum of Glass (Corning) and other major museum collections in the USA and Czechoslovakia. Galleries: Vespermann Gallery, Atlanta GA, Sarah Squeri Gallery, Cincinnati OH, Traver Sutton Gallery/William Traver Gallery, Seattle WA and Wilson and Gough, London. Photographic credit: Michael Seidl.

Jan Blum p.119
Educated: Rozelle School of Visual Arts, Sydney, Australia; Sydney College of the Arts; Pilchuk School and Glass Center, Stanwood WA, USA. Exhibitions: mainly in Australia, also in Germany and Holland. Collections: City Art Gallery (Wagga Wagga), Australian National Gallery (Canberra) and other major museum collections in Australia, Denmark and the USA. Galleries: Meat Market Craft Centre, Melbourne. Photographic credit: Rebecca Thomas.

Philip Boas p.63
Born 1949, Jakarta, Indonesia. Educated: Gerrit Rietveld Akademie, Amsterdam, Holland; Rijksakademie voor Beeldende Kunsten, Amsterdam. Exhibitions: various, in Western Europe and Indonesia. Collections: Stedelijk Museum (Amsterdam), Rijksmuseum (The Hague) and other major museum collections in Holland. Galleries: Néotu and Étamine, Paris and Elders Special Productions and Stichting, Kunst & Bedrijf, Amsterdam.

Susan Bosence p.61
Born 1913, UK. Educated: learned from the pioneer British blockprinters, Phyllis Barron and Dorothy Larcher. Teaching: includes visiting lectureships at Camberwell School of Art and Crafts, London and West Surrey College of Art and Design, Farnham. Exhibitions: various, in the UK and the USA. Solo exhibition at Arts Centre, Plymouth in 1990. Collections: Victoria and Albert Museum, Crafts Council Collection (London) and Crafts Study Centre, Holburne of Menstrie Museum (Bath). Galleries: Crafts Council Shop at the V&A, London. Photographic credit: Richard Davies.

Rudolf Bott p.101
Born 1956, Stockstadt am Main, Germany. Educated: Zeichenakademie Hanau; Akademie der Bildenden Künste, Munich, Germany. Exhibitions: various since 1982 in Germany, the UK and the USA. Awards: Dannerpreis, Germany in 1990. Galleries: Galerie Rezac, Chicago. Photographic credit: Jochen Grün.

Kristoffel Boudens p.177
Born 1958, Bruges, Belgium. Educated: after completing studies in fine arts, lettercutting apprenticeship with his brother, Pieter Boudens (see

below), and calligraphy with Gaynor Goffe and Tom Perkins (see below). Teaching: currently teaching lettering at the Royal Academy of Fine Arts, Antwerp.

Pieter Boudens p.176
Born 1955, Belgium. Educated: studied with his calligrapher father, Jef Boudens, Sepp Jakob in Germany, David Kindersley (see below) in the UK and Jean-Claude Lamborot (see below) in France. Exhibitions: various. Photographic credit: Jan Demylle.

Marsha Brady p.173
Educated: Northern University of Colorado. Teaching: since 1979, calligraphy instructor in the Graphics Communications Department, California State University, Long Beach CA. Exhibitions: various, in the USA, Eastern and Western Europe. Galleries: ITC Galleries, New York.

Michael Brennand-Wood p.69
Born 1952, Bury, Lancashire, UK. Educated: Bolton College of Art; Manchester Polytechnic; Birmingham Polytechnic. Teaching: currently part-time lecturer at Goldsmiths College, London. Exhibitions: numerous, international. Solo exhibition at Galerie Ra, Amsterdam in 1990. Awards: include a Fine Art Award, 1989, International Textile Competition, Kyoto. Collections: Victoria and Albert Museum, Crafts Council Collection (London) and other major museum collections in the UK, Australia and Japan. Galleries: Contemporary Textile Gallery, London and Galerie Ra, Amsterdam. Photographic credit: Chris Gomershall.

Alison Britton p.39
Born 1949, London, UK. Educated: Leeds College of Art; Central School of Art and Design, London; Royal College of Art, London. Teaching: currently tutor at the Royal College of Art, London. Exhibitions: numerous, international. Solo exhibitions at Contemporary Applied Arts, London and Aberystwyth Arts Centre (and touring) in 1990–91. Collections: Victoria and Albert Museum, Crafts Council Collection (London), Ulster Museum (Belfast), Shipley Art Gallery (Gateshead), Cleveland Crafts Centre (Middlesbrough) and other major international museum collections. Galleries: Contemporary Applied Arts, London. Photographic credit: David Cripps and Andrew Greaves (portrait on p.15).

Caroline Broadhead p.56
Born 1950, Leeds, West Yorkshire, UK. Educated: Leicester School of Art; Central School of Art and Design, London. Teaching: currently at

Middlesex Polytechnic, London. Exhibitions: various, international. Collections: Crafts Council Collection, Worshipful Company of Goldsmiths (London), Shipley Art Gallery (Gateshead) and other major museum collections in the UK, Holland, Israel, Australia and Japan. Galleries: Contemporary Applied Arts, London. Photographic credit: David Cripps/ *Crafts* magazine.

Floris van den Broecke p.206
Born 1945, Harlingen, Holland. Educated: Akademie voor Beeldende Kunsten, Arnhem; Royal College of Art, London. Teaching: since 1985, Professor of Furniture at Royal College of Art, London. In 1990, Visiting Professor at Fachhochschule, Düsseldorf. Exhibitions: various, in the UK and Holland. Collections: Crafts Council Collection (London) and Van Reekum Museum (Apeldoorn). Galleries: Contemporary Applied Arts, London. Photographic credit: National Garden Festival, Gateshead.

Pini Brokmann pp.14, 151
Born 1956, Bielefeld, Germany. Educated: Fachhochschule, Bielefeld, Germany. Exhibitions: in Germany only. Galleries: Anthologie Quartett, Bad Essen. Photographic credit: Klaus-Dieter Braun.

Sigurd Bronger p.86
Born 1957, Oslo, Norway. Educated: Elvebakken Goldsmiths School, Oslo; Vakschool, Schoonhoven, Holland. Exhibitions: various since 1980, international. Collections: Museums of Applied Art in Oslo, Bergen and Trondheim in Norway and other major museum collections in Scandinavia and the USA. Galleries: Galerie Ra, Amsterdam and Kunstnerforbundet, Oslo. Photographic credit: Terje Agnalt.

Denis Brown p.175
Educated: College of Marketing and Design, Dublin; Roehampton Institute, London. Exhibitions: since 1988, mainly in Ireland and the UK, also in Germany. Awards: include the California Gold Medal for craftsmanship of outstanding merit and a Crafts Council of Ireland Award, 1989. Commissions: most recently (1991) *The Great Book of Clashganna*.

Santiago Brugalla pp.160, 162
Born 1929, Barcelona, Spain. Educated: School of Arts and Crafts, Barcelona; Escuela Massana, Barcelona. Apprenticed in bookbinding to his father, Emilio Brugalla. Exhibitions: numerous, in Spain, France, Switzerland and the USA. Collections: Museo Picasso, Fondation Joan Miró, Biblioteca de Catalunya (Barcelona) and other major museum

and library collections in Spain and the USA. Represented by: Center for Book Arts, New York and Designer Bookbinders, London.

Jaroslava Brychtova p.129
Born 1924, Železný Brod, Czechoslovakia. Educated: Academy of Applied Arts and Academy of Fine Arts, Prague. Exhibitions: numerous, international; works with her husband, Stanislav Libensky. Collections: Uměleckoprůmyslové Muzeum (Prague), Muzeum Skla a Bižuterie (Jablonec nad Nisou) and many other major international museum collections. Galleries: Heller Gallery, New York, Habatat Galleries, Boca Raton FL and Galerie Clara Scremini, Paris.

Werner Bünck p.99
Born 1943, Einswarden in Oldenburg, Germany. Educated: Werkkunstschule, Düsseldorf. Teaching: since 1981, lecturer in metalwork at the Fachhochschule, Hildesheim. Exhibitions: numerous, international. Awards: include the Exempla-Preis, Munich, 1977. Collections: Kunstgewerbemuseum (Berlin), Museum für Kunsthandwerk (Frankfurt), Kunstgewerbemuseum (Cologne) and other major museum collections in Germany, the UK and the USA. Photographic credit: G. Sudgen.

Pauline Burbidge p.64
Born 1950, Bridport, Dorset, UK. Educated: London College of Fashion; St Martin's School of Art, London. Exhibitions: various, in the UK, Gibraltar and the USA. Solo exhibitions at Ruskin Crafts Gallery, Sheffield and Costume and Textile Museum, Nottingham in 1989. Founder-member of Quilt Art in the UK. Collections: Victoria and Albert Museum, Crafts Council Collection (London), Shipley Art Gallery (Gateshead) and other collections in the UK and the USA. Galleries: Contemporary Applied Arts, Contemporary Textile Gallery and Crafts Council Shop at the V&A, London. Photographic credit: Keith Tidball.

Gordon Burnett p.106
Born 1951, Fraserburgh, Scotland, UK. Educated: Grays School of Art, Aberdeen, Scotland; Royal College of Art, London; Camberwell School of Art and Crafts, London. Teaching: since 1988, Head of Jewelry, Grays School of Art. Exhibitions: various, including the UK, Germany, the USA, Japan. Commissions: numerous commissions in the UK, also in Holland and Qatar. In 1990, a clock for the Scottish Development Agency. Galleries: Miharudo Gallery, Tokyo. Photographic credit: Masaaki Sekiya.

Daisy Cameron p.139
Born New Zealand. A member of the Te Ati Haunai a Paparangi tribe.

Ken Campbell p.170
Born 1939, London, UK. Educated: printing apprenticeship, taught by Harry Beck and Rolf Brandt; studied at London College of Printing. Since 1962, produces his own books and also works as a painter, designer, printmaker, visualizer and poet. Exhibitions: various, in Western Europe and the USA. Solo exhibitions at Granary Books, New York and Victoria and Albert Museum, London in 1990. Collections: Victoria and Albert Museum (London), Library of Congress (Washington D.C.) and other major museum and library collections in the UK. Galleries: Granary Books, New York.

Lida Lopes Cardozo p.176
Born 1954, Holland. Educated: Royal Academy, The Hague. Met David Kindersley (see below) in 1975, joined his workshop in 1976, married him. They jointly run the workshop and a publishing company, Cardozo Kindersley.

William Carlson p.130
Born 1950, Dover OH, USA. Education: Cleveland Institute of Art OH; Alfred University NY; Pilchuk School and Glass Center, Stanwood WA. Teaching: currently Professor of Art, University of Illinois. Exhibitions: numerous, international. Solo exhibition at Betsy Rosenfield Gallery, Chicago IL in 1990. Collections: Corning Museum of Glass (Corning), Leigh Yawkey Woodson Art Museum (Wausau), Metropolitan Museum of Art (New York) and other major museum collections in the USA, Switzerland and Japan. Galleries: Betsy Rosenfield Gallery, Chicago IL, Heller Gallery, New York, Maurine Littleton Gallery, Washington D.C., Habatat Galleries, Farmington Hills MI and Holsten Galleries, Palm Beach FL. Photographic credit: Betsy Rosenfield Gallery.

Nino Caruso p.39
Teaching: many courses and workshops in the USA, Canada and Japan. Exhibitions: numerous, in Italy, the USA, Canada, Korea and Japan. Solo exhibitions at Piazza delle Conserve, Cesenatico and Santo Stefano di Camastra, Messina in 1989. Awards: numerous. Commissions: many public environmental and sculptural works. Collections: Museo Internazionale della Ceramica (Faenza), Museum of Modern Art (Tokyo) and other major international museum collections. Galleries: Galleria Incontro d'Arte, Rome. Photographic credit: Massimiliano Ruta.

Claudi Casanovas i Sarsanedas p.43
Born 1956, Barcelona, Spain. Educated: Escuela Massana, Barcelona. Exhibitions: numerous in Western Europe, Scandinavia and Japan. Solo exhibitions at Galleri Lejonet, Stockholm and Galeria Caramany, Girona in 1990. Awards: include a Grand Prix at Vallauris in 1986. Collections: Museo de Ceramica (Madrid), Museo de Cerámica (Manises) and other major museum collections in Western Europe and Sweden. Galleries: Galerie Besson, London, etc. Photographic credit: Hisao Susuki.

Pino Castagna p.51
Born 1932, Castelgomberto, Vicenza, Italy. Exhibitions: numerous, in Western Europe and Japan. Solo exhibition at Palazzo Pisani, Lonigo in 1990. Galleries: Galleria Dé Serpenti, Rome and Galleria Forni, Bologna.

Wendell Castle pp.178, 187
Born 1932, Emporia KA, USA. Educated: University of Kansas, Lawrence KA. Teaching: since 1984, Artist-in-Residence at Rochester Institute of Technology. Exhibitions: numerous, mainly in the USA, also in Western Europe. Solo exhibition at Delaware Art Museum and Virginia Museum of Fine Arts in 1990. Awards: include a Golden Plate from American Academy of Achievement, 1988. Collections: Metropolitan Museum of Art, American Craft Museum (New York), Renwick Gallery, Smithsonian Institution (Washington D.C.), Museum of Fine Arts (Boston) and other major museum collections in the USA and Norway. Galleries: Snyderman Gallery, Philadelphia PA, Alexander Milliken Gallery, New York, Hokin/Kaufman Gallery, Chicago IL and Judy Youens Perception Galleries, Houston TX. Photographic credit: Calgari Corp.

John Cederquist p.184
Born 1946, Altadena CA, USA. Educated: California State University at Long Beach CA. Teaching: 1976–86 at Saddleback Community College, Mission Viejo CA. Exhibitions: various, mainly in the USA, also in the UK. Collections: Renwick Gallery, Smithsonian Institution (Washington D.C.), Museum of Fine Arts (Boston), Craft and Folk Art Museum (Los Angeles) and other major museum collections in the USA and the UK. Galleries: Franklin Parrasch Gallery, New York. Photographic credit: Mike Sasso.

Anton Cepka p.87
Exhibitions: various, in Czechoslovakia, Western Europe, Canada, Japan and Australia. Awards: include the Ehrenring der Gesellschaft für

Goldschmiedekunst in 1990. Galleries: Galerie am Graben, Vienna.

Claude Champy p.42
Born 1944, Paris, France. Educated: École des Métiers d'Art. Exhibitions: many, in Western Europe and Japan. Solo exhibition at Gallery Ueda Ginza, Tokyo in 1990. Awards: Grand Prix from the Suntory Museum, Tokyo in 1988. Collections: Musée des Arts Décoratifs (Paris) and many others. Galleries: Galerie D.M. Sarver, Paris, Galerie Charlotte Hennig, Darmstadt and Galerie Ueda Ginza, Tokyo.

Kai Chan p.90
Born 1940, China. Emigrated to Canada 1966. Educated: Ontario College of Art; Banff Centre School of Fine Arts, Canada. Exhibitions: numerous since 1972, international. Solo exhibitions at Prime Canadian Crafts, Toronto, and Gallery Lynda Greenberg, Ottawa in 1990. Collections: Ontario Craft Council Collection and other major museum collections in Canada and Norway. Galleries: Prime Canadian Crafts, Toronto, Gallery Lynda Greenberg, Ottawa, Galerie Trois Points, Montreal and Galerie Ra, Amsterdam. Photographic credit: K. Kembry.

Peter Chang p.93
Born 1944, London, UK. Educated: Liverpool School of Art; Slade School of Fine Art, University College, London. Exhibitions: since 1984 as a jeweler, in the UK, Holland, France and the USA. Collections: Crafts Council Collection (London), National Museums of Scotland and Aberdeen Art Gallery. Galleries: Contemporary Applied Arts, London, Scottish Gallery, Edinburgh, Helen Drutt Gallery, PA and Galerie Ra, Amsterdam. Photographic credit: B.J. Santos-Shaw.

Édouard Chapallaz p.33
Born 1921, Yverdon, Switzerland. Educated: École de Céramique de Chavennes-Renens. Exhibitions: numerous, international. Awards: include a Grand Prix for applied arts from the Fondation Vaudoise in 1988. Collections: major international museum collections. Photographic credit: Peter Friedli.

Peter Chatwin p.150
Born 1945, Birmingham, UK. Educated: Birmingham College of Art and Design. Formed partnership with Pamela Martin (see below) in 1981. Exhibitions: various since 1981, in Western Europe, the USA and Japan. Collections: Victoria and Albert Museum, Crafts Council Collection (London), Shipley Art Gallery (Gateshead), Ulster Museum (Belfast), City Museum and Art Gallery (Birmingham) and other major

museum collections in the UK and Japan. Galleries: Crafts Council Shop at the V&A, London, Oxford Gallery, Oxford and Hand and the Spirit, Scottsdale AR. Photographic credit: Keith Tidball.

Dale Chihuly p.125
Born 1941, Tacoma WA, USA. Educated: University of Washington, Seattle WA; University of Wisconsin, Madison WI; Rhode Island School of Design, Providence RI. Exhibitions: numerous, international. Solo exhibitions at Azabu Museum, Tokyo and at Hudson River Museum, Yonkers NY in 1990. Awards: include an Honorary Doctorate from the California College of Arts and Crafts, Oakland CA (1988). Collections: American Craft Museum, Cooper-Hewitt Museum, Metropolitan Museum of Art (New York), Renwick Gallery, Smithsonian Institution (Washington D.C.), Corning Museum of Art (Corning) and many other major international museum collections. Represented by: Chihuly Studio, Seattle WA.

Chunghi Choo p.99
Born 1938, Inchon, Korea. Educated: Ewha Women's University, Seoul; Cranbrook Academy of Art, Bloomfield Hills MI, USA. Teaching: University of Iowa, Iowa City IA. Exhibitions: various, mainly in the USA, also in Western Europe. Collections: American Craft Museum, Cooper-Hewitt Museum, Smithsonian Institution, Museum of Modern Art, Metropolitan Museum of Art (New York) and other major museum collections in the USA, France and the UK.

Theodora Chorafa p.41
Born 1959, London, UK; now lives in Greece. Educated: Camberwell School of Art and Crafts, London; Centro di Addestramento Professionale, Faenza, Italy; École des Arts Décoratifs, Geneva. Exhibitions: since 1983, in Western and Eastern Europe. Collections: Musée des Ursulines (Maçon) and Conseil Général de l'Yonne (Auxerre), France. Galleries: ORA Gallery, Athens.

Brian Clarke p.135
Born 1953, Oldham, Lancashire, UK. Educated: Oldham School of Art; Burnley College of Art; North Devon College, Bideford. Commissions: numerous stained glass works in the UK (including the new Stansted Airport), Germany, Saudi Arabia and Japan. Many exhibitions of stained glass designs; also paintings.

Ewan Clayton p.173
Educated: St Andrews University, Scotland; Roehampton Institute, London. Teaching: Lecturer at

Roehampton Institute, London. Exhibitions: various, in Europe and North America. Commissions: include work for the British Royal family, the College of Arms, University College at Buckingham and the British Broadcasting Corporation in the UK. Also works as a consultant for the Xerox corporation at their Palo Alto Research Center CA, USA. Photographic credit: Jeanne Masoero.

Jane Burch Cochran p.69
Educated: Centre College of Kentucky, Danville KY; Cincinnati Art Academy, Cincinnati OH, USA. Exhibitions: various, mainly in the USA, also in Japan. Solo exhibition at Triangle Gallery, Lexington KY in 1990. Galleries: Great American Gallery, Atlanta GA, Mariposa Gallery, Santa Fé NM and Albuquerque NM, and Triangle Gallery, Lexington KY.

Susan Cohn p.90
Born 1952, Australia. Educated: Royal Melbourne Institute of Technology; Swinburne Institute of Technology, Melbourne. Exhibitions: mainly in Australia, also in Germany, Holland and the UK. Solo exhibition at City Gallery, Melbourne in 1991. Collections: Australian National Gallery (Canberra), Art Gallery of Victoria (Melbourne), Powerhouse Museum (Sydney) and other major museum collections in Australia. Photographic credit: Kate Gollings.

David Colwell p.181
Born 1944, Surbiton, Surrey, UK. Educated: Kingston School of Art, Kingston-upon-Thames; Royal College of Art, London. Exhibitions: various, in the UK only. Collections: Victoria and Albert Museum (London) and Temple Newsam House (Leeds). Commissions: in 1990, seating for the West Wing Picture Gallery, National Museum of Wales. Galleries: Contemporary Applied Arts and David Colwell, London.

Lia Cook p.65
Born 1942, Ventura CA, USA. Educated: University of California, Berkeley CA. Teaching: Professor of Art at California College of Arts and Crafts, Oakland CA. Exhibitions: numerous, international. Solo exhibition at National Academy of Sciences, Washington D.C. in 1990. Awards: include an Excellence Award at the International Textile Competition '89, Kyoto. Collections: Renwick Gallery, Smithsonian Institution (Washington D.C.), Metropolitan Museum, Museum of Modern Art, American Crafts Museum (New York) and other major museum collections in the USA, Denmark and France. Galleries: Allrich Gallery, San Francisco CA and Bellas

Artes Gallery, Santa Fé NM and New York.

Paula Crespo p.86
Born 1947, Lisbon, Portugal. Educated: Lisbon University; Centre de Arte e Comunicação Visual (AR.CO), Lisbon. Became a partner in workshop/gallery Artefacto 3 in 1987. Exhibitions: some, in Portugal, Japan, Holland, Germany and Brazil. Solo exhibition at the Museu Nacional do Traje, Lisbon in 1990. Galleries: Artefacto 3, Lisbon. Photographic credit: Álvaro Rosendo.

Marinette Cueco p.73
Born Argentat (Corrèze), France. Exhibitions: in Western Europe, South America, Africa, Australia and NZ. Solo exhibition at Jardin d'Entrelacs, Uzerche in 1990. Collections: Musée d'Art Moderne de la Ville de Paris and other major international museum collections.

Anne Currier p.37
Born 1950, Louisville KA, USA. Educated: Art Institute of Chicago School; University of Washington, Seattle WA. Teaching: since 1985, Associate Professor, New York State College of Ceramics, Alfred University, NY. Exhibitions: various, in the USA and Canada. Solo exhibition at Helen Drutt Gallery in 1990. Galleries: Helen Drutt Gallery, Philadelphia PA.

D4Design – Bill MacMahon, Stephen Roberts, Michael Scott-Mitchell p.182
Born 1959, 1959 and 1960 respectively. D4Design formed 1987, bringing together the directors' different fields of interest: architecture, interior design and theatre design. Commissions: include interior design, lighting design and graphics for the Rockpool Resturant, Sydney and various other projects for restaurants, businesses, theatres and museums in Australia.

Dan Dailey p.124
Born 1947, Amesbury PA, USA. Educated: Philadelphia College of Art; Rhode Island School of Design, Providence RI. Teaching: currently Head of Glass Program, Massachusetts College of Art. Exhibitions: numerous, international. Solo exhibition at Betsy Rosenfield Gallery, Chicago IL and Leo Kaplan Gallery, New York in 1990. Collections: American Craft Museum, Metropolitan Museum of Art (New York), Corning Museum of Glass (Corning), Renwick Gallery, Smithsonian Institution (Washington D.C.) and other major museum collections in Germany, Australia and Japan. Galleries: Betsy Rosenfield Gallery, Chicago IL, Leo Kaplan Gallery, New York, Habatat Galleries, Boca Raton FL, Kurland/Summers Gallery, Los Angeles CA, Sanske

Galerie, Zürich and Yamaha Galleries, Tokyo. Photographic credit: Betsy Rosenfield Gallery.

William Daley p.37
Born 1925, Hastings-on-Hudson NY, USA. Educated: Massachusetts College of Art, Boston MA; Columbia University, New York NY. Teaching: formerly Professor of Art/Ceramics at Philadelphia College of Art and Design. Exhibitions: numerous, mainly in the USA, also in the UK, Korea, Japan and France. Solo exhibition at Helen Drutt Gallery in 1990. Collections: Renwick Gallery, Smithsonian Institution (Washington D.C.), Everson Museum of Art (Syracuse) and other major museum collections in the USA, the UK, Holland and Korea. Galleries: Helen Drutt Gallery, Philadelphia PA and Braunstein Gallery, San Francisco CA. Photographic credit: James Quail.

Dick Dankers p.186
Born 1950, Amsterdam, Holland. Founder-member of the design gallery Frozen Fountain, Amsterdam. Awards: include the Dutch Classic Design Prize in 1990 for furniture.

Pierre Degen p.108
Born 1947, La Neuveville, Switzerland. Educated: École des Arts Appliqués, La Chaux-de-Fonds; Kunstgewerbe Schule, Lucerne. Jeweler and metalworker. Teaching: 1973–90, part-time lecturer, jewelry department, Middlesex Polytechnic, London. Exhibitions: numerous, international. Collections: Crafts Council Collection (London), Shipley Art Gallery (Gateshead) and other major international museum collections. Galleries: Crafts Council Shop at the V&A, London. Photographic credit: Ros Perry.

Roseline Delisle p.30
Born 1952, Quebec, Canada. Educated: Collège du Vieux Montréal. Exhibitions: mainly in the USA, also in Canada and Japan. Collections: Everson Museum of Art (Syracuse), San Francisco Museum of Modern Art (San Francisco) and other major museum collections in the USA. Galleries: Garth Clark Gallery, Los Angeles and New York, Gallery Koyanagi, Tokyo. Photographic credit: Susan Einstein.

Paul Derrez p.10
Born 1950, Sittard, Holland. Educated: Academy of Industrial Design, Eindhoven; Vakschool, Schoonhoven. Exhibitions: many since 1975, international. Founder/Director of Galerie Ra since 1976. Collections: Stedelijk Museum (Amsterdam), Centraal Museum (Utrecht), Gemeente Museum (The Hague) and other major

museum collections in Holland, the UK, Norway, Australia and Japan. Galleries: Galerie Ra, Amsterdam. Photographic credit: Ton Werkhoven.

Richard DeVore p.33
Born 1933, Toledo OH, USA. Educated: University of Toledo; Cranbrook Academy of Art, Bloomfield Hills MI. Exhibitions: numerous, international. Solo exhibition at Max Protetch Gallery, New York in 1989. Collections: American Craft Museum (New York), Everson Museum of Art (Syracuse), Los Angeles County Museum of Art (Los Angeles) and many other major museum collections in the USA and Western Europe. Galleries: Max Protetch Gallery, New York and Greenberg Gallery, St Louis MO. Photographic credit: The Greenberg Gallery.

Carmen Dionyse p.18
Born 1921, Belgium. Educated: Koninklijke Akademie, Ghent. Exhibitions: numerous, in Western Europe and Australia. Photographic credit: R. Heirman.

Tom Dixon p.197
Born 1959, Fax, Tunisia. Educated: self-taught furniture-maker. Exhibitions: in Western Europe and Japan. Collections: Victoria and Albert Museum (London), Musée des Arts Décoratifs (Paris) and other major museum collections in France and Switzerland. Galleries: Crafts Council Shop at the V&A, The Collection, Themes and Variations and Tom Dixon, Portobello, London, Galerie Yves Gastou, Paris, Galerie Théorème, Brussels and Galerie Face, Tokyo. Photographic credit: Cindy Palmano.

Julienne Dolphin-Wilding p.206
Born 1960. Educated: London College of Fashion; Middlesex Polytechnic. Exhibitions: in the UK and the USA. Solo exhibition at Joseph, Brompton Road, London in 1989. Galleries: Joseph, Brompton Road, London and Furniture of the 20th Century Gallery, New York. Photographic credit: Monika Zarolin.

John Donoghue p.29
Born 1952, Rochester MN, USA. Educated: Memphis Academy of Arts TN; Cranbrook Academy of Art, Bloomfield Hills MI. Exhibitions: various, mainly in the USA, also in Holland. Solo exhibition at Pro-Art, St Louis MO in 1990. Collections: American Craft Museum (New York), St Louis Art Museum (St Louis) and other major museum collections in the USA and Holland. Photographic credit: Susan Dougan.

215

Mark Douglass p.199
Born 1964, Victoria, Australia.
Educated: Chisholm Institute of
Technology, Melbourne. Set up
Whitehall Enterprises with five other
artists in 1987. Exhibitions: since 1985,
in Australia only. Solo exhibition at
Remo Gallery, Sydney in 1989.
Commissions: various since 1986, in
Australia. Galleries: Riddoch Art
Gallery, Mount Gambier and Melbourne
Contemporary Art Gallery, Melbourne.
Photographic credit: Pilkingtons.

André Dubreuil p.198
Born 1951, Lyons, France. Educated:
Inchbald School of Design, London.
Exhibitions: various, in Western Europe,
the USA and Japan. Solo exhibition at
Hamiltons Gallery, London in 1989.
Galleries: Hamiltons Gallery, London,
Galerie Gladys Mougin, Galerie Yves
Gastou, Paris and Galerie Théorème,
Brussels.

Marie Ducate p.118
Born 1954, Lille, France. Exhibitions:
various, mainly in France, also in
Germany, Belgium and the USA. Solo
exhibitions at Galerie Axe Art Actuel,
Toulouse and Éklair Diffusion, Brussels
in 1990. Collections: Fodor Museum
(Amsterdam). Galleries: Galerie Axe Art
Actuel, Toulouse, Art Sérédiac, Lyons
and Éklair Diffusion, Brussels.
Photographic credit: Y. Gallois.

Ruth Duckworth p.23
Born 1919, Hamburg, Germany.
Educated: Liverpool School of Art;
Hammersmith School of Art; Central
School of Art and Crafts, London.
Exhibitions: numerous, international.
Solo exhibition at Garth Clark Gallery,
New York in 1990. Collections:
American Craft Museum (New York),
Renwick Gallery, Smithsonian
Institution (Washington D.C.), Museum
of Contemporary Art (Chicago),
Museum of Art (Philadelphia) and other
major international museum collections.
Galleries: Garth Clark Gallery, New
York. Photographic credit: John White/
Garth Clark Gallery.

Ken Eastman p.39
Born 1960, UK. Educated: Edinburgh
College of Art; Royal College of Art,
London. Exhibitions: various since
1982, mainly in the UK, also in the USA,
Germany and Japan. Solo exhibition at
Contemporary Applied Arts, London in
1990. Collections: Victoria and Albert
Museum and Crafts Council Collection
(London) and other major museum
collections in the UK. Galleries:
Contemporary Applied Arts and Crafts
Council Shop at the V&A, London.
Photographic credit: David Cripps.

Andreas Eckhardt p.182
Born 1965, Cologne, Germany.
Educated: trained as a stonemason and
sculptor at the Dombauhütte and at the
Fachhochschule, Cologne. Member of
Gruppe X99 since 1987. Exhibitions:
various, in Germany and Italy. Galleries:
RTL Galerie and Galerie Nada,
Cologne.

Thomas Eisl p.194
Born 1947, Tyrol, Austria. Moved to
London in 1969. Educated: Falmouth
School of Art; St Martin's School of Art,
London. Exhibitions: various. Galleries:
Contemporary Applied Arts and One
Off Ltd, London.

Lillian Elliott pp.13, 139, 145
Born 1930, Detroit MI, USA. Educated:
Wayne State University, Detroit MI;
Cranbrook Academy of Art, Bloomfield
Hills MI. Teaching: instructor at John F.
Kennedy University, Orinda CA since
1983 and at other art colleges and
universities. Exhibitions: various, in the
USA, Western Europe and the Far East.
Collections: American Craft Museum
(New York), Renwick Gallery,
Smithsonian Institution (Washington
D.C.), Institute of Arts (Detroit), City Art
Collection (San Francisco) and other
major museum collections in the USA,
Hungary and Switzerland. Galleries:
Miller/Brown Gallery, San Francisco.
Photographic credit: Scott McCue.

Timothy C. Ely p.163
Educated: University of Washington,
Seattle WA. Exhibitions: various, mainly
in the USA, also in Canada, the UK and
France. Solo exhibition at Granary
Books, New York in 1991. Collections:
Toledo Art Museum (Toledo), New York
Public Library and other major museum
and library collections in the USA, the
UK, Germany and Switzerland.
Represented by: Granary Books, New
York.

Bern Emmerichs p.197
Born 1961, Victoria, Australia.
Educated: Prahran College of
Advanced Education, Victoria; Phillips
Institute of Technology, Melbourne.
Exhibitions: since 1983, in Australia.
Collections: Australian National Gallery
(Canberra), Art Gallery of Western
Australia (Perth) and other major
museum collections in Australia.
Galleries: Meat Market Craft Centre,
Devise Gallery, Melbourne and
Artspace, Adelaide. Photographic
credit: Tim Griffith.

Sita Falkena p.88
Born 1955, Curaçao, Netherlands
Antilles. Education: Akademie voor
Beeldende Kunsten, Arnhem; Gerrit
Rietveld Akademie, Amsterdam.
Exhibitions: in Western Europe,
Scandinavia, the USA and Japan.

Collections: Kostuum Museum, State
Collection (The Hague) and
Nordenfjeldske Kunstindustrimuseum
(Trondheim). Galleries: Galerie Ra,
Amsterdam and Galerie Marzee,
Nijmegen. Photographic credit: Ton
Werkhoven.

Kaffe Fassett p.66
Born 1937, San Francisco CA, USA.
Educated: Museum of Fine Arts School,
Boston. Exhibitions: various, in the UK,
Scandinavia, the USA, Canada and
Australia. Retrospective at the Victoria
and Albert Museum 1989, touring
internationally through 1991.
Collections: Victoria and Albert
Museum, Crafts Council Collection
(London), Aberdeen Art Gallery and
other major museum collections in the
UK, Norway, Denmark and Australia.
Galleries: Ehrman, London.
Photographic credit: Susan Wakeford.

Anne Fewlass p.58
Born 1944, Hull, East Yorkshire, UK.
Educated: Birmingham College of Art;
Leicester College of Art. Exhibitions:
various, mainly in the UK, also in Japan.
Collections: Victoria and Albert
Museum, Crafts Council Collection
(London) and other major museum
collections in the UK. Galleries:
Contemporary Applied Arts, London
and Crafts Council Shop at the V&A,
London. Photographic credit: Ian
Sumner.

Arline Fisch p.89
Born 1931, Brooklyn NY, USA.
Educated: Skidmore College, Saratoga
Springs NY; University of Illinois,
Urbana IL; Kunsthandvaerkerskolen,
Copenhagen; Apprentice School for
Gold and Silversmiths, Copenhagen.
Teaching: since 1961, Professor of Art
at San Diego State University CA.
Exhibitions: numerous since 1955,
international. Solo exhibition at Plum
Gallery, Kensington MD in 1990.
Awards: include an Outstanding Solo
Exhibition Award from the Association
International de Criticos de l'Arte,
Montivideo, Uruguay in 1989.
Collections: Renwick Gallery,
Smithsonian Institution (Washington
D.C.), American Craft Museum (New
York) and many other major
international museum collections.
Galleries: Plum Gallery, Kensington
MD, Katie Gingrass Gallery, Milwaukee
WI and Galerie am Graben, Vienna.
Photographic credit: William Gullette.

Ulla Forsell p.126
Born 1944, Stockholm, Sweden.
Educated: Swedish State College of
Arts, Crafts and Design, Stockholm;
Glass School, Orrefors, Sweden;
Gerrit Rietveld Akademie, Amsterdam,
Holland. Exhibitions: various,
international. Awards: include a

Coburger glass prize in 1985.
Collections: National Museum
(Stockholm), Museum of Arts and
Crafts (Gothenburg) and other major
international museum collections.
Galleries: Blas & Knada, Stockholm.
Photographic credit: Anders
Qwarnström.

Robert Foster p.101
Born 1962, Kyneton, Australia.
Educated: Canberra School of Art.
Exhibitions: some, mainly in Australia,
also in Germany. Collections: Victoria
State Crafts Collection and Australian
National Gallery (Canberra). Galleries:
Meat Market Craft Centre, Melbourne.
Photographic credit: Penny Morrison.

Susie Freeman p.58
Born 1956, London, UK. Educated:
Manchester Polytechnic; Royal College
of Art, London. Exhibitions: various,
international. Collections: Crafts
Council Collection, Victoria and Albert
Museum (London), Shipley Art Gallery
(Gateshead) and other major museum
collections in the UK. Galleries:
Contemporary Applied Arts, Crafts
Council Shop at the V&A, London,
Galerie V&V, Vienna and Rennweg
Galerie, Zürich. Photographic credit:
Tom Lee.

Viola Frey p.47
Born 1933, Lodi CA, USA. Educated:
Stockton Delta College CA; California
College of Arts and Crafts, Oakland
CA; Tulane University, New Orleans
LO. Exhibitions: numerous, mainly in the
USA, also in Canada, Japan and
Western Europe. Solo exhibition at
Rena Bransten Gallery, San Francisco
CA in 1990. Collections: Everson
Museum of Art (Syracuse), Los Angeles
County Museum of Art (Los Angeles)
and other major museum collections in
the USA and France. Galleries: Rena
Bransten Gallery, San Francisco CA,
Nancy Hoffman Gallery, New York and
Asher/Faure Gallery, Los Angeles CA.
Photographic credit: Rena Bransten
Gallery.

Christoph Friedrich p.7
Born 1952, Bülach, Switzerland.
Educated: Kunstgewerbeschule,
Zürich. Exhibitions: various since 1978,
in Switzerland and abroad.

Bert Frijns p.112
Born 1953, Kerkrade, Holland.
Educated: Gerrit Rietveld Akademie,
Amsterdam. Exhibitions: various,
international. Awards: include the
Hokkaido Museum of Modern Art Prize,
World Glass Now '88. Collections:
Stedelijk Museum (Amsterdam),
Museum Boymans-van Beuningen
(Rotterdam), National Glasmuseum
(Leerdam) and other major museum
collections in Holland, Germany,

Australia and the USA. Galleries: Galerie het Kapelhuis, Amersfoort and Galerie Rob van den Doel, The Hague.

Elizabeth Fritsch p.31
Born 1940, Whitchurch, Shropshire UK. Educated: Royal College of Art, London. Exhibitions: various, international. Solo exhibition at Hetjens-Museum, Düsseldorf in 1991. Collections: Crafts Council Collection, Victoria and Albert Museum (London), City Art Gallery (Bristol, Manchester and Leeds) and other major international collections. Galleries: Fischer Fine Art, London.

Kyohei Fujita p.120
Born 1921, Tokyo, Japan. Educated: Tokyo Academy of Fine Arts. Exhibitions: numerous, international. Solo exhibition at Heller Gallery, New York in 1990. Awards: include the Imperial Award and the Japan Academy Award in 1989. Collections: National Museum of Modern Art (Tokyo), Hokkaido Museum of Modern Art (Sapporo), Corning Museum of Glass (Corning NY) and other major international museum collections. Galleries: Takashimaya Galleries, Tokyo, Osaka and Yokahama, and Heller Gallery, New York.

Sueharu Fukami p.25
Born 1947, Kyoto, Japan. Educated: Kyoto Arts and Crafts Training Centre. Exhibitions: various since 1967, in Japan and Eastern and Western Europe. Awards: include a prize at Faenza in 1985. Collections: National Museum of Modern Art (Tokyo), Japan Foundation and other major international museum collections. Photographic credit: Koyanagi Gallery.

Morio Funakushi p.94
Born 1950, Ibaraki, Japan. Educated: Rikkio University, Tokyo; Staatlichen Zeichenakademie, Hanau. Exhibitions: various, international. Awards: include a Grand Prix at the 1979 Japan Jewelry Exhibition and at the 1982 Modern Jewelry Design Contest. Collections: National Museum of Modern Art (Kyoto). Galleries: Galerie Ra, Amsterdam.

György Fusz p.45
Born 1955, Hungary. Educated: Academy of Applied Arts, Budapest. Teaching: currently at Academy of Applied Arts Master School. Photographic credit: Sandor Sajnovits.

Jette Valeur Gemzøe pp.52, 53
Born 1942, Copenhagen, Denmark. Educated: John Becker's Weaving Workshop, Copenhagen; Royal Academy of Fine Arts, Copenhagen. Teaching: since 1976, at Skolen for Brugskunst, Copenhagen. Exhibitions:

various, international. Collections: Danish Stock Exchange and the National Bank of Denmark (Copenhagen) and other institutions in Denmark, Norway, Germany and Jordan. Photographic credit: Toto Wohlert.

Liliane Gérard p.165
Born 1946, Mont-sur-Marchienne, Belgium. Educated: École Supérieure d'Architecture et des Arts Visuels, La Cambre, Brussels. Teaching: since 1987, head of the bookbinding studio at École de la Cambre. Exhibitions: various, in Belgium, Germany, France and the USA. Collections: Bibliothèque Royale (Brussels), Musée Royal de Mariemont (Morlanwelz) and other major museum and library collections in Belgium, Luxembourg, France and the USA.

Wolfgang Gessl p.99
Born 1949, Vienna, Austria. Educated: trained in goldsmithing in Austria; Swedish State College of Arts, Crafts and Design, Stockholm. Teaching: since 1978, part-time teacher in metalwork and jewelry at Swedish State College of Arts, Crafts and Design, Stockholm. Exhibitions: various, in Sweden, Finland, Germany, Japan, etc. Solo exhibition at Gallery Metallum, Stockholm in 1990. Collections: National Swedish Museum of Fine Arts (Stockholm) and other major museum collections in Scandinavia. Galleries: Galerie Metallum, Galerie NFS and Galerie Konsthantverkarna, Stockholm. Photographic credit: Sune Sundahl.

Katrine Giæver p.60
Born 1960, Tromsø, Norway. Educated: National College of Art and Design, Oslo; Visva Bharati University, West Bengal, India. Exhibitions: some, in Norway, Sweden and Germany. Galleries: RAM Galleri, Oslo and Galleri Ratatosk, Gothenburg. Photographic credit: Yann Aker.

Maggi Giles p.46
Born 1938, Newquay, Cornwall, UK. Educated: Bromley Art School, Kent. Exhibitions: numerous, in Western Europe. Collections: Stedelijk Museum (Amsterdam), Haags Gemeentemuseum (The Hague), Museum Boymans-van Beuningen (Rotterdam) and other major museum collections in Holland, the UK and USA. Photographic credit: Mieke H. Hille.

Eleanor Glover p.159
Born 1952, UK. Educated: Sir John Cass College of Art and Design, London; Manchester College of Art and Design, Manchester. Apprenticed to Ron Fuller in toymaking. Teaching: since 1986, part-time lecturer at Gwent College of Higher Education.

Exhibitions: various, in the UK only. Galleries: Contemporary Applied Arts, Crafts Council Shop at the V&A, London and Oxford Gallery, Oxford.

Vladimir Gorislavtsev p.26
Born 1939, USSR. Educated: V.I. Mukhina Institute of Applied Art and Industrial Design. Exhibitions: various since 1969, in Eastern and Western Europe and North America. Awards: first prizes at Faenza in 1979 and 1982. Collections: Russian Museum (Leningrad), Museo Internazionale delle Ceramiche (Faenza) and other major museum collections in the USSR.

Goudji p.107
Born 1941, Georgia, USSR. Educated: Academy of Fine Art, Tbilisi. Left the USSR for France in 1974. Exhibitions: numerous, in France, Western Europe and North America. Solo exhibitions at Musée d'Orfèvrerie F. Mandet de Riom, Galerie Claude Bernard at Salon du Mars and Fine Art Society, London in 1991. Awards: include the Grand Prix Régional des Métiers d'Art, Région Île de France, Paris in 1988. Collections: Musée des Arts Décoratifs (Paris) and other major museum collections in France. Commissions: numerous, including Academicians' swords for Robert Turcan and Félicien Marceau. Galleries: Galerie Claude Bernard, Paris, Galerie Place des Arts, Montepellier, Galerie Capazza, Nançay and Fine Art Society, London. Photographic credit: Marc Wittmer.

Hermann Gradinger p.205
Born 1936, Mainz, Germany. Educated: Meisterschule für Bau- und Kunstschlosser, Stuttgart, Germany. Exhibitions: various, in Western Europe and the USA. Commissions: numerous, distinguished, in private and public buildings in Germany.

Angkuna Graham (Ernabella Arts) p.62
Born 1934, Ernabella, South Australia. Educated: Ernabella Arts. The Ernabella Arts Inc. workshop was set up in 1949 to channel the creative talents of the Aboriginal women of Ernabella into such activities as spinning, dyeing, weaving, woodcarving and batik dyeing. Ernabella batik is designed and produced by the women of the Pitjantjatjara tribe of Central Australia.

Giorgio Gregori p.7
Born 1957, Rome, Italy. Educated: studied architecture in Milan. Joined Alchimia design group in 1978 and has been involved in numerous projects including furniture design. Commissions: include (with Alchimia) 'Casa della felicità' for Alberto Alessi, 'Casa roll' for Zanussi Edilizia Industrializzata and a project for the new Museum of the City in Gröningen.

Albrecht Greiner-Mai p.110
Born 1932, Lausche, Germany. Educated: Glasblaserfachschule, Lausche; Fachschule für Angewandte Kunst, Schneeburg. Exhibitions: numerous, international. Awards: include a Gold Medal at the Second International Glass and Porcelain Exhibition, Jablonec nad Nisou, Czechoslovakia in 1976. Collections: Kunsthandwerksmuseum, Schloss Köpenik (Berlin), Museum des Kunsthandwerks (Leipzig), Sammlung der Veste Coburg (Coburg) and other major museum collections in Germany, Belgium and the USA.

Marco de Gueltzl p.198
Born 1958, Roanne, France. Exhibitions: since 1981, in France, the UK, Sweden and the USA. Solo exhibitions at Pixi and Galerie Via, Paris, in 1990. Galleries: Galerie Via, Galerie Différences, Paris and Heller Gallery, New York. Photographic credit: Ian Patrick.

Jacqueline Guille p.63
Born 1951, London, UK. Educated: Leeds University; Central School of Art and Design, London. Teaching: currently at the Norfolk Institute of Art and Design. Exhibitions: various, in the UK, Switzerland and the USA. Solo exhibitions at Contemporary Textile Gallery, London and Vorpal Gallery, New York in 1991. Galleries: Contemporary Applied Arts, Contemporary Textile Gallery, London and Vorpal Gallery, New York. Photographic credit: David Whitworth.

Christine Kluge Haberkorn p.40
Born 1945, Oberhof/Thüringen, Germany. Educated: Akademie für Werkkunst und Mode, Berlin. Exhibitions: various, in Germany, Spain, Finland and the USA. Awards: include a Preis des Landes Berlin für das Gestaltende Handwerk in 1987. Collections: Kunstgewerbemuseum (Berlin), Museum für Kunsthandwerk (Frankfurt) and Württembergisches Landesmuseum (Stuttgart). Galleries: Galerie Hensellek, Frankfurt, Muffendorfer Keramikgalerie, Bonn and Messe-Galerie, Coblenz.

Alfred Habermann Jnr p.203
Born 1953, Jihlava, Czechoslovakia. Educated: apprenticed to his father, the master blacksmith Alfred Habermann; studied at Kunstgewerbeschule, Turnov. Has participated in many distinguished symposia and congresses in Europe.

Helmut Hahn p.75
Born 1928, Mönchengladbach, Germany. Educated: Staatliche Kunstakademie, Düsseldorf. Teaching: since 1970, Professor of Textile Design

at Fachhochschule Niederrhein, Krefeld. Exhibitions: various, in Western Europe, including the Lausanne Biennale. Collections: Württembergisches Landesmuseum (Stuttgart) and Schloss Rheydt (Mönchengladbach).

Walter Hamady p.171
Born 1940, Flint MI, USA. Educated: Wayne State University; Cranbrook Academy of Art, Bloomfield Hills MI. Teaching: since 1981, Professor, University of Wisconsin, Madison WI. Exhibitions: numerous, mainly in the USA, also in Canada and Western Europe. Retrospective at Wustum Museum of Fine Arts, Racine WI in 1991 and travelling. Collections: Whitney Museum of American Art, New York Public Library (New York), Library of Congress, Archives of American Art (Washington D.C.) and many other major international library and museum collections. Galleries: Perimeter Gallery, Chicago IL.

Jiří Harcuba p.128
Born 1928, Harrachov, Czechoslovakia. Educated: apprenticeship in the Harrachian Glassworks; studies at Glassmaking School, Nový Bor; Academy of Applied Arts, Prague. Teaching: a long association with the Prague Academy of Applied Arts was interrupted, on political grounds, for some years; in 1990, was rehabilitated and made a Professor. Exhibitions: numerous, international. Solo exhibitions at Augustinermuseum, Freiburg im Breisgau and Sam Davidson Gallery, Seattle WA in 1990. Collections: Uměleckoprůmyslové Muzeum (Prague), Muzeum Skla a Bižuterie (Jablonec nad Nisou), Sklárske Muzeum (Nový Bor) and other major international museum collections. Galleries: Mährische Galerie, Brünn, Galerie Monica Turjen, Bremen, Sam Davidson Gallery, Seattle WA, etc. Photographic credit: Gabriel Urbánek.

Jane Harris p.58
Born 1965, Glasgow, UK. Educated: Chelsea School of Art, London; Duncan of Jordanstone School of Art, Dundee; Glasgow School of Art. Exhibitions: some, in the UK and Germany. Awards: Jugend Gestaltet Prizewinner, Munich in 1990. Galleries: Scottish Gallery, Edinburgh.

Kaija Sanelma Harris p.77
Born 1939, Turkku, Finland. Educated: Åbo Hemslöjdslärinne Institut, Turku; Architectural Tapestry Workshop, Banff Centre, Canada. Exhibitions: numerous, in North America and the UK. Awards: include Handweavers' Guild of America Merit Award, 1986–90. Collections: Canadian Crafts

Council, Saskatchewan Crafts Council and other major museum collections in Canada. Galleries: Craftspace, Winnipeg, Mendel Art Gallery and Saskatchewan Craft Gallery, Saskatoon.

Fritz Harstrup p.35
Born 1951, Sandefjord, Norway. Educated: National College of Craft and Design, Oslo. Teaching: National Colleges of Craft and Design in Oslo and Bergen. Exhibitions: various, mainly in Norway, also in Japan and the USA. Solo exhibition at Gallery Nota Bene, Oslo in 1990. Collections: Kunstindustrimuseums in Oslo, Trondheim and Bergen. Galleries: Gallery Nota Bene and Gallery Føyner, Oslo. Photographic credit: Blue Line.

Hans-Joachim Härtel p.107
Born 1956, Weimar, Germany. Educated: Institut für Architekturemail, Thale; Hochschule für Industrielle Formgestaltung, Halle. Exhibitions: various, mainly in Germany, also in Eastern and Western Europe. Collections: Kunsthandwerksmuseum, Schloss Köpenik (Berlin) and Angermuseums (Erfurt). Galleries: Schmuckforum, Zürich and Galerie V&V, Vienna.

Elisabet Hasselberg-Olsson p.76
Born 1932, Gothenburg, Sweden. Education: Self-taught. Exhibitions: numerous since 1965, international. Commissions: many, including for the Plenary Hall of the Swedish Parliament. Photographic credit: Anders Quarnström.

Gay Hawkes p.200
Born 1942, Burnie, Tasmania. Educated: University of Tasmania; Tasmanian School of Art. Exhibitions: various, in Australia, New Zealand and Norway. Solo exhibitions at Bathhouse Museum, Rotorua, Dowse Gallery, Wellington and touring NZ in 1990. Collections: Powerhouse Museum (Sydney), Museum of Contemporary Art (Brisbane), Art Gallery of South Australia (Adelaide) and other major museum collections in Australia and Norway. Galleries: Australian Galleries, Melbourne. Photographic credit: Evan Clark.

Shokosai Hayakawa p.141
Born 1932, Osaka, Japan. Exhibitions: numerous. First exhibited at Dento Kogei Ten (Traditional Crafts Exhibition) in 1966. In 1967, became 5th generation Shokosai.

Ann Hechle p.172
Born 1939, Calcutta, India. Educated: Reigate School of Art; Central School of Art and Crafts, London. Exhibitions: various. Commissions: numerous.

Collections: Victoria and Albert Museum (London), Crafts Study Centre, Holburne of Menstrie Museum (Bath) and other major museum collections in the UK and USA. Photographic credit: Colin Wilson.

Axel Heibel p.168
Born 1943, Lahnstein/Rheinlandpfalz, Germany. Educated: Werkkunstschule, Offenbach/Main; Hochschule für Bildende Künste, Hamburg. Exhibitions: numerous, international. Solo exhibition at Gutenberg-Museum, Mainz in 1990. Collections: Kunstmuseum (Düsseldorf), Hamburg Kunsthalle and other major museum and library collections in Western Europe and North America. Galleries: Galerie Achim Overmann, Münster.

Sibyl Heijnen p.81
Born 1961, Kerkrade, Holland. Educated: Gerrit Rietveld Akademie, Amsterdam. Exhibitions: since 1982, mainly in Holland, also in Germany, Poland and Japan. Solo exhibition at Nederlands Textielmuseum, Tilburg in 1990. Photographic credit: Simon Bodens.

Anna Heindl p.97
Born 1950, Perg, Austria. Educated: Hochschule für Angewandte Kunst, Vienna. Exhibitions: various since 1972, in Western Europe, Japan and Australia. Galleries: Galerie Krinzinger, Galerie am Graben, Vienna, Werkstättgalerie, Berlin and Galerie Farel, Aigle. Photographic credit: Christoph Schorff.

Ewen Henderson p.41
Born 1934, Staffordshire, UK. Educated: Goldsmiths College, University of London; Camberwell School of Art and Crafts, London. Teaching: since 1968, at Camberwell School of Art and Crafts. Exhibitions: numerous since 1969, international. Solo exhibitions at Garth Clark Gallery, New York and Galerie Besson, London in 1990. Collections: Victoria and Albert Museum, Crafts Council Collection (London), Ulster Museum (Belfast), Cleveland Museum (Middlesbrough) and other major international museum collections. Galleries: Galerie Besson, Crafts Council Shop at the V&A, Contemporary Applied Arts, London, Galerie Marianne Heller, Heidelberg, Miharudo Gallery, Tokyo and Garth Clark Gallery, New York. Photographic credit: David Cripps.

Wayne Higby p.40
Born 1943, Colorado Springs, USA. Educated: University of Colorado, Boulder CO; University of Michigan, Ann Arbor MI. Teaching: since 1973, at New York State College of Ceramics, Alfred University. Exhibitions: numerous

since 1965, mainly in the USA, also in Western Europe and the Far East. Solo exhibition at Helen Drutt Gallery in 1990. Collections: American Craft Museum, Metropolitan Museum of Art (New York), Everson Museum of Art (Syracuse), Museum of Fine Arts (Boston), Renwick Gallery, Smithsonian Institution (Washington D.C.) and other major museum collections in the USA, Japan and the UK. Galleries: Helen Drutt Gallery, Philadelphia.

Pavel Hlavá p.130
Born 1924, Semily, Czechoslovakia. Educated: Glass Industry School, Železný Brod; Academy of Fine Arts, Prague. Exhibitions: numerous, international. Awards: include a gold medal at the International Glass Exhibition, Kanazawa, Japan in 1988. Collections: Uměleckoprůmyslové Muzeum (Prague) and other major international museum collections. Photographic credit: Gabriel Urbánek.

Ladislav Hodný p.164
Born 1943, Týn nad Vltavou, Czechoslovakia. Educated: apprenticed in bookbinding to his father; Ocnovská škola kníharská (bookbinders school), Nový Jičín; Uměleckoprůmyslová skola, Brno. Exhibitions: various, mainly in Czechoslovakia, also in Germany, Switzerland and Austria. Awards: include the Prix de la Reliure Originale, at the Concours Reliures Décorées, Paris in 1989. Collections: Národní Muzeum, Uměleckoprůmyslové Muzeum (Prague) and other major library and museum collections in Czechoslovakia. Galleries: Galerie 'K', Horice v Podkronosí. Member of the Book Art Center, New York. Photographic credit: Fotoatelier Hanácek.

Bev Hogg p.46
Born Australia. Educated: Canberra School of Art, Canberra. First solo exhibition at Crafts Council Gallery, Watson in 1990.

Michael Hosaluk p.157
Born 1954, Invermay, Saskatchewan, Canada. Educated: Kelsey Institute of Applied Arts and Sciences, Saskatoon, Saskatchewan. Exhibitions: various, in North America, Japan and Australia. Collections: Royal Ontario Museum (Toronto) and other major museum collections in Canada, the USA and Japan. Galleries: Saskatchewan Craft Gallery, Saskatoon. Photographic credit: Grant Kernan.

Erhard Hössle p.106
Born 1929, Memmenhausen, Schwaben, Germany. Educated: Akademie der Bildenden Künste, Munich. Maker of all kinds of objects, from teapots to kites. Teaching:

currently, professor at the Akademie der Bildenden Künste, Nuremberg. Exhibitions: numerous. Commissions: wideranging, in Germany.

Maria Hössle p.57
Born 1961, Munich, Germany. Educated: after an apprenticeship in ecclesiastical decoration, studied at Akademie der Bildenden Künste, Nuremberg. Exhibitions: since 1987, in Eastern and Western Europe. Awards: include a Dannerpreis in 1987. Galleries: Heim + Handwerk, Munich. Photographic credit: Stefan Hössle.

Patrice Hugues p.61
Born 1930, Courbevoie, France. Educated: studies at Atelier Fernand Léger. Exhibitions: since 1973 as a textile artist, international. Touring solo exhibition, ending at Galerie Alain Oudin, Paris in 1991. Collections: Musée des Arts Décoratifs, Musée d'Art Moderne et de la Ville de Paris and Musée National d'Art Moderne (Paris) and other major museum collections in France. Galleries: Galerie Alain Oudin, Paris.

Ulrica Hydman-Vallien p.11
Born 1938, Stockholm, Sweden. Educated: Swedish State College of Arts, Crafts and Design, Stockholm. Employed as a designer for Kosta-Boda AB since 1972. Exhibitions: various, international. Collections: Nationalmuseum, King Gustav VI Adolf's Collection (Stockholm), Corning Museum of Glass (Corning NY), Kunstsammlungen der Veste Coburg (Coburg) and other major international museum collections. Galleries: Galleri Malen, Helsingborg, Galerie Trois, Geneva and Heller Gallery, New York. Photographic credit: Heller Gallery.

Toshio Iezumi pp.131, 135
Born 1954, Ashikaga-shi, Japan. Exhibitions: various, mainly in Japan, also in the USA and Czechoslovakia. Solo exhibition at Gallery Genka, Tokyo in 1990. Collections: Tokyo Glass Institute (Kawasaki) and Corning Museum of Glass (Corning). Galleries: Gallery Genka, Tokyo.

Shokansai Iizuka p.139
Born 1919, Tokyo, Japan. Educated: Tokyo Bijutsu Gakko. Exhibitions: numerous, in Japan. First exhibited in Nitten in 1947 and in Dento Kogei Ten (Traditional Crafts Exhibition) in 1974. Designated a Living National Treasure in 1982.

Kazumi Ikemoto p.127
Born 1954, Kyoto, Japan. Educated: Kyoto City University of Arts. Teaching: currently part-time lecturer at Tama Art University. Exhibitions: some since

1977, mainly in Japan, also in the USA and Korea. Solo exhibition at Gallery Genka, Tokyo in 1990. Awards: a Fine Work Prize at the Tokyo Glass Art '90 exhibition, Hankyu Department Store, Tokyo in 1990. Collections: Hokkaido Museum of Modern Art (Sapporo). Galleries: Gallery Genka, Tokyo and Heller Gallery, New York.

Wahei Ikezawa p.84
Born 1946, Shimane-ken, Japan. Educated: Kanazawa Arts and Crafts University. Exhibitions: various, in Japan, Formosa and Western Europe. Collections: Schmuckmuseum (Pforzheim). Galleries: Lynn McAllister Gallery, Seattle WA, Habatat Galleries, Boca Raton FL and Gallery Tomoedo, Tokyo.

Bryan Illsley p.109
Born 1937, Surbiton, Surrey, UK. Educated: apprenticed as a stonemason; evening classes at Kingston School of Art, Kingston-upon-Thames; worked at the Leach Pottery and subsequently with Breon O'Casey at St Ives. Painter, jeweler, sculptor in metal and wood. Exhibitions: numerous, mainly in the UK, also in Japan and the USA. Solo exhibition at Jamison Thomas Gallery, Portland OR in 1990. Collections: Crafts Council Collection, Contemporary Art Society, Arts Council of Great Britain (London), Kettles Yard (Cambridge) and other major museum collections in the UK. Commissions: two large wooden pieces for Chiltern Sculpture Trail funded by Southern Arts in 1990. Galleries: Contemporary Applied Arts, Electrum Gallery, Crafts Council Shop at the V&A, London, New Craftsmen, St Ives and Jamison Thomas Gallery, Portland OR. Photographic credit: Masaaki Sekiya.

Kado Isaburo p.152
Born 1940, Japan. Lives and works in Wajima, where there has been an important lacquer industry since the eighteenth century.

Makoto Ito p.125
Born 1940, Tairyien, Japan. Educated: Tama Art University, Tokyo. Teaching: since 1972, at Tama Art University. Exhibitions: various, mainly in Japan, also in Western Europe, Australia, New Zealand, North America and Brazil. Collections: Musée des Arts Décoratifs (Paris) and other major museum collections in France, Germany and the USA. Galleries: Gallery Maronie, Kyoto and Green Gallery, Tokyo.

Hisatoshi Iwata p.121
Born 1925, Tokyo, Japan. Educated: Tokyo National University of Fine Arts and Music; Tokyo Institute of Technology. Exhibitions: numerous since 1949, mainly in Japan, also in

North America and Australia. Awards: the 38th Japan Art Academy Prize, 1982. Collections: National Museum of Modern Art (Tokyo), National Museum of Modern Art (Kyoto), Hokkaido Museum of Modern Art (Sapporo) and other major museum collections in Japan and the USA.

Ritzi Jacobi p.78
Born 1941, Bucharest, Rumania. Educated: Academy of Arts, Bucharest. Exhibitions: various, international. Collections: Kunstgewerbemuseum (Berlin), Museum für Kunsthandwerk (Frankfurt), Badisches Landesmuseum (Karlsruhe), Museum für Kunst and Gewerbe (Hamburg) and other major museum collections in Western Europe, the USA and Japan. Commissions: various, in Germany and the USA.

Ferne Jacobs p.143
Born 1942, Chicago IL, USA. Educated: Arts Center College of Design, Los Angeles CA; California State University at Long Beach; Claremont Graduate School, Claremont CA. Exhibitions: various since 1967, mainly in the USA, also in Western and Eastern Europe. Solo exhibition at Sybaris Gallery, Royal Oak MI in 1989. Collections: American Craft Museum (New York), Erie Art Museum (Erie PA) and other major museum collections in the USA. Galleries: Franklin Parrasch Galleries, New York. Photographic credit: Susan Einstein.

Michael James p.65
Born 1949, New Bedford MA, USA. Educated: Southeastern Massachusetts University, North Dartmouth MA; Rochester Institute of Technology, Rochester NY. Exhibitions: various, in the USA, Western Europe, Japan and Turkey. Solo exhibitions at Clark University, Worcester MA and Galerie Jonas, Petit-Cortaillod, Switzerland in 1990. Collections: Newark Museum (Newark) and Ball State University Gallery of Art (Muncie), USA. Galleries: Galerie Jonas, Petit-Cortaillod. Photographic credit: David Caras.

Hansína Jensdóttir p.108
Born 1954, Reykjavík, Iceland. Educated: trained as a jeweler with her father, Jens Gudjónsson; studied at the Technical School of Iceland, the Icelandic School of Art, and the School of Art, Reykjavík; also at S.A.I.T., Calgary, Alta, Canada. Exhibitions: since 1981 in Canada, Scandinavia and Iceland.

Gilles Jonemann p.91
Born 1944, Geneva, Switzerland. Educated: Ateliers des Fontblanches; École des Beaux-Arts, Aix-en-Provence; École des Arts Appliqués, Paris.

Exhibitions: since 1969, in Western Europe, Scandinavia and Japan. Collections: Musée des Arts Décoratifs, Paris and other museum collections in France. Galleries: Galerie Contempo-Art, Nice, Schmuckforum, Zürich and Sternthaler Galerie, Bonn.

Trevor Jones p.163
Born 1931, Wembley, Middlesex, UK. Educated: Harrow School of Art; Hornsey College of Art. Teaching: 1959–84, taught bookbinding at St John's College, York (now College of Rippon and York St John). A member of Designer Bookbinders since its inception in 1955 and President 1983–85. Exhibitions: numerous since 1956, in Western and Eastern Europe, Scandinavia, the USA and Brazil. Two-person show at Dunkeld and Birnam Arts Festival, Scotland in 1990. Collections: Victoria and Albert Museum, British Library (London), Royal Library (Copenhagen) and other major museum and library collections in the USA. Photographic credit: Jim Kershaw.

Hermann Jünger p.89
Born 1928, Hanau, Hesse, Germany. Educated: Staatliche Zeichenakademie, Hanau; Akademie der Bildenden Künste, Munich. Teaching: Lecturer at Akademie der Bildenden Künste, Munich. Exhibitions: numerous, international. Solo exhibition at Galerie If, Tokyo in 1990. Collections: Schmuckmuseum (Pforzheim), Museum für Kunsthandwerk (Frankfurt), Museum für Kunst und Gewerbe (Hamburg), Kestner-Museum (Hanover) and other major museum collections in Germany, Czechoslovakia and Australia. Galleries: Galerie Lalique, Berlin, Galerie am Nerotal, Wiesbaden, Galerie Helga Malten, Dortmund and Galerie Map, Cologne.

Ikkei Kakutani p.105
Born 1904, Osaka, Japan. Learned tea-ceremony kettle casting from his father and later from Hozuma Katori. Exhibitions: numerous, in Japan. Has exhibited frequently in Dento Kogei Ten (Traditional Japanese Crafts Exhibition). Designated a Living National Treasure in 1978.

Karen Karnes p.23
Born 1925, New York, USA. Educated: New York State College of Ceramics, Alfred University NY. Exhibitions: numerous, mainly in the USA, also in the UK and Italy. Solo exhibition at Garth Clark Gallery, New York in 1990. Awards: include the Society of Arts and Crafts Medal for Excellence, 1990. Collections: Metropolitan Museum of Art, American Crafts Museum (New York), Everson Museum of Art (Syracuse) and other major museum

exhibitions at Musée Bellerive, Zürich and Heller Gallery, New York in 1990. Collections: Uměleckoprůmyslové Muzeum (Prague), Muzeum Skla a Bižuterie (Jablonec nad Nisou) and other major international museum collections. Galleries: Galerie Clara Scremini, Paris, Heller Gallery, New York and Habatat Galleries, Boca Raton FL. Photographic credit: Russell Johnson.

Jacqueline Liekens p.172
Born 1947, Brussels, Belgium. Educated: École Nationale Supérieure d'Architecture et des Arts Visuels, La Cambre. Teaching: 1981–90 at Institut des Arts et Métiers, Brussels. Exhibitions: various, in Belgium and Western Europe. Awards: include three silver medals at the Concours Paul Bonet, Ascona, Switzerland in 1975. Collections: Bibliothèque Royale Albert 1er, Bibliotheca Wittockiana (Brussels) and other major museum and library collections in Belgium, Luxembourg and Canada. Commissions: distinguished commissions for H.M. Queen Fabiola, H.M. King Baudouin and the Association Belgo-Hispanique.

Stefan Lindfors p.201
Born 1962, Mariehamn, Finland. Educated: University of Industrial Arts, Helsinki. Exhibitions: various in Europe, in 1991 in Paris. Awards: include a silver medal at the Milan Triennale in 1986. Commissions: include furniture for the Café at the Helsinki Industrial Arts Museum in 1989.

Mark Lindquist pp.148, 157
Born 1949, Oakland CA, USA. Educated: New England College, Henniker NH; Pratt Institute, Brooklyn NY; Florida State University. Exhibitions: various, mainly in the USA, also in France and the UK. Collections: American Craft Museum and Metropolitan Museum of Art (New York), Renwick Gallery, Smithsonian Institution (Washington D.C.), Museum of Fine Arts (Boston) and other major museum collections in the USA. Galleries: Franklin Parrasch Gallery, New York and Wilson and Gough Gallery, London.

Nel Linsen p.93
Born 1935, Mook, Holland. Educated: Akademie voor Beeldende Kunsten, Arnhem. Exhibitions: various, in Holland, Western Europe and North America. Solo exhibition at Galerie Trits, Delft in 1989. Collections: Gemeentemuseum (Arnhem), Costuummuseum (The Hague), Stedelijk Museum (Amsterdam) and other major museum collections in Western Europe. Galleries: Galerie Trits/Sieraden, Delft and Schmuckforum, Zürich.

Harvey Littleton p.123
Born 1922, Corning NY, USA. Educated: Brighton School of Art, UK; University of Michigan; Cranbrook Academy of Art, Bloomfield Hills MI. Teaching: 1951–77 at University of Wisconsin. Exhibitions: numerous, in the USA and abroad. Awards: include an Honours Diploma from the Glass Museum, Frauenau, and the American Craft Council Gold Medal in 1983. Collections: Museum of Modern Art (New York), Corning Museum of Glass (Corning) and other major museum collections in the USA, Germany and Japan. Galleries: Holsten Galleries, Palm Beach FL, Heller Gallery, New York and Maurine Littleton Gallery, Washington DC.

Joan Livingstone p.70
Born 1948, Portland OR, USA. Educated: Beloit College WI; Portland State University OR; Cranbrook Academy of Art, Bloomfield Hills MI. Teaching: since 1983, Associate Professor at Art Institute of Chicago School. Exhibitions: various, mainly in the USA, also in Canada, Colombia and Switzerland. Solo exhibition at Artemisia Gallery, Chicago IL in 1990. Galleries: Roy Boyd Gallery, Chicago IL.

Alex Locadia p.189
Born 1958, Brooklyn NY, USA. Educated: Parsons School of Design, New York. Exhibitions: in the USA, France, Belgium and Japan. Solo exhibition at Art et Industrie, New York in 1989. Galleries: Art et Industrie, New York and Brutus Gallery, Osaka, Japan. Photographic credit: Joseph Coscia Jr./ Art et Industrie.

Thomas Loeser p.190
Born 1956, Boston MA, USA. Educated: Haverford College PA; Boston University, Boston MA. Teaching: 1991, instructor at University of Wisconsin, Madison WI. Exhibitions: numerous since 1981, in North America, Europe and Finland. Collections: Cooper-Hewitt Museum (New York), Museum of Fine Arts (Boston) and other major museum collections in the USA. Galleries: Snyderman Gallery, Philadelphia PA, Gallery Naga, Boston MA and Meredith Gallery, Baltimore MD.

Dona Look p.138
Born 1948, Mequon WI, USA. Educated: University of Wisconsin, Oshkosh WI. Teaching: 1976–78, Sydney and Tamworth High Schools, NSW, Australia. Exhibitions: various, mainly in the USA, also in Europe. Awards: include an American Craft Museum Design Award in 1985. Collections: American Craft Museum (New York), Philadelphia Museum of Art (Philadelphia) and other major museum

collections in the USA. Galleries: Perimeter Gallery, Chicago IL. Photographic credit: Dedra Walls.

Ingeborg Lorenz p.81
Born 1955, Nuremberg, Germany. Educated: Fachhochschule, Münchberg; Akademie der Bildenden Künste, Nuremberg. Exhibitions: various, since 1983, in Western Europe and Japan. Awards: First Prize at the Fifth Deutsche Biennale der Textilkunst, Krefeld in 1987. Galleries: Galerie Kunst und Handwerk, Munich and Galerie Kohlenhof, Nuremberg.

Marie-Rose Lortet p.68
Born 1945, Strasbourg, France. Exhibitions: various since 1969, international. Solo exhibition at Imago, Bègles, France in 1990. Collections: Musée d'Art Brut (Lausanne).

Susan Low-Beer p.47
Born Montreal, Canada. Educated: Mount Allison University, Canada; Cranbrook Academy of Art, Bloomfield Hills MI. Teaching: since 1982, an Instructor at Art Gallery of Ontario, Toronto. Exhibitions: numerous, mainly in Canada, also in the USA and Japan. Solo exhibition at Prime Gallery, Toronto in 1990. Collections: Museum of Art (Montreal), Canada Council Art Bank (Ottawa) and other major museum collections in Canada and Japan. Galleries: Prime Gallery, Toronto and Galerie Barbara Silverberg Contemporary Ceramics, Montreal.

Helmut Lueckenhausen p.184
Born 1950, Cologne, Germany. Educated: Royal Melbourne Institute of Technology, Australia; State College of Victoria, Hawthorn, Australia. Teaching: currently Senior Lecturer at Swinburne Institute of Technology, Australia. Exhibitions: various, mainly in Australia, also in the USA. Solo exhibition at Genoa Gallery, Skaneateles NY in 1990. Collections: Powerhouse Museum (Sydney), Art Gallery of Western Australia (Perth), Australian National Gallery (Canberra) and other major museum collections in Australia. Galleries: Meat Market Craft Centre, Melbourne and Genoa Gallery, Skaneateles NY. Photographic credit: Peter Jeffs.

Judy McCaig p.95
Born 1957, Edinburgh, UK. Educated: Duncan of Jordanstone College of Art, Dundee; Royal College of Art, London; also studied printmaking and etching at Central Institute and Chelsea School of Art, London. Exhibitions: various, international. Collections: Crafts Council Collection (London) and Scottish Crafts Collection. Galleries: Galerie Hipotesi, Barcelona and Miharudo Gallery, Tokyo.

Carol McNicoll p.27
Born 1943, Birmingham, UK. Educated: Solihull College of Technology; Leeds Polytechnic; Royal College of Art, London. Exhibitions: numerous since 1969 in Western Europe, Norway, Australia and Japan. Collections: Victoria and Albert Museum, Crafts Council Collection (London), Cleveland Craft Centre (Middlesbrough) Shipley Art Gallery (Gateshead) and other major museum collections in Western Europe and Australia. Commissions: several tableware projects, both retail (Next, Designers' Guild) and private (e.g. for architect Piers Gough). Galleries: Crafts Council Shop at the V&A, London. Photographic credit: Carolina Benshamesh.

John McQueen p.142
Born 1943, Oakland IL, USA. Educated: University of South Florida, Tampa FL; Tyler School of Art, Temple University, Philadelphia PA. Exhibitions: numerous, mainly in the USA, also in Japan. Collections: Cooper-Hewitt Museum, Smithsonian Institution (New York), Museum of Art (Philadelphia) and other major museum collections in the USA. Galleries: Garth Clark Gallery, New York.

Fritz Maierhofer p.86
Born 1941, Vienna, Austria. Exhibitions: various, international. Solo exhibition at Kunstgalerie Knokke Heist, Belgium in 1990. Collections: Österreichisches Museum für Angewandte Kunst (Vienna) and other major museum collections in Western Europe. Galleries: Galerie Michèle Zeller, Bern, Kunstgalerie Knokke Heist, Belgium and Galerie IBO, Klagenfurt, Germany.

John Makepeace p.186
Born 1939. Founder of the John Makepeace School for Craftsmen in Wood, Parnham, Dorset in 1979. Exhibitions: many, mainly in the UK, also in Germany, Belgium and the USA. Collections: Fitzwilliam Museum (Cambridge), Victoria and Albert Museum (London), Royal Museum of Scotland (Edinburgh) and other major museum collections in the UK and Germany. Commissions: numerous, for museums, corporations and private clients. Work on view at Parnham House, Beaminster, Dorset.

Anna Malicka-Zamorska p.44
Born 1942, Lvov, USSR. Educated: State College of Fine Arts, Wroclaw, Poland. Exhibitions: numerous since 1965, in Eastern and Western Europe, Australia and the USA. Collections: museum collections in Poland, Czechoslovakia, Hungary, Italy, Australia and the USA.

Kate Malone p.27
Born 1959, London, UK. Educated: Bristol Polytechnic; Royal College of Art, London. Exhibitions: various since 1982, mainly in the UK, also in Japan, Germany, Canada and the Bahamas. Solo exhibition at Aberystwyth Arts Centre in 1990. Collections: Leeds City Art Gallery Collection (Leeds). Galleries: Contemporary Applied Arts, London. Photographic credit: Peter Chatterton.

Sam Maloof p.180
Born 1916, Chino CA, USA. Educated: Chino High School. Exhibitions: numerous, international. Collections: American Craft Museum (New York), Crafts and Folk Art Museum (Los Angeles), Minnesota Art Museum (St Paul), Museum of Fine Arts (Boston), Philadelphia Museum of Art (Philadelphia PA) and other major museum collections in the USA.

Jack Mankiewicz p.155
Born 1947, Warsaw, Poland. Has lived in the USA, Israel, Denmark and, currently, in Germany. Exhibitions: various. Commissions: custom-made pens and desk sets.

Irena Mareckova pp.158, 159
Born 1956, Prague, Czechoslovakia. Educated: Academy of Applied Arts, Prague and Theatre Academy, Prague. Exhibitions: various, in Eastern and Western Europe. Productions: designed sets, costumes, puppets, props and masks for numerous theatre, puppet-theatre and film productions. Awards: Czech Literary Fund Award in 1987 for her work on a production of 'Mowgli', based on the Rudyard Kipling Jungle Books. Photographic credit: Josef Piacek.

Pamela Martin p.150
Born 1949, London, UK. Educated: Loughborough College of Art and Design. Formed partnership with Peter Chatwin in 1981 (see above). Photographic credit: Keith Tidball.

Paolo Martinuzzi p.128
Born 1933, Venice, Italy. Exhibitions: numerous, mainly in Western Europe, also in Japan. Solo exhibition at Kunsthaus an Museum Carola van Ham in 1989. Awards: Coburger Glass Prize, Prix d'honneur 2e in 1985. Collections: Museo Vetrario (Murano), Musée des Arts Décoratifs (Paris and Lausanne), Glasmuseum (Immenhausen) and other major international museum collections. Galleries: Galerie Clara Scremini, Paris, Galerie Rob van den Doel, The Hague, Galerie J & L Lobmeyr, Vienna, etc. Photographic credit: Kunstmuseum, Düsseldorf.

Monique Mathieu-Frenaud p.9
Born 1927, Paris, France. Educated: Université de la Sorbonne, Paris; courses at the Cercle de la Librairie; studies with various bookbinders. Exhibitions: various, in Western Europe. Awards: the Rose Adler prize presented by the Société de la Relieure Originale in 1961. Collections: Bibliothèque Nationale (Paris), Bibliothèque Municipale (Rheims), Bibliotheca Wittockiana (Brussels), Harvard University Library (Cambridge MA) and other major museum and library collections in Western Europe.

Fédérica Matta p.191
Born 1955, Neuilly-sur-Seine, France. Exhibitions: various, in Western Europe, the USA and Australia. Galleries: Galerie Cremniter-Laffanour, Caroline Corre, Paris, Gallery of Functional Art, Los Angeles CA and Tolarno Gallery, Victoria.

Wilhelm Mattar p.95
Born 1946, Schlangen/Detmold, Germany. Educated: Fachhochschule für Gestaltung, Pforzheim. Closely involved in the Forum für Schmuck und Design in Cologne. Exhibitions: various, in Western Europe, Denmark, Japan and the USA. Collections: Schmuckmuseum (Pforzheim), Kunstgewerbemuseum (Berlin), Museum für Angewandte Kunst (Cologne) and other major museum collections in Germany and Denmark. Galleries: Werkstättegalerie, Berlin, Galerie Hipotesi, Barcelona, Galerie Metal, Copenhagen, Galerie Marzee, Nijmegen and Galerie Tragart, Basel. Photographic credit: Rüdiger Flöter.

Edward Paraumati Maxwell p.74
Born 1939, New Zealand, a member of the Te Arawa, Tuhoe and Ngati Awa tribes. Weaving is traditionally women's work in Maori culture but some men are now acquiring and practising this skill. The 'Paki' shown is based on a traditional raincape made for everyday, rather than ceremonial, use.

Ulla Mayer p.98
Born 1948, Germany. Educated: Akademie der Bildenden Künste, Nuremberg. Exhibitions: in Western Europe. Awards: a Bayerischer Staatsförderpreis in 1982. Collections: Badisches Landesmuseum (Karlsruhe) and Neue Sammlung (Munich).

Richard Meitner p.118
Born 1949, Philadelphia PA, USA. Lives and works in Holland. Educated: University of California, Berkeley CA; Gerrit Rietveld Akademie, Amsterdam. Teaching: since 1980, at the Gerrit Rietveld Akademie, Amsterdam. Exhibitions: various, international. Awards: include a special prize, 2.

Coburger Glaspreis, Coburg in 1985. Collections: Stedelijk Museum (Amsterdam), Musée des Arts Décoratifs (Paris and Lausanne), Corning Museum of Glass (Corning) and other major international museum collections. Photographic credit: Robert Schlingemann.

Enrique Mestre Estelles p.36
Born 1936, Alboraia, Valencia, Spain. Educated: Escuela Practica de Cerámica de Manises; Escuela de Artes Applicadas de Valencia; Escuela Superior de Bellas Artes de San Carlos, Valencia. Exhibitions: numerous, international. Solo exhibition at Galerie Macula, Alicante in 1990. Awards: include a Gold Medal from the State of Bavaria in 1976. Collections: Museo de Manises (Manises), Museo de Arte Contemporaneo (Madrid), Museu de Ceràmica (Barcelona) and other major museum collections in Western and Eastern Europe and the USA. Galleries: Galerie Macula, Alicante and Galerie Punto, Valencia. Photographic credit: Enrique Carrazani.

Bruce Metcalf p.95
Born 1949, Amherst, Massachusetts, USA. Educated: Tyler School of Art, Temple University, Philadelphia PA; Syracuse University NY. Teaching: currently Professor of Art at Kent State University OH. Exhibitions: various, mainly in the USA, also in Mexico and Korea. Collections: Cranbrook Academy of Art (Bloomfield Hills MI), Museum of Art (Philadelphia) and other major museum collections in the USA and in Holland. Galleries: Susan Cummins Gallery, Mill Valley CA, Perimeter Gallery, Chicago IL, Jewelers Werk, Washington DC and V & V Galerie, Vienna.

Floris Meydam p.114
Born 1919, Leerdam, Holland. Educated: Leerdam Glass School. Exhibitions: numerous since 1947, international. Awards: include a 'Good Design Award' from the Museum of Modern Art, New York in 1952. Collections: Museum Boymans-Van Beuningen (Rotterdam), Stedelijk Museum (Amsterdam), Nationaal Glasmuseum (Leerdam) and many other major museum collections in Western Europe and the USA. Photographic credit: Photo Schaart, Rotterdam.

Monique Middelhoek p.22
Born 1959, Emmen, Holland. Educated: Akademie voor Beeldend Kunstonderwijs, Kampen. Exhibitions: various, mainly in Holland, also in Switzerland. Awards: 'Complimenti' at Ornaris, Berne in 1986. Collections: Gemeentemuseum (Arnhem). Galleries: Galerie de Vis, Harlingen and Galerie Terra, Delft.

Jon Mills p.201
Born 1959, Birmingham, UK. Educated: Hereford College of Art; Wolverhampton Polytechnic. Founder member of Red Herring Studios and Gallery, Brighton. Exhibitions: various, in Western Europe, Japan and the USA. Solo exhibition at Crafts Council Shop at the V&A, London in 1990. Collections: Design Council and Crafts Council Collections (London). Galleries: Crafts Council Shop at the V&A, London and Red Herring Gallery, Brighton. Photographic credit: Jon Pratty.

Martin Mindermann p.32
Born 1960, Bremen, Germany. Educated: Hochschule für Künste, Bremen. Exhibitions: various, since 1986. Awards: Second Prize, Richard Bampi Prize 1987. Collections: Kunstgewerbemuseum (Berlin), Keramion (Frechen). Württembergisches Landesmuseum (Stuttgart) and other major museum collections in Germany. Galleries: Galerie Hauptsache Keramik, Hamburg, Galerie Kunsthandwerk Schnoor, Bremen and Galerie Terra, Arnhem. Photographic credit: Wurthmann.

Kyusetsu Miwa p.20
Born 1910, Hagi City, Japan. Exhibitions: numerous, in Japan. Has exhibited in Dento Kogei Ten (Traditional Crafts Exhibition) since 1957. In 1967, became 11th generation Kyusetsu. Designated a Living National Treasure in 1983.

Gertraud Möhwald p.45
Born 1929, Dresden, Germany. Educated: Hochschule für Industrielle Formgestaltung, Halle. Teaching: 1970–89 at Akademie der Künste, Boden, Austria. Exhibitions: numerous, mainly in Germany, also abroad. Collections: include major museum collections in Berlin, Dresden, Leipzig, Stuttgart. Photographic credit: G. Kilian.

Klaus Moje p.116
Born 1936, Hamburg, Germany; now lives in Australia. Educated: apprenticeship in the family studio; Glasfachschule, Rheinbach and Hadamar. Teaching: since 1982, in charge of the glass department at Canberra School of Art, Australia. Exhibitions: numerous, international. Solo exhibition at Galerie Sanske, Zürich in 1990. Awards: include a prize from Suntory Museum of Art, Tokyo in 1984. Collections: Kunstgewerbemuseum (Berlin), Kunstsammlungen der Veste Coburg (Coburg), Glasmuseum (Frauenau), Kunstmuseum (Düsseldorf) and many other major international museum

collections. Galleries: Galerie Sanske, Zürich, Galerie L, Hamburg and Habatat Galleries, Farmington Hills MI.

Odrun Molnar-Chiodera p.150
Born 1962, Switzerland; now lives in Norway. Educated: National College of Art, Crafts and Design, Oslo. Exhibitions: since 1986, in Scandinavia and Germany. Collections: Kunstindustrimuseet (Oslo) and other museum collections in Scandinavia. Photographic credit: T. Agnalt.

Platt Monfort p.144
Born 1921, Huntington NY, USA. Educated: Pratt Institute, Brooklyn NY. Teaching: various seminars and workshops in the USA. Exhibitions: in the USA and Europe. Photographic credit: Peter Jones.

Simon Moore p.112
Born 1959, Hull, UK. Educated: West Surrey College of Art and Design, Farnham. Maker of one-offs, also does production work with Steven Newell (see below). Set up Glass-Works Studio, London with Steven Newell and Catherine Hough. Exhibitions: some, in Western Europe, Japan and the USA. Solo exhibition at Galerie Midi Pile, Lausanne in 1989. Collections: Victoria and Albert Museum, Crafts Council Collection (London), Ulster Museum (Belfast) and Musée des Arts Décoratifs (Paris). Galleries: Contemporary Applied Arts, London and Galerie Midi Pile, Lausanne. Photographic credit: David Cripps.

Heike Mühlhaus pp.28, 195
Born 1954, Wiesbaden, Germany. Educated: Fachhochschule, Wiesbaden. Since 1981, has collaborated with Renate von Brevern on 'Cocktail' projects. Exhibitions: various, in Western Europe and Scandinavia. Galleries: Galerie UND, Düsseldorf, Design Galerie, Berlin and Galerie 5A, Munich. Photographic credit: Idris Kolodziej.

Tchai Munch p.117
Born 1954. Educated: School of Crafts and Design, Copenhagen, Denmark; Pilchuk School and Glass Center, Stanwood WA, USA. Exhibitions: various since 1987, international. Awards: Hempel's Glaspris 1988. Collections: Glasmuseum (Ebeltoft), Rohsska Konstslojdmuseet (Gothenburg) and other major museum collections in Scandinavia and Germany. Galleries: Galerie Ewers an Gross St Martin, Cologne and Galerie L, Hamburg. Photographic credit: Tchai Munch.

Forrest Myers p.200
Born 1941, Long Beach CA, USA. Educated: California School of Fine Arts, San Francisco CA. Exhibitions: various since 1960, mainly in the USA, also in Mexico, Japan and Holland. Solo exhibition at Art et Industrie, New York in 1989. Collections: Art Institute of Chicago (Chicago), Museum of Fine Arts (Dallas TX) and other major museum collections in the USA. Galleries: Art et Industrie, New York and Brutus Gallery, Osaka, Japan. Photographic credit: Joseph Coscia Jr./ Art et Industrie.

Jan Myers-Newbury p.65
Born 1950, Greenville PA, USA. Educated: St Olaf College, Northfield MN; University of Minnesota, St Paul MN. Exhibitions: various, in the USA only. Solo exhibition at Sonia's Gallery, Minneapolis MN in 1989. Collections: Minneapolis Institute of Arts (Minneapolis), Minnesota Historical Society (St Paul) and other museums in the USA. Galleries: Sonia's Gallery, Minneapolis MN.

Thomas Naethe p.23
Born 1954, Berlin, Germany. Educated: Fachschule für Keramik, Höhr-Grenzhausen. Exhibitions: various since 1980, mainly in Germany, also in France. Awards: Second Prize, Richard Bampi Prize, 1984. Collections: Museum für Kunsthandwerk (Frankfurt), Keramion (Frechen), Kestner-Museum (Hanover) and other major museum collections in Germany. Galleries: Galerie Kunst + Keramiek, Deventer. Photographic credit: Strengler Atelier, Osnabruck.

Risë Nagin p.67
Born 1950, Norwalk CT, USA. Educated: Carnegie-Mellon University, Pittsburgh PA. Exhibitions: various, mainly in the USA, also in Western and Eastern Europe. Collections: Museum of Art (Philadelphia). Galleries: Helen Drutt Gallery, Philadelphia.

Zuishin Nakadai p.146
Born 1912, Chiba City, Japan. Exhibitions: numerous, in Japan. First exhibited in Dento Kogei Ten (Traditional Crafts Exhibition) in 1962. Designated a Living National Treasure in 1984.

Kimpei Nakamura pp.48, 49
Born 1935, Kanazawa, Ishikawa-ken Japan. Educated: Kanazawa Art University; Japanese Government Industrial Research Institute. Teaching: Professor at Tama Art University, Toyko. Exhibitions: many, mainly in Japan, also in the USA, Italy, France, the UK and the USSR. Awards: include the Cultural Prize of Northern Japan in 1967. Collections: National Museum of Modern Art, Suntory Museum of Art (Tokyo) and other major museum collections in Japan, the USA, France

and Switzerland. Galleries: Fujii Gallery Modern, Tokyo.

Anthony Natsoulas p.46
Born 1959. Educated: University of California; Maryland Institute College of Art; California State University. Exhibitions: numerous in the USA. Solo exhibition at James Snidle Gallery, Chico CA in 1990. Galleries: James Snidle Gallery, Chico CA and Natsoulas Novelozo Gallery, Davis CA. Photographic credit: Eddie Hood.

Eduardo Nery p.51
Born 1938, Figueira da Foz, Portugal. Educated: Academy of Fine Arts, Lisbon; studied with Jean Lurçat at Saint-Céré in France. Exhibitions: numerous, international. Collections: Centro de Arte Moderna, Museu Nacional de Arte Moderna (Porto) and other major museum collections in Portugal. Photographic credit: José Veneno.

Steven Newell p.112
Born 1948, Massachusetts, USA; now lives in London. Educated Kansas City Institute; Carnegie-Mellon University; Royal College of Art, London. Founder-member of Glass-Works with Simon Moore (see above) and Catherine Hough. Makes one-off and production work. Exhibitions: various since 1974, international. Awards: 1977 European Glass Prize, Coburg. Collections: Victoria and Albert Museum, Crafts Council Collection (London), Shipley Art Gallery (Gateshead), Broadfield House (West Midlands) and other major museum collections in Germany and the USA. Galleries: Contemporary Applied Arts, London, Galerie d'Amon, Paris and Galerie Charlotte Hennig, Darmstadt. Photographic credit: David Cripps.

Peter Niczewski p.10
Born 1948, London, UK. Educated: Chelsea School of Art, London. Exhibitions: various, in Western Europe, Japan and the USA. Collections: Crafts Council Collection (London), Shipley Art Gallery (Gateshead) and other major museum collections in the UK and Holland. Galleries: Contemporary Applied Arts, Crafts Council Shop at the V&A, Collier Campbell, London, Galerie Ra, Amsterdam and Jewelers Werk, Washington DC.

Guido Niest p.101
Born 1958, Ciudad Ojeda, Venezuela. Moved to Europe in 1979. Educated: Fachhochschule, Munich. Since 1986, has worked at the Sabattini Argentana as Assistant to Lino Sabattini (see below), but also accepts jewelry commissions.

Yohei Nishimura p.169
Born 1947, Kyoto, Japan. Educated: Tokyo National University. Teaches ceramics at a school for the blind. Exhibitions: various, mainly in Japan, also in Korea, Canada, Germany, Belgium and Denmark. Solo exhibition at Gallery Mori, Tokyo in 1990. Collections: Metropolitan Museum of Art (Tokyo), Yamaguchi Prefectural Museum of Art, Kure Museum of Art and Musée des Arts Décoratifs (Paris). Galleries: Gallery Mori, Gallery Pousse, etc. in Tokyo.

Osamu Noda p.133
Educated: Tama Art University, Tokyo, Japan; Illinois State University, USA. Teaching: 1986–90, at Tama Art University, Tokyo. Exhibitions: various, in Japan, Korea, the USA, Germany and Switzerland. Solo exhibition at Ikebukoro Seibu Department Store, Tokyo in 1989. Awards: First Prize (student) 'Fragile Glass Art '84', *Glass Art Magazine*, USA. Galleries: Plus-Minus Gallery, Tokyo and Lynn McAllister Gallery, Seattle WA.

Yumiko Noda p.114
Educated: Tama Art University, Tokyo, Japan; Illinois State University, USA. Exhibitions; various, in Japan, Korea, the USA, Germany and Switzerland. Galleries: Lynn McAllister Gallery, Seattle WA and Heller Gallery, New York.

Norelene (Hélène and Nora Ferruzzi) p.59
Hélène Ferruzzi and her step-daughter, Nora Ferruzzi, collaborate in the production of hand-printed fabrics. Exhibitions: in Western Europe and North America. Collections: Musée de la Mode et du Costume (Paris), Musée de l' Impression sur Étoffes (Mulhouse), Museum Boymans-Van Beuningen (Rotterdam) and other major museum collections in Western Europe. Galleries: Norelene, Venice, Nobilis – Fontan, Paris, Panache, Toronto and Trompe l'Oeil Gallery, New York.

Magdalene N Odundo p.35
Born Nairobi, Kenya. Educated: West Surrey College of Art and Design, Farnham; Royal College of Art, London. Exhibitions: various, in Western Europe, North America and Kenya. Solo exhibitions at Anthony Ralph Gallery, New York and Museum für Kunst und Gewerbe with Galerie L, Hamburg in 1991. Collections: Victoria and Albert Museum, British Museum, Crafts Council Collection (London), Cleveland Crafts Centre (Middlesbrough) and other major museum collections in the UK, Germany, Kenya and the USA. Galleries: Oxford Gallery, Oxford and Anthony Ralph Gallery, New York. Photographic credit: Duncan Ross.

Maria José Oliviera p.56
Born 1943, Lisbon, Portugal. Educated: IADE, Lisbon. Exhibitions: since 1979, mainly in Portugal, also in Spain. Solo exhibition at Sociedade Nacional des Belas-Artes, Lisbon in 1990. Galleries: Artefacto 3, Lisbon and Galerie Gu, Barcelona.

Ingrid Olsson p.38
Born Sweden. Educated: Swedish State College of Arts, Crafts and Design, Stockholm. Exhibitions: various, mainly in Sweden, also abroad. Awards: Swedish Form, Prize of Honour 1983. Collections: National Museum (Stockholm), Museum of Malmö and other major museum collections in Sweden. Galleries: Konsthantverkarna, Stockholm. Photographic credit: Bengt Videgård.

Michael Olszewski p.64
Born 1950, Baltimore MD, USA. Educated: Maryland Institute College of Art, Baltimore MD; Kansas City Art Institute MO; Cranbrook Academy of Art, Bloomfield Hills MI. Teaching: currently, Associate Professor at Moore College of Art and Design, Philadelphia PA. Exhibitions: various, mainly in the USA, also in Austria. Solo exhibition at Helen Drutt Gallery in 1990. Galleries: Helen Drutt Gallery, Philadelphia PA.

Yoichi Onagi p.83
Born 1931, Tokyo, Japan. Educated: Doshisya University; Kyoto Gakugei University. Exhibitions: numerous, in Japan, Korea, Taiwan and Western and Eastern Europe. Collections: Kyoto Municipal Museum. Photographic credit: Yasu Suzuka.

Showasai Ono p.146
Born 1912, Okayama Prefecture, Japan. Exhibitions: numerous, in Japan. First exhibited in Dento Kogei Ten (Traditional Crafts Exhibition) in 1965. Designated a Living National Treasure in 1984.

Judy Onofrio p.96
Born New London CO, USA. Educated: Sullins College, Bristol VI. Exhibitions: various, mainly in the USA, also in Holland. Collections: include Museum voor Hedendagse Kunst Het Kruithuis (Den Bosch). Galleries: Helen Drutt Gallery, Philadelphia PA.

Kodo Otomaru p.152
Born 1898, Japan, Educated: began learning *choshitsu* lacquer technique at the age of thirteen with Keido Ishii. Exhibitions: numerous since 1932, in Japan. Awards: numerous, distinguished. Has been designated a Living National Treasure.

Pekka Paikkari p.50
Born 1960, Somero, Finland.

Educated: Kuopio Institute for Craft and Industrial Design. Exhibitions: since 1983, mainly in Finland, also in Germany, France and the UK. Solo exhibitions at Jyväskylä in 1989. Collections: Taideteollisuus Museo, Arabia Museo (Helsinki) and other major museum collections in Finland and the UK. Represented by: Oy Arabia AB, Helsinki. Photographic credit: Wärtsilä, Finland.

Albert Paley pp.204–205
Born 1944, Philadelphia PA, USA. Educated: Tyler School of Art, Temple University, Philadelphia PA. Teaching: since 1984, Artist-in-Residence at College of Fine and Applied Art, Rochester Institute of Technology, Rochester NY. Exhibitions: numerous, international. Solo exhibitions at Gerald Peters Gallery, Santa Fé NM and Dawson Gallery, Rochester NY in 1990. Collections: Cooper-Hewitt Museum, Smithsonian Institution and Metropolitan Museum of Art (New York), Museum of Fine Arts (Boston), Renwick Gallery, Smithsonian Institution (Washington D.C.) and other major museum collections in the USA. Commissions: numerous, in the USA. Galleries: Fendrick Gallery, Washington D.C., Gerald Peters Gallery, Santa Fé NM, Dawson Gallery, Rochester NY and Walter Gallery, Santa Monica CA.

Jim Partridge pp.149, 207
Born 1953. Educated: John Makepeace School for Craftsmen in Wood, Dorset, UK. Since 1986, has collaborated with Liz Walmsley on site-specific outdoor woodworks. Exhibitions: various, in Western and Eastern Europe and Japan. Solo exhibition at Crafts Council Gallery, London in 1989. Awards: Prizewinner, World Crafts Council, Bratislava in 1986. Collections: Crafts Council Collection, Contemporary Arts Society (London) and the National Museum of Modern Art (Kyoto). Galleries: Contemporary Applied Arts, London and Scottish Gallery, Edinburgh.

Katarzyna Paszkowska p.78
Born 1961, Poland. Educated: Academy of Art, Poznan; studies in the studios of M. Abakanowicz and W. Sniercy. Teaching: at the Tapestry Studio of the Academy of Art, Poznan until 1981. Exhibitions: various, in Eastern and Western Europe.

Jiří Pelcl pp.104, 201
Born 1950, Brno, Czechoslovakia. Educated: Brno Art School; Academy of Applied Arts, Prague; Royal College of Art, London. Founding member of the ATIKA Design group. Exhibitions: various, in Western Europe. Commissions: Václav Havel's study,

Prague Castle, in 1990. Galleries: Gallery Na Mustku, Prague, Galerie Néotu and Galerie Via, Paris, Galerie Ambiente, Frankfurt and Galerie Binnen, Amsterdam.

Sibylle Peretti p.118
Born 1964, Mulheim-Ruhr, Germany. Educated: Glasfachschule, Zwiesel. Teaching: since 1987 at the Fachhochschule, Cologne. Exhibitions: in Germany and the USA. Solo exhibition at Galerie Herrmann, Drachselsried in 1989. Galleries: Galerie Herrmann, Drachselsried and Galerie Monica Trüjen, Bremen.

Tom Perkins p.8
Born 1957, Plymouth, Devon, UK. Educated: Plymouth College of Art and Design; Reigate School of Art and Design. Assistant to Richard Kindersley. Teaching: visiting lecturer at Digby Stuart College, Roehampton Institute, London. Exhibitions: various since 1979, mainly in the UK, also in Belgium and the USA. Collections: Crafts Council Collection (London) and Crafts Study Centre, Holburne of Menstrie Museum (Bath). Commissions: various, clients include the Crafts Council, Ely Cathedral, Magdalen College Chapel, Oxford, etc. in the UK.

Ruudt Peters p.104
Born 1950, Naaldwijk, Holland. Educated: Gerrit Rietveld Akademie, Amsterdam. Teaching: since 1984 at Kunstakademie Kampen. Exhibitions: various since 1983, mainly in Holland, also in Western Europe. Collections: Stedelijk Museum (Amsterdam) and other major museums in Holland and the USA. Galleries: Galerie Marzee, Nijmegen, Galerie het Kapelhuis, Amersfoort and Galerie V&V, Vienna. Photographic credit: Bob Versluys.

Kajsa Af Petersens p.70
Born 1941. Educated: Swedish State College of Arts, Crafts and Design, Stockholm. Exhibitions: mainly in Scandinavia, also in Poland and the USA. Productions: various collaborations with the dance group, Tiger. Collections: Rohsska Konstslojdmuseet (Gothenburg) and other major museum collections in Sweden. Photographic credit: Peter Af Petersens.

Gloria Petyarre – Utopia Batik p.62
Born 1938, of the Anmatyewe language group, Northern Territory, Australia. In 1978, a batik group was organized at Utopia Station as part of an adult education programme. The production and sale of fabrics helps provide the community with a measure of economic independence.

Gwyn Hanssen Pigott p.23
Born 1935, Ballarat, Australia. Educated: University of Melbourne. Teaching: University of New South Wales, Kelvin Grove College, Brisbane and Australian Flying Arts School. Exhibitions: numerous, mainly in Australia, also in NZ, Japan, the UK, France and the USA. Collections: Powerhouse Museum (Sydney), Art Gallery of Western Australia (Perth), National Gallery of Victoria (Melbourne), Art Gallery of South Australia (Adelaide) and major museum collections in Japan, the UK and France. Galleries: Gary Anderson Gallery, Sydney. Photographic credit: Victor France.

Jochem Poensgen p.135
Born 1931, Düsseldorf, Germany. Educated: self-taught. Exhibitions: numerous, international. Collections: Hessisches Landesmuseum (Darmstadt), Kunstmuseum (Düsseldorf), Museum für Kunsthandwerk (Frankfurt-am-Main) and other major museum collections in Germany, the UK and the USA. Commissions: numerous architectural projects. In 1990, St Vincentiuskirche, Bersenbruck, Germany and Ornaskyrkogarden, Lulea, Sweden. Galleries: Galerie Handwerk, Munich.

David Pottinger p.21
Born 1965, Dalby, Queensland, Australia. Educated: Kelvin Grove College, Brisbane. Exhibitions: various, in Australia. Collections: Australian National Gallery (Canberra). Photographic credit: Nick Ainford.

Ramon Puig Cuyas p.97
Born 1953, Mataró/Barcelona, Spain. Educated: Escuela Massana, Barcelona. Teaching: lecturer in Jewelry Design at Escuela Massana, Barcelona, since 1978. Exhibitions: various since 1972, international. Solo exhibition at Helen Drutt Gallery in 1990. Collections: numerous international public collections. Galleries: Helen Drutt Gallery, Philadelphia PA and Hilde Leis Galerie, Hamburg.

David Pye p.146
Born 1914, UK. Educated: Architectural Association School of Architecture, London. Teaching: taught for 26 years, for the last ten as Professor of Furniture Design at the Royal College of Art, London, retired 1974. Author of the key design texts, *The Nature and Art of Workmanship* and *The Nature and Aesthetics of Design*. Exhibitions: numerous, international. A retrospective in 1984 at Crafts Council Gallery, London. Collections: Victoria and Albert Museum, Crafts Council Collection (London), Crafts Study Centre, Holburne of Menstrie Museum (Bath) and other major museum collections in

the UK. Galleries: Crafts Council Shop at the V&A, London. Photographic credit: David Cripps.

Robin Quigley p.102
Born 1947, New York, USA. Educated: Tyler School of Art, Temple University, Philadelphia PA; Rhode Island School of Design, Providence RI. Teaching: since 1981, Assistant Professor at Rhode Island School of Design. Exhibitions: various, international. Solo exhibition at Garth Clark Gallery, New York in 1990. Galleries: Garth Clark Gallery, New York.

Wendy Ramshaw p.88
Born 1939, Sunderland, County Durham, UK. Educated: College of Art and Industrial Design, Newcastle upon Tyne; Central School of Art and Design, London. Exhibitions: numerous, international. Solo exhibitions at Hand and the Spirit Gallery, Scottsdale AR and City Art Gallery, Birmingham in 1990. Awards: include the De Beers 'Diamond Today' Prize and a De Beers Diamond International Award. Collections: Victoria and Albert Museum, Crafts Council Collection, Goldsmiths Hall Permanent Collection and Museum of London (London) and other major international museum collections. Galleries: Hand and the Spirit Gallery, Scottsdale AR and Electrum Gallery, London. Photographic credit: Bob Cramp.

Puti Rare p.55
Born New Zealand, a member of the Ngati Maniapoto tribe. Her 'korowai' is a garment worn by people of rank on ceremonial occasions and features several traditional Maori techniques, being made entirely by hand at every stage of construction.

Ursula Rauch p.66
Born 1944, Salem/Bodensee, Germany. Educated: Bodensee Kunstschule, Konstanz; Hochschule für Bildende Künste, Berlin; Staatliche Akademie der Bildenden Künste, Karlsruhe. Exhibitions: various, in Germany and France. Collections: Regierungspräsidium (Karlsruhe). Galleries: Galerie im Blauen Haus, Karlsruhe.

Howard Raybould p.191
Born 1046, London, England. Educated: Ravensbourne College of Art and Design; Hammersmith School of Art. Exhibitions: various, mainly in the UK, also in France, the USA and Canada. Collections: Crafts Council Collection (London), Shipley Art Gallery (Gateshead) and other museum collections in the UK. Commissions: numerous. Galleries: Thumb Gallery, Contemporary Applied Arts, Crafts Council Shop at the V&A, London and

Oxford Gallery, Oxford. Photographic credit: Melanie Cox.

Mary Restieaux p.7
Born 1945, Norwich, UK. Educated: Cambridge College of Art and Technology; Royal College of Art, London. Teaching: currently part-time at Goldsmiths College, London. Exhibitions: various, international. Collections: Victoria and Albert Museum, Crafts Council Collection (London), Shipley Art Gallery (Gateshead), Crafts Study Centre, Holburne of Menstrie Museum (Bath) and other major museum collections in the UK, Germany and Japan. Galleries: Crafts Council Shop at the V&A, Contemporary Applied Arts, London and Hand and the Spirit Gallery, Scottsdale AR. Photographic credit: Ed Barber.

Lucie Rie p.25
Born 1902, Vienna, Austria. Educated: Kunstgewerbeschule, Vienna. Moved to the UK in 1938. Taught at Camberwell School of Art and Crafts. Collaborated with the late Hans Coper. Exhibitions: numerous, international. Solo exhibition (including new work) at Sogetsu in 1990. Awards: numerous. Became a Dame of the British Empire (DBE) in 1991. Collections: Crafts Council Collection (London) and numerous other major international museum collections. Galleries: Galerie Besson, London.

Gérard Rigot p.191
Born 1929. Educated: studied painting; self-taught toy- and furniture-maker. Exhibitions: various, in Western Europe, Scandinavia and the USA. Solo exhibition at Camden Arts Centre and two-person exhibition at Contemporary Applied Arts, London in 1989. Collections: Musée des Arts Décoratifs (Paris). Galleries: Contemporary Applied Arts, London and Galerie Ahlmer, Paris.

Faith Ringgold p.67
Born 1930, New York NY, USA. Educated: City College of New York; City University of New York. Teaching: University of California, San Diego CA. Exhibitions: numerous in the USA. Collections: Children's Museum (New York), Newark Museum (Newark) and other major museum collections in the USA. Photographic credit: Fabric Workshop, Philadelphia.

Kristina Riska p.50
Born 1960, Finland. Educated: University of Industrial Arts, Helsinki. Exhibitions: since 1984, in Finland. Collections: Arabia Museum Collection, State of Finland Collection, Taideteollisuus Museo (Helsinki) and

other major museum collections in Finland. Galleries: Arabia Gallery, Helsinki. Photographic credit: Kimmo Triman.

Christopher Robertson p.188
Born 1957, Norseman, Western Australia. Educated: Curtin University of Technology, Australia; Royal College of Art, London. Exhibitions: since 1984, in Australia and the UK. Exhibition with Jennifer Robertson (see below) at the Crafts Council Gallery, Perth in 1989. Collections: Art Gallery of Western Australia (Perth) and Powerhouse Museum (Sydney).

Jennifer Robertson p.188
Born 1962, Weston-Super-Mare, Avon, UK. Educated: West Surrey College of Art and Design, Farnham; Royal College of Art, London. Exhibitions: some, in the UK and Australia. Exhibition with Christopher Robertson (see above) at the Crafts Council Gallery, Perth in 1989.

Marta Rogoyska p.76
Born 1950, Beckenham, Kent, UK. Educated: Leeds Polytechnic; Royal College of Art, London; training periods in Warsaw, Aubusson and Nuremberg. Teaching: since 1980, part-time at Morley College, London. Exhibitions: many, international. Collections: Victoria and Albert Museum, Crafts Council Collection (London) and other major museum collections in the UK, France and Japan. Commissions: many corporate and private, including the BBC, the British Medical Association and various schools in the UK. Galleries: Contemporary Applied Arts and Crafts Council Shop at the V&A, London.

José Luis Romanillos p.154
Born 1932, Madrid, Spain. Educated: apprenticed to a cabinetmaker at the age of thirteen, otherwise self-taught. Moved to the UK in 1956. Commissions: an internationally respected luthier, his waiting-list for guitars and related instruments stretches into the next century. He is technical advisor for musical instruments to the Crafts Council. Photographic credit: Nic Dixon.

Aldo Rontini p.11
Born 1947, Brisighella, Italy. Teaching: at the Istituto d'Arte Ceramica 'G. Ballardini', Faenza. Since the early 1980s, associated with the Cooperativa Ceramica d'Imola. Exhibited in *Metamorphosis*, Shigaraki Ceramic Cultural Park, Japan.

Dick Roose p.182
Born 1952. Educated: Akademie voor Beeldende Vorming, Tilburg. Exhibitions: since 1983, in Holland only.

Galleries: Gallery Novis, Utrecht and Town Gallery, Schiedam.

Roland Rouré p.108
Born 1940. Works in mixed media and best known for his large-scale mobiles and toy sculptures. Exhibitions: various, in France. Collections: Musée des Arts Décoratifs (Paris).

Michael Rowe pp.14, 104
Born 1948, High Wycombe, Buckinghamshire, UK. Educated: High Wycombe College of Art; Royal College of Art, London. Teaching: currently, Head of Metalwork and Jewelry at Royal College of Art, London. Exhibitions: numerous, international. Awards: include Sotheby Decorative Arts Award (1988). Collections: Victoria and Albert Museum, Crafts Council Collection (London), Shipley Art Gallery (Gateshead) and other major museum collections in the UK, Germany and Australia. Galleries: Contemporary Applied Arts and Crafts Council Shop at the V&A, London. Photographic credit: Ian Haigh.

Christian Rudolph p.106
Born 1959, Aschaffenburg, Germany. Educated: Akademie der Bildenden Künste, Nuremberg (1986–91). Exhibitions: some, since 1987, in Germany only. Collections: Museum für Kunsthandwerk (Frankfurt-am-Main). Galleries: Galerie Kunsthandwerk, Berlin and Galerie Decus, Nuremberg.

Desmond Ryan p.155
Born 1941, Dublin, Ireland. Educated: Beckenham School of Art; Royal College of Art, London. Exhibitions: various, in Western Europe and Japan. Collections: Crafts Council Collection, Victoria and Albert Museum (London) and other major museum collections in the UK and Germany. Galleries: Crafts Council Shop at the V&A, London. Photographic credit: Jeremy McCabe.

Johanna Rytkölä p.12
Born 1956, Helsinki, Finland. Educated: University of Industrial Arts. Exhibitions: in Scandinavia and Western Europe. Solo exhibitions at Galleria Bronda, Helsinki in 1990. Collections: Paulo Foundation, State of Finland Collection and other museum collections in Finland. Galleries: Galleria Bronda, Helsinki and Galleri Blås & Knåda, Stockholm. Photographic credit: Kalevi Rytkölä.

Lino Sabattini p.100
Born 1925, Correggio, Italy. Exhibitions: various, in Western Europe, Japan and the USA. Solo exhibition at Corso Monforte, Milan in 1989. Awards: include a Compasso d'Oro in 1979. Collections: Museum of Modern Art, Cooper-Hewitt Museum,

Smithsonian Institution (New York), Museum of Contemporary Art (La Jolla CA), Victoria and Albert Museum, British Museum (London) and other major museum collections in Western Europe and the USA. Represented by: Sabattini Argentaria S.p.A., Bregnana/Como.

Naja Salto p.78
Born 1945, Educated: School of Decorative Art, Copenhagen; National Danish Theatre School; Danish Academy of Art Architectural School. Exhibitions: various since 1967, in Scandinavia, Western and Eastern Europe and the USA. Solo exhibition at Konstmuseet, Lund in 1990. Collections: Kunstindustrimuseet (Copenhagen) and other major museum collections in Denmark.

Arturo Alonzo Sandoval p.79
Born 1942, Espanola NM, USA. Educated: California State College, Los Angeles CA; Cranbrook Academy of Art, Bloomfield Hills MI. Teaching: currently Professor at College of Fine Arts, University of Kentucky, Lexington KY. Exhibitions: numerous, mainly in the USA, also in Switzerland, Japan and Korea. Solo exhibition at Harlequin Gallery, San José CA in 1990. Collections: Museum of Modern Art (New York). Galleries: Yaw Gallery, Birmingham AL and Eve Mannes Gallery, Atlanta GA. Photographic credit: Mary S. Rezny.

Shimpei Sato pp.131, 132
Born 1953, Fukushima Prefecture, Japan. Educated: San Francisco Academy of Art College. Exhibitions: various, mainly in Japan, also in Austria.

Wolfgang Sattler p.206
Born in Germany. Works as a designer in Milan. Since 1982 a member of Rastlos, a loosely connected group of fourteen kindred designers (among them Andreas Brandolini, Jasper Morrison and Massimo Iosa Ghini) who occasionally work and exhibit together.

Jane Sauer p.143
Born 1937, St Louis MO, USA. Educated: Washington University, St Louis MO. Exhibitions: numerous, mainly in the USA, also in the UK, Australia, NZ, Canada, Zimbabwe, etc. Collections: Nordenfjeldske Kunstindustrimuseum (Trondheim) and other major museum collections in the USA, China and Japan. Galleries: Bellas Artes, Santa Fé NM and Works Gallery, Philadelphia PA. Photographic credit: Mark Katzman.

Mike Savage p.102
Born 1962, Hampshire, UK. Educated: Camberwell School of Art and Crafts; Royal College of Art, London.

Exhibitions: some, in the UK, Germany and Japan. Collections: Crafts Council Collection (London). Galleries: Contemporary Applied Arts, London. Photographic credit: V. Brown.

David Sawyer p.154
Born 1942, Derby, UK. Educated: Exeter College of Art and Design. Exhibitions: in the UK only. Commissions: various in the UK and Belgium, including Sound Playgrounds at Bethnal Green and Islington and various musical instruments for theatre productions. Collections: Musical Instrument Museum (Brussels). Photographic credit: Nick Rogers.

Adrian Saxe pp.27, 29
Born 1943, Glendale CA, USA. Educated: Chouinard Art Institute, Los Angeles CA; California Institute of the Arts, Valencia CA. Teaching: Associate Professor of Art at University of California since 1973. Exhibitions: many in the USA, France, Japan and Korea. Solo exhibition at Garth Clark Gallery, New York in 1990. Collections: Renwick Gallery, Smithsonian Institution (Washington D.C.), Everson Museum of Art (Syracuse), Los Angeles County Museum of Art (Los Angeles) and other major museum collections in the USA, the UK and France. Galleries: Garth Clark Gallery, New York and Los Angeles. Photographic credit: John White/Garth Clark Gallery.

Ludwig Schaffrath p.134
Born 1924, Alsdorf, Germany. Educated: Rheinisch-Westfälischen Technischen Hochschule, Aachen. Teaching: since 1985, Professor at the Akademie der Bildenden Künste, Stuttgart. Exhibitions: numerous since 1948, in Germany and abroad. Commissions: numerous, international. Photographic credit: W. Derix Tannusstein.

Karl Scheid p.6
Born 1929, Lengfeld/Odenwald, Germany. Educated: Werkkunstschule, Darmstadt. Exhibitions: numerous, in Germany, Scandinavia and Japan. Collections: Kunstgewerbemuseum (Berlin), Sammlungen der Veste Coburg (Coburg), Hetjens-Museum, (Düsseldorf) and other major museum collections in Western and Eastern Europe and Japan.

Marjorie Schick p.92
Born 1941, Illinois, USA. Educated: University of Wisconsin, Madison WI; Indiana University, Bloomington IN; Sir John Cass School of Art, London. Teaching: since 1967, Professor of Art at Pittsburg State University, Pittsburg KA. Exhibitions: numerous, international. A Retrospective at School of Fine Arts Gallery, Indiana University,

Bloomington IN in 1990. Awards: include a Fine Works Award, Isetan Art Museum, Tokyo in 1983. Collections: National Museum of Modern Art (Kyoto), Nordenfjeldske Kunstindustrimuseum (Trondheim), Kunstindustrimuseet (Oslo) and other major museum collections in the USA, Korea, Holland and the UK. Galleries: Gallery Ra, Amsterdam, Contemporary Applied Arts, London and Helen Drutt Gallery, Philadelphia and New York. Photographic credit: Malcolm Turner.

Cynthia Schira p.77
Born 1934, Pittsfield MA, USA. Educated: Rhode Island School of Design, Providence RI; University of Kansas; École d'Art Décoratif, Aubusson, France. Teaching: currently Professor of Design, University of Kansas. Exhibitions: various, in the USA, Western and Eastern Europe, Finland and Japan. Collections: Renwick Gallery, Smithsonian Institution (Washington D.C.), Metropolitan Museum of Art, Cooper-Hewitt Museum (New York) and other major museum collections in the USA and Switzerland. Galleries: Miller/Brown Gallery, San Francisco CA.

Peter Schmitz p.102
Born 1959, Duisberg, Germany. Educated: Fachhochschule, Hildesheim/Holzminden. Runs Galerie Pande. Exhibitions: various since 1984, mainly in Germany, also in the USA, the UK and France. Collections: Römer und Pelizaeus Museum (Hildesheim). Galleries: Galerie Pande, Hildesheim, Galerie Form + Gefäss, Würzberg and Möbel Per Du, Hamburg.

Werner Schneider p.174
Born 1935, Marburg/Lahn, Germany. Educated: Werkkunstschule, Wiesbaden. Teaching: since 1971, Professor at Fachhochschule, Wiesbaden. Exhibitions: numerous, international. Collections: various major museum collections in Western Europe. Photographic credit: Katharina Pieper.

Johannes Schreiter p.134
Born 1930, Buchholz/Erzgebirge, Germany. Educated: in Münster/Westphalia, Mainz and Berlin. Teaching: 1963–87, Professor at Hochschule für Bildende Künste, Frankfurt. Exhibitions: numerous, international. Awards: include a Medal of Honour at the second *Kleine Grafische Formen* exhibition in Lódź, Poland in 1981. Collections: major museum collections in more than fifty countries, including Germany. Commissions: numerous, in Germany, France, the UK and Sweden. Photographic credit: Renée v. Falkenburg.

June Schwarcz p.102
Born 1918, Denver, Colorado, USA. Educated: University of Colorado; University of Chicago; Pratt Institute, Brooklyn NY. Exhibitions: numerous, international. Solo exhibition at Franklin Parrasch Gallery, New York in 1990. Collections: American Crafts Museum (New York), Everson Museum (Syracuse), Renwick Gallery, Smithsonian Institution (Washington D.C.) and other major museum collections in the USA, Norway and Switzerland. Galleries: Franklin Parrasch Gallery, New York.

Robert Schwarz p.168
Born 1951, Ludwigshafen, Germany. Educated: University of Heidelberg; University of Mainz. Exhibitions: various, mainly in Germany, also in France, Spain, Belgium and Yugoslavia. Solo exhibition at Gutenberg-Museum, Mainz in 1989. Often collaborates with Johannes Strugalla. Collections: Universitätsbibliothek (Heidelberg), Württembergische Landesbibliothek (Stuttgart), Bayerische Staatsbibliothek (Munich) and other major museums and library collections in Western Europe and the USA. Represented by: Editions F. Despalles, Paris and Mainz. Photographic credit: Françoise Despalles.

Tereza Seabra p.89
Born 1944, Alcobaça, Portugal. Educated: Escola Superior de Belas Artes, Lisbon; Craft Institute of America and Art Centre Y, New York; Hochschule für Bildenden Künste, Hamburg. Teaching: Head of Jewelry Department, AR.CO, Lisbon. Exhibitions: various, in Western Europe, South America and Japan. Galleries: Galeria de Arte, Vilamoura, Galerie Marzee, Nijmegen and Galerie Koppel, Hamburg. Photographic credit: Paul Valente.

Warren Seelig p.80
Born 1946, Abington PA, USA. Educated: Kutztown State College, Kutztown PA; Philadelphia College of Textiles and Science; Cranbrook Academy of Art, Bloomfield Hills MI. Teaching: currently professor and head of fibers programme at University of the Arts, Philadelphia PA. Exhibitions: various, in the USA and Western Europe. Collections: American Craft Museum (New York) and Greenville County Museum of Art, North Carolina.

Teresa Segurado p.156
Born 1957, Lisbon, Portugal. Educated: António Arroio School, IADE School and AR.CO, Lisbon. A member of '3.4.5' group of Portuguese weavers, founded by Gisella Santi. Exhibitions: various, mainly in Portugal also in Western Europe. Solo exhibition at Museu Naçional do Traje, Lisbon in 1990.

Hisako Sekijima p.144
Educated: studied with Akimichi Hashimoto in Japan and with Sandra Newman, John McQueen and Ken and Kathleen Dalton in the USA. Teaching: at Tokyo Textile Kenkyujo and Kawashima Textile School, Kyoto. Exhibitions: various, in Japan and the USA. Solo exhibitions at Gallery Isogaya and Axis Gallery, Tokyo in 1990. Collections: Erie Art Museum, Pennsylvania, USA. Galleries: Bellas Artes Gallery, Santa Fé NM and New York, and Gallery Isogaya and Axis Gallery, Tokyo. Photographic credit: Masaaki Sekiya.

Kay Sekimachi p.142
Born 1926, San Francisco CA, USA. Educated: Haystack Mountain School of Crafts, Liberty ME; California College of Arts and Crafts, Oakland CA. Exhibitions: numerous, international. Collections: American Craft Museum (New York), Renwick Gallery, Smithsonian Institution (Washington D.C.) and other major museum collections in the USA, Japan, France and the UK. Galleries: Miller/ Brown Gallery, San Francisco and Bellas Artes Gallery, Santa Fé NM.

Sunao Sera p.94
Educated: Women's Junior College of Art, Japan. Exhibitions: mainly in Japan, also in Germany. Awards: 'Fine works awards' at the Japan Jewelry Exhibition in 1988 and 1990.

Fukumi Shimura p.54
Born 1924, Kyoto, Japan. Educated: Bunka Gakuin. Exhibitions: numerous, in Japan. First exhibited in Dento Kogei Ten (Traditional Crafts Exhibition) in 1957. Designated a Living National Treasure in 1990. Collections: Crafts Gallery, National Museum of Modern Art (Tokyo), Victoria and Albert Museum (London), etc.

Peter Shire p.125
Born 1947, Los Angeles CA, USA. Educated: Chouinard Art Institute, Los Angeles CA. Exhibitions: various, in the USA, Eastern and Western Europe and Japan. Solo exhibitions at Art et Industrie, New York, Galerie Clara Scremini, Paris, Design Gallery Milano, Milan, etc. in 1989. Collections: Everson Museum of Art (Syracuse), Los Angeles County Museum of Art (Los Angeles), San Francisco Museum of Modern Art (San Francisco), Art Institute of Chicago (Chicago) and other major museum collections in the USA, the UK and Poland. Galleries: Modernism, San Francisco, Saxon-Less Gallery, San Francisco, etc. in the USA and Western Europe.
Photographic credit: William Nettles.

Helen Shirk p.103
Born 1942, Buffalo NY, USA. Educated: Skidmore College, Saratoga Springs NY; Kunsthandvaerkerskolen, Copenhagen; Indiana University, Bloomington IN. Teaching: since 1975, Professor of Art at San Diego State University CA. Exhibitions: numerous, mainly in the USA, also in Canada, Western Europe and Japan. Awards: include a Meritorious Performance and Professional Promise Award from San Diego State University. Collections: Carnegie Museum of Art (Pittsburgh), Minnesota Museum of Art (St Paul) and other major museum collections in the USA, Japan and Germany. Galleries: Helen Drutt Gallery, Philadelphia PA, Hand and the Spirit Gallery, Scottsdale AR and Joan Robey Gallery, Denver CO.

Verena Sieber-Fuchs p.92
Born 1943, Zürich, Switzerland. Educated: Kunstgewerbeschule, Basel and Zürich. Exhibitions: various, in Western Europe, the USA and Japan. Awards: First Prize at the 6th International Jewelry Exhibition, Tokyo 1986. Collections: major museum collections in Amsterdam, The Hague and Lausanne. Galleries: Galerie Ra, Amsterdam. Photographic credit: Ton Werkhoven.

Jan Siebers p.187
Born 1960. Educated: Akademie voor Beeldende Kunsten, Arnhem. Exhibitions: since 1988, in Holland, France and Belgium. Collections: Gemeente Museum (The Hague), Gemeente Museum (Arnhem) and other major museum collections in Holland. Galleries: Théorèmes, Brussels, Galerie Intermezzo, Galerie Coumans, Dordrecht, Pand 102, The Hague and Aspects, Arnhem. Photographic credit: R. Schropp.

Alev Ebuzziya Siesbye p.22
Born 1938, Istanbul, Turkey. Educated: Academy of Fine Arts, Istanbul. Exhibitions: numerous, international. Solo exhibition at Galerie Jonas, Cortaillod, Switzerland in 1990. Collections: Kunstindustrimuseet (Copenhagen), Museum Boymans-Van Beuningen (Rotterdam), Kestner-Museum (Hanover), Los Angeles County Museum of Art (Los Angeles) and numerous other major international museum collections. Galleries: Galerie Amphora, Oosterbeek, Holland, Galérie Jonas, Cortaillod, Switzerland, Galeri Nev/Urart, Istanbul, etc. Photographic credit: Carrebye.

Sinclair Till (Suzie Sinclair and Alastair Till) p.186
Both born 1958, UK. Educated: Suzie Sinclair at Goldsmiths College of Art.

Set up the Sinclair Till Flooring Company in 1986. Commissions: many, including the floor for Wilson Hale Gallery, London.

Karyl Sisson pp.136, 141
Born 1948, Brooklyn NY, USA. Educated: New York University, New York; University of California, Los Angeles CA. Exhibitions: various, mainly in the USA, also in Japan. Collections: American Craft Museum (New York) and other museum collections in the USA. Galleries: Katie Gingrass Gallery, Santa Fé NM. Photographic credit: Susan Einstein.

Ingunn Skogholt p.75
Educated: National College of Art and Design, Oslo, Norway; Academy of Arts, Bratislava, Czechoslovakia; Edinburgh College of Art; Royal College of Art, London. Exhibitions: various, in Scandinavia and the UK. Collections: Crafts Council Collection (London) and major museum collections in Norway. Commissions: major corporate commissions in Norway. Photographic credit: A.M. Andreassen.

Keith A. Smith p.169
Born 1938, USA. Teaching: Art Institute of Chicago School and Visual Studies Workshop. Has made 155 books since 1967, about 130 of which are one-of-a-kind. Has published 23 books to date, all but one since 1982. Awards: include two Guggenheim Fellowships and a National Endowment for the Arts grant. All books available directly from the author, Keith A. Smith, Rochester NY.

Martin Smith p.37
Born 1950, Braintree, Essex, UK. Educated: Ipswich School of Art; Bristol Polytechnic; Royal College of Art, London. Exhibitions: various since 1975, international. Solo exhibition at Galerie de Witte Voet, Amsterdam in 1990. Collections: Victoria and Albert Museum, Crafts Council Collection (London), Cleveland Crafts Centre (Middlesbrough), Shipley Art Gallery (Gateshead) and other major museum collections in the UK, Holland, the USA and Japan. Galleries: Crafts Council Shop at the V&A, London and Galerie de Witte Voet, Amsterdam. Photographic credit: David Cripps.

Philip Smith p.167
Born 1928, Southport, Lancashire, UK. Educated: School of Art and Craft, Southport; Royal College of Art, London. Exhibitions: numerous, international. Collections: British Museum, Victoria and Albert Museum, Crafts Council Collection (London) and many other major museum and library collections in the UK, Holland, the USA, Colombia, Australia and South Africa. Photographic credit: Michael Barnett.

Romilly Saumarez Smith p.164
Born 1954. Educated: Camberwell School of Art and Crafts, London. Exhibitions: in Western Europe and the USA. Collections: Victoria and Albert Museum (London) and other major museum and library collections in the USA. Commissions: numerous. Committee-member and Fellow of Designer Bookbinders, London. Photographic credit: Nick Nicholson.

Richard Snyder p.193
Born 1951, New York, USA. Educated: Philadelphia College of Art; Museum of Fine Arts School, Boston. Teaching: guest lecturer at Rhode Island School of Design, Providence RI in 1989. Exhibitions: in the USA and Japan only. Solo exhibition at Art et Industrie, New York in 1990. Collections: Art Institute of Chicago. Galleries: Art et Industrie, New York, David Gill, London and Brutus Gallery, Osaka.

Jan Sobota p.166
Born Czechoslovakia. Educated: Apprenticeship with Karel Silinger; Academy of Applied Arts, Prague, Czechoslovakia. Moved to the USA in 1984. Exhibitions: numerous since 1957, in Eastern and Western Europe and the USA. Collections: Museum of Applied Arts (Pilzen), National Museum of Books (Strahov, Prague) and other major museum and library collections in Czechoslovakia, Western Europe and the USA.

Monika Speyer p.64
Born 1959, Augsburg, Germany. Educated: Fachhochschule, Augsburg. Exhibitions: since 1985, in Germany only. Solo exhibition at Treppenhausgalerie, Augsburg in 1990. Galleries: Galerie Smend, Cologne and Treppenhausgalerie, Augsburg. Photographic credit: Richter & Spink, Augsburg.

Kurt Spurey p.25
Born 1941, Vienna, Austria. Exhibitions: various, international. Solo exhibitions at Galerie Zürich-Kosmos, Vienna and Galerie Terranga, Dornbirn in 1989. Awards: include Gold Medals at Faenza in 1971, 1976, 1977 and 1979. Collections: Museum für Angewandte Kunst (Vienna and Prague), Hetjens Museum (Düsseldorf), Museum für Kunst und Gewerbe (Hamburg), Museo della Ceramica (Faenza), Victoria and Albert Museum (London) and many other major international museum collections. Has participated in many international symposia and conferences.

Rudolf Staffel p.24
Born 1911, San Antonio TX, USA. Exhibitions: numerous, mainly in the USA, also in Japan and the UK.

Collections: American Craft Museum (New York), Everson Museum of Art (Syracuse), Museum of Fine Arts (Boston), Renwick Gallery, Smithsonian Institution (Washington D.C.) and other major museum collections in the USA, Canada and the UK. Galleries: Helen Drutt Gallery, Philadelphia PA.

Stiletto Studios p.194
Born 1959 (a one-man studio), Rüsselsheim, Germany. Educated: Technische Universität and Hochschule der Künste, Berlin; Kunstakademie, Düsseldorf. Exhibitions: various, in Western and Eastern Europe and the USA. Solo exhibition at Galerie Quo Vadis, Stüttgart, Germany in 1990. Collections: Kunstmuseum (Düsseldorf), Vitra Museum (Weil-am-Rhein), and Prodomo (Vienna). Galleries: Galerie Quo Vadis, Stüttgart, Pentagon Möbelgalerie, Cologne, Willoughby Sharp Gallery, New York, Galerie Néotu, Paris and Galerija SKUC, Ljubljana. Photographic credit: Idris Kalodziés.

Walter Suter p.202
Born 1948, Muttenz, Switzerland. Educated: Kunstgewerbeschule in Basel and Zürich. Teaching: for five years at the Gewerbeschule Muttenz. Exhibitions: since 1970, in Switzerland, Germany, Italy and Morocco.

Tore Svensson p.103
Educated: Hogskolan for Konsthantverk och Design, Gothenburg, Sweden. Teaching: since 1989 at Hogskolan for Konsthantverk och Design, Gothenburg. Exhibitions: in Sweden only. Galleries: Nutida Svenskt Silver, Stockholm, Rista Konsthantverk, Umea, and Guld & Silversmederna K I & Cecilia Johansson AB, Gothenburg. Photographic credit: Anders Jiràs.

K. Szekeres p.33
Born 1940.

Yoshihiko Takahashi pp.113, 133
Born 1958, Tokyo, Japan. Educated: Tama University of Art, Tokyo. Exhibitions: various, mainly in Japan, also in Korea, Germany, the USA and Brazil. Solo exhibition at Shibuya Seibu, Tokyo in 1989. Collections: National Museum of Modern Art (Tokyo), Hokkaido Museum of Art (Sapporo), Corning Museum of Glass (Corning NY) and other major museum collections in Germany and Switzerland. Galleries: Shibuyu Seibu, Tokyo and Habatat Galleries, Farmington Hills MI.

Kazuo Takiguchi p.14
Born 1953, Gojo-zaka, Kyoto, Japan. Educated: Kyoto City University of Fine Arts. Exhibitions: various, mainly in Japan, also in Italy. Solo exhibition at

Gallery Koyanagi, Tokyo in 1989. Awards: Kazuo Yagi Prize for Contemporary Ceramics, 1986. Collections: National Museum of Modern Art (Tokyo), the Japan Foundation and other major museum collections in Japan and the UK. Galleries: Gallery Koyanagi, Tokyo.

Guy Taplin p.153
Born 1939, London, UK. Educated: self-taught, began carving birds in 1975. Exhibitions: various, in the UK, Holland and the USA. Solo exhibition at Andrew Usiskin Contemporary Art Gallery, London in 1990. Collections: Contemporary Art Society, Arts Council of Great Britain (London). Galleries: Contemporary Applied Arts, Crafts Council Shop at the V&A, Andrew Usiskin Contemporary Art Gallery, London, Oxford Gallery, Oxford, Courcoux & Courcoux Contemporary Art, Salisbury, etc. Photographic credit: Nigel Arter (Andrew Usiskin Gallery).

David Taylor p.126
Born 1949, Oxford, UK. Educated: Oxford Polytechnic; Central School of Art and Design, London. Member of the Glasshouse studio, London; makes one-off and production pieces. Exhibitions: numerous, international. Collections: Victoria and Albert Museum, Crafts Council Collection (London), Ulster Museum (Belfast) and other major museum collections in Western Europe, Japan and the USA. Galleries: The Glasshouse, Contemporary Applied Arts, London, Galerie L, Hamburg, Galerie Transparence, Brussels and Heller Gallery, New York.

Janice Tchalenko p.28
Born 1942, Rugby, Warwickshire, UK. Educated: Harrow College of Art. Teaching: part-time teaching at Camberwell School of Art and Crafts and tutoring at the Royal College of Art, London. Exhibitions: numerous, international. Awards: include the Manchester Prize for Art in Production, 1988. Collections: Victoria and Albert Museum, Crafts Council Collection (London), Cleveland Crafts Centre (Middlesbrough), Ulster Museum (Belfast), Shipley Art Gallery (Gateshead) and other major museum collections in the UK, Germany, Sweden, Finland and the USA. Galleries: Crafts Council Shop at the V&A, London.

Naoji Terai p.152
Born 1912, Japan. Educated: Tokyo Academy of Fine Arts; subsequent studies with Gonroku Matsuda. Teaching: professor at Ishikawa Prefectural Art and Craft High School, then Director of the Institute for Lacquer Art, Wajima. Exhibitions: numerous, in

Japan. Awards: include Special Selection Prize at Nitten on two occasions and the Hokuto Prize. Has served as a jury member of the Nitten and the Dento Kogei Ten (Traditional Crafts Exhibition).

Rita Ternes p.31
Born 1955, Neuwied, Germany. Educated: Fachschule für Keramik-Gestaltung, Höhr-Grenzhausen. Exhibitions: various since 1982, mainly in Germany, also in Italy. Awards: include the 'Youth Forms – Ceramics' awarded by Rosenthal AG in 1985. Collections: Museum für Kunsthandwerk (Frankfurt), Keramion (Frechen), Kestner-Museum (Hanover) and other major museum collections in Germany. Photographic credit: Strenger Atelier, Osnabrück.

Heinrich Thein p.6
Born 1947, Bremen, Germany. Educated: apprenticeship in brass instrument-making with Herbert Lätzsch in Bremen; studies at Handwerkskammer für Oberbayern, Munich. Has shared a studio with Max Stein (see below) since 1974. Awards: Bremen Prize for Crafts in 1979. Collections: Focke Museum, Graphothek (Bremen) and Museum für Kunst und Gewerbe (Hamburg). Commissions: for Concentus Musicus, Vienna, Deutscher Oper, Berlin, British Broadcasting Corporation, London, Royal Danish Opera House, Copenhagen, Chicago Orchestra, Sydney Opera House and numerous other major international orchestras, opera houses and musicians. Represented by: Max & Heinrich Thein, Bremen. Photographic credit: Monika Thein-von Plottnitz.

Max Thein p.16
Born 1956, Bremen, Germany. Educated: studied brass instrument-making in Heinrich Thein's (see above) Musikstudium with Joachim Mittelacher, Bremen. Has shared a workshop with Heinrich Thein since 1974. Awards: Auguste Papendieck Prize in 1984.

Deborah Thomas p.135
Born 1956, Swansea, UK. Educated: Wolverhampton College; Slade School of Fine Art, University College, London. Exhibitions: in the UK and the USA. Commissions: in the UK, Iceland, Morocco and the USA. Galleries: Themes and Variations, London. Photographic credit: Daniel Faoro.

Maisa Tikkanen p.71
Born 1952, Oulujoki, Finland. Educated: Kunstgymnasiet, Nyslott; Kunstindustrielle Hojskolen, Helsinki. Exhibitions: various, mainly in Finland, also international. Solo exhibition at Savonlinna Art Museum, Savonlinna in 1990. Awards: include the Finland

State Prize for Craft, 1989. Collections: Kunstindustrimuseet (Helsinki), Savonlinna Art Museum (Savonlinna) and other major museum collections in Finland. Galleries: Gallery 25, Helsinki. Photographic credit: P.J. Turtiainen.

Xavier Toubes p.48
Born 1947, La Coruna, Spain. Educated: New York State College of Ceramics, Alfred University, NY. Teaching: currently Associate Professor of Art at University of North Carolina at Chapel Hill NC. Exhibitions: numerous in the USA, Western and Eastern Europe and Japan. Solo exhibition at Galerie van Mourik, Rotterdam in 1990. Collections: museum collections in Spain, Holland and the USA. Galleries: Galerie van Mourik, Rotterdam.

Jaime Tressera Clapés p.183
Born 1943, Barcelona, Spain. Educated: Escuela Massana, Barcelona. Exhibitions: various, international. Awards: include the international Design Review Awards 1990, from International Design Editions New York. Commissions: numerous, international.

Karla Trinkley p.115
Born 1956, Boyertown PA, USA. Educated: Tyler School of Art, Temple University, Philadelphia PA; Rhode Island School of Design, Providence RI. Exhibitions: various, mainly in the USA, also in Czechoslovakia, Australia and Japan. Collections: Los Angeles County Museum (Los Angeles), Corning Museum of Glass (Corning) and other major museum collections in the USA, Japan and Australia. Galleries: Betsy Rosenfield Gallery, Chicago IL.

Richard la Trobe-Bateman p.207
Born 1938, London, UK. Educated: St Martin's School of Art, London; Royal College of Art, London. Exhibitions: various, in the UK, Denmark, Austria, the USA and Japan. Collections: Victoria and Albert Museum, Crafts Council Collection (London), Crafts Study Centre, Holburne of Menstrie Museum (Bath) and other major museum collections in the UK. Commissions: many, including work for Oxford Colleges and a high chair given to the first son of the Prince of Wales. Galleries: Contemporary Applied Arts, London.

Bob Trotman pp.188, 190
Born 1947, Winston-Salem NC, USA. Exhibitions: various since 1980, in the USA, Scandinavia, Western and Eastern Europe. Solo exhibition at Hodges/Taylor Gallery, Charlotte NC in 1989. Collections: Arizona State University Museum of Art and Rhode Island School of Design Museum of Art.

Collection (London), and other major museum collections in Western Europe, Norway, Australia, Hong Kong and Japan. Commissions: include custom-made lighting for the Victoria and Albert Museum, London. Galleries: Contemporary Applied Arts, London and Helen Drutt Gallery, Philadelphia PA. Photographic credit: Bob Cramp.

Liz Williamson p.57
Educated: Melbourne College of Textiles; Royal Melbourne Institute of Technology, Australia. Teaching: 1990, part-time lecturer at University of Technology, Sydney. Exhibitions: various, mainly in Australia, also in Indonesia, Japan and the UK. Collections: Powerhouse Museum (Sydney), Victorian State Craft Collection (Melbourne), Australian National Gallery (Canberra) and other major museum collections in Australia. Galleries: Meat Market Craft Centre, Melbourne. Photographic credit: Ashley Barber.

Christina Hurihia Wirihara p.73
Born 1949, New Zealand, a member of the Tanui/Ngati Rangiunuora tribe. Her 'whariki' is based on the traditional 'fine' mats used in the Wharenui (Maori meeting houses). The weaving technique, 'raranga', is also used in Maori basket-making.

Sami Wirkkala p.192
Born 1948, Helsinki, Finland. Educated: University of Industrial Arts, Helsinki. Has worked for Design Tapio Wirkkala & Co. since 1971. Exhibitions: various, in Scandinavia and Western Europe. Awards: Macef Prize in Italy in 1975.

Lam de Wolf p.95
Born 1949, Badhoevedorp, Holland. Educated: Gerrit Rietveld Akademie, Amsterdam. Teaching: at Gerrit Rietveld Akademie, Amsterdam. Exhibitions: various, international. Solo exhibition at Galerie Ra, Amsterdam in 1991. Galleries: Galerie Ra, Amsterdam, Galerie Mooi, Utrecht and Positura, Barcelona. Photographic credit: Ton Werkhoven.

Maria Ka Pick Wong p.91
Born 1962, Hong Kong. Educated: Middlesex Polytechnic, UK; Royal College of Art, London. Exhibitions: various, in the UK, Germany, Switzerland, the USA and Japan. Awards: include First Prize at the 1988 International Jewelry Competition 'Amulet and Talisman', Schwabisch Gmund, Germany. Commissions: 1990, a piece of jewelry for the Lancashire Museum service private collection. Galleries: Electrum Gallery and Contemporary Applied Arts, London.

Betty Woodman p.26
Born 1930, Norwalk CT, USA. Educated: School for American Craftsmen, Alfred University, Alfred NY. Teaching: since 1979, Professor, University of Colorado at Boulder CO. Exhibitions: numerous, international. Solo exhibitions at Max Protetch Gallery, New York, Francesca Pia Gallery, Bern and Museum het Kruithuis, Den Bosch in 1990. Collections: Metropolitan Museum of Art (New York), Museum of Fine Arts (Boston), Los Angeles County Museum of Art and other major museum collections in the USA and Western Europe. Galleries: Max Protetch Gallery, New York.

Jozan Yamada p.20
Born 1924, Tokohame City, Japan. Educated: ceramic department at Tokoname Kogyo Gakko. Exhibitions: numerous, in Japan and Western Europe. First exhibited in Dento Kogei Ten (Traditional Crafts Exhibition) in 1968. Awards: include a Grand Prix at Expo, Brussels.

Mitsugi Yamada p.60
Born 1912, Gifu City, Japan. Exhibitions: numerous, in Japan. First exhibited in Dento Kogei Ten (Traditional Crafts Exhibition) in 1958.

Shinya Yamamura p.6
Born 1960, Tokyo, Japan. Educated: Kanazawa Art and Crafts University. Exhibitions: since 1985, in Japan only. Solo exhibition at Miharudo Gallery, Tokyo in 1990. Galleries: Miharudo Gallery and Gallery Isogaya, Tokyo.

Mutsuo Yanagihara p.35
Born 1934, Kochi, Japan. Educated: Kyoto City University of Arts. Teaching: since 1968, Professor at Osaka University of Arts. Exhibitions: numerous, international. Awards: include the *Camera di Commercio di Ravenna*, 1972. Collections: National Museum of Modern Art (Kyoto), National Art Museum (Tokyo), Japan Foundation and other major museum collections in Japan, Brazil, the USA and Western Europe.

Naito Yokoyama p.124
Born 1937, Taipei, Taiwan. Educated: Tokyo University of Fine Arts. Exhibitions: numerous, international. Collections: Corning Museum of Glass (Corning NY), Musée des Arts Décoratifs (Lausanne) and other major museum collections in Japan. Member of Tokyo Designers Space.

Alexander Zadorin p.44
Born 1941, USSR. Educated: V.I. Mukhina Institute of Applied Art and Industrial Design, Leningrad. Exhibitions: in Russia and Western

Europe. Solo exhibition at Leningrad Artists Union Exhibition Hall in 1988. Collections: Russian Museum (Leningrad), Museum of Russian Decorative Art, Kuskovo Museum of Ceramics and Glass (Moscow) and other major museum collections in the USSR.

Jan Zalud pp.158, 159
Born 1955, Prague, Czechoslovakia. Left Czechoslovakia in 1968. Educated: studied fine art at Sunderland Polytechnic; started wood-carving in 1979. Exhibitions: some, in the UK, Germany, France and Japan. Awards: Jugend Gestaltet prize, Munich in 1983. Collections: Crafts Council Collection (London), Shipley Art Gallery (Gateshead), Leeds City Art Gallery and other museum collections in the UK. Galleries: Contemporary Applied Arts, London, Royal Exchange Craft Centre, Manchester and Craft Centre and Design Gallery, Leeds.

Dana Zámecníková p.128
Born 1945, Prague, Czechoslovakia. Educated: Czechoslovakian Technical University; Academy of Applied Arts, Prague; Pilchuk School and Glass Center Summer School, Stanwood WA, USA. Exhibitions: numerous since 1980, international. Solo exhibitions at Galerie Gottschalk-Betz, Frankfurt, Galerie Clara Scremini, Paris and Sanske Galerie, Zürich in 1990. Collections: Uměleckoprůmyslové Muzeum (Prague), Glasmuseum (Ebeltoft), Corning Museum of Glass (Corning) and many other major international museum collections. Galleries: Galerie Gottschalk-Betz, Frankfurt, Galerie Clara Scremini, Paris, Sanske Galerie, Zürich, Heller Gallery, New York, Habatat Galleries, Farmington Hills MI, Yamaha Galleries, Tokyo, etc. Photographic credit: Kunstmuseum, Düsseldorf.

Dieter Zimmermann p.192
Born 1948. Educated: studied industrial design. Painter and designer. Exhibitions: in Germany and Switzerland only. Galleries: Galerie UND, Düsseldorf and Galerie Quovadis, Stuttgart. Photographic credit: Vollmer-Freiburg.

Paul Zimmermann p.203
Educated: Schüler von Heijo Pfingsten, Bildhauer, Luisenschule, Munich; Berufspädagogischen Institut, Munich. Exhibitions: numerous, in Eastern and Western Europe and the USA. Awards: include Staatspreis Baden-Württemberg.

Yan Zoritchak p.122
Born 1944, Zdiar, Czechoslovakia. Educated: Glass Industry School, Železný Brod; Academy of Applied Arts,

Prague. Moved to France in 1970. Exhibitions: various, in Eastern and Western Europe, the USA and Japan. Awards: include 1st prize, Hokkaido Museum of Modern Art, Sapporo in 1985. Collections: Uměleckoprůmyslové Muzeum (Prague), Kunstmuseum (Düsseldorf), Kunstsammlungen der Veste Coburg (Coburg) and other major museum collections in Europe and Japan.

Czeslaw Zuber p.127
Born 1948, Poland. Educated: Academy of Fine Arts, Wroclaw. Moved to France in 1982. Exhibitions: numerous, international. Solo exhibitions at Habatat Galleries, Farmington Hills MI, and Galerie D.M. Sarver, Paris in 1989. Collections: National Museum (Wroclaw) and Glass Museum (Jelenia Gora) in Poland, and other major international museum collections. Galleries: Galerie D.M. Sarver, Paris, Habatat Galleries, Farmington Hills MI, Braggiotti Galerie, Rotterdam, Galerie L, Hamburg and Galerie Gottschalk-Betz, Frankfurt. Photographic credit: Alexis Terzief.

Edward Zucca p.185
Born 1946, Philadelphia PA, USA. Educated: Philadelphia College of Art. Exhibitions: numerous since 1967, in the USA only. Collections: Museum of Fine Arts (Boston) and other museum collections in the USA. Galleries: Snyderman Gallery, Philadelphia PA and Naga Gallery, Boston MA. Photographic credit: Museum of Fine Arts, Boston.

Toots Zynsky p.117
Born 1951, Massachusetts, USA. Educated: Haystack Mountain School of Crafts, Deer Isle ME; Pilchuk School and Glass Center, Stanwood WA; Rhode Island School of Design, Providence RI. Exhibitions: various, mainly in the USA, also in Japan and Western Europe. Collections: Cooper-Hewitt Museum, Smithsonian Institution, Metropolitan Museum of Modern Art (New York), Corning Museum of Glass (Corning), Renwick Gallery, Smithsonian Institution (Washington D.C.) and other major international museum collections. Photographic credit: Betsy Rosenfield Gallery.

ORGANIZATIONS

AUSTRALIA

Crafts Council of Australia
35 George Street, The Rocks, Sydney NSW 2000
☎ (+61) 2 241 1701 Fax (+61) 2 247 6143
The national body for the crafts. Disseminates information, organizes professional association activites and market development, mediates between the industry and government, concerns itself with matters of national and international significance while maintaining links through the State Craft Councils with local issues.

Crafts Council of ACT
1 Aspinal Street, Watson ACT 2602
☎ (+61) 6 241 2373
A corporate member of the Crafts Council of Australia with the responsibility of representing, promoting and developing the crafts in its state.

Crafts Council of NSW
88 George Street, The Rocks, Sydney NSW 2000
☎ (+61) 2 247 9126 Fax (+61) 2 247 2641
See Crafts Council of ACT above.

Crafts Council of Northern Territory
Conacher Street, Bullocky Point, Darwin NT 0800
☎ (+61) 89 81 6615
See Crafts Council of ACT above.

Crafts Council of Queensland
166 Ann Street, Brisbane QD 4000
☎ (+61) 7 229 2661 Fax (+61) 7 229 2243
See Crafts Council of ACT above.

Crafts Council of South Australia
169 Payneham Road, St Peters SA 5069
☎ (+61) 8 363 0383 Fax (+61) 8 363 0551
See Crafts Council of ACT above.

Crafts Council of Tasmania
11/65, Salamanca Place, Hobart TAS 7000
☎ (+61) 02 23 5622
See Crafts Council of ACT above.

Crafts Council of Victoria
7 Blackwood Street, North Melbourne VIC 3051
☎ (+61) 3 329 0611 Fax (+61) 3 329 2272
See Crafts Council of ACT above.

Crafts Council of Western Australia
1st Floor, Perth City Railway Station, Wellington Street, Perth WA 6000
☎ (+61) 9 325 2799 Fax (+61) 9 325 1221
See Crafts Council of ACT above.

Jam Factory Craft Centre
169 Payneham Road, St Peters SA 5069
☎ (+61) 8 362 5661 Fax (+61) 8 363 0551
An integrated centre for South Australian crafts, incorporating retail shops and wholesaling facilities, galleries and workshops in ceramics, hot glass, leather and wood. Works closely with the Crafts Council of South Australia.

Meat Market Craft Centre
42 Courtney Street, North Melbourne VIC 3051
☎ (+61) 3 329 9966 Fax (+61) 3 329 2272
Incorporates retail shops, galleries, the State of Victoria Crafts Collection and houses a number of craft organizations. Has workshops in leather, hot glass, cold glass, ceramics, textiles and wood. Works in conjunction with the Crafts Council of Victoria.

Sale Regional Arts Centre
P O Box 396, Sale VIC 3850
☎ (+61) 51 442 829 Fax (+61) 51 445 130

BELGIUM

Aksent Vzw
Hoogstraat 36, B 3600 Genk
☎ (+32) 11 36 39 16 or 11 35 09 45
President: L.M.M. Thijs
Founded 1985, aims to raise the standard of education, in both artistic and scientific fields. Organizes exhibitions, seminars and workshops. Flemish community.

Athena Brabant
Lage Steenweg 41, B 1850 Grimbergen
☎ (+32) 2 26 92 390
President: Willy Coorman
Secretary: Ebba Schucht
Aims to promote and teach crafts of the highest quality, publishes a quarterly newsletter, organizes a yearly exhibition. Flemish community.

Le Domaine de la Lice
Rue Poulet 12, B 1440 Braine le Château
☎ (+32) 2 366 93 12
President: Maurice Duwaerts
Gobelin association. French community.

Esim – Economisch en Sociaal Instituut voor de Middenstand
Congresstraat 33, B 1000 Brussels (new address from May 1991)
Director: Eddy Gheysen
Secretary: Johan Valcke
Serves the Flemish community, covers every craft, publishes a newsletter.

Euro Glass Club
Rue des Brasseurs 175, B 5000 Namur
☎ (+32) 81 24 11 64
President: Françoise Delmont
Director: Jean-Pierre Umbenstock

Fibre & Fil
c/o Louise Dolphijn, Rue Éloi Bouvier, B 1474 Ways
☎ (+32) 2 633 27 33
Textile artists' association.

Fondation de la Tapisserie, des Arts du Tissu et des Arts Muraux
Place Reine Astrid 2, B 7500 Tournai
☎ (+32) 69 23 42 85
President: Norbert Gadenne
Association promoting tapestry and the textile arts, aims to disseminate information, organizes a triennial, assembling work from French-speaking countries all over the world.

Interieur Vzw
Casinoplein 10, B 8500 Kortrijk
☎ (+32) 56 21 66 03 Fax (+32) 56 21 85 64
President: Hubert Sap
Secretary: Jo Libeer
Covers the field of interior design, modern style, interior decoration, crafts for the home. Publishes a newsletter, organizes exhibitions and a major design fair every two years.

National Entity WCC
WCC – Belgique francophone, rue de Longs Près 3, B 7079 Mignault
☎ (+32) 64 44 39 76
Executive Manager: Anne Leclercq

National Entity WCC
WCC – Flemish speaking, PO Box 10, B 1000 Brussels 23
☎ (+32) 2 219 3434
WCC Delegate: Johan Valcke

CANADA

Artists in Stained Glass
35 McCaul Street, Toronto ON M5T 1V7

Canadian Crafts Council
189 Laurier Avenue E, Ottawa ON K1N 6P1
☎ (+1) 613 235 8200 Fax (+1) 613 235 7425
Director: Peter Weinrich
National body concerned with the crafts industry, maintains links through regional Crafts Associations.

Canadian Guild of Crafts Quebec
2025 Peel Street, Montreal PQ H3A 1T6
☎ (+1) 514 849 6091
Administrator: Nainz Kalemkerian

Crafts Association of British Columbia
1386 Cartwright Street, Granville Island, Vancouver BC V6H 3R8
☎ (+1) 607 687 6511
Executive Director: Gail Rogers
Publishes *Crafts Contacts*, runs a shop/gallery, has a portfolio registry and provides a resource centre.

Crafts Guild of Manitoba Inc.
183 Kennedy Street, Winnipeg MB R3C 1S6
☎ (+1) 204 943 1190
Chairman: G.G. Habib
Publishes a monthly newsletter, disseminates information.

Fusion
Ontario Clay and Glass Association, 140 Yorkeville Avenue, Toronto ON M5R 1C2
☎ (+1) 416 923 7406
Administrator: Eliu Racine
Publishes *Fusion*, runs the Pottery Shop.

Newfoundland and Labrador Crafts Development Association
265 Duckworth Street, P O Box 5295, St John's NF A1C 5W1
☎ (+1) 709 753 2749
Director: Anne Mamiel
Publishes a newsletter, *Crafts*.

Ontario Crafts Council
35 McCaul Street, Toronto ON M5V 1E7
☎ (+1) 416 977 3551
Executive Director: Joan Foster
Publishes *Ontario Crafts* and *Craft News*, runs the Craft Gallery and the Guild Shop in Toronto, disseminates information, houses a library, has a slide portfolio system.

Ontario Woodcarvers Association
33 Toulon Road, Scarborough ON M1G 1V6
☎ (+1) 416 439 0716
Membership Convenor: James C. Williams

CZECHOSLOVAKIA

Československý Výbor Světovej Rady Remesiel
Czechoslovak Committee of the World Crafts Council, Technicka 7, CZ 823 51 Bratislava
☎ (+42) 7 23 85 40 Fax (+42) 7 23 66 49
Chairman: Matej Turcer
Secretary: Eva Gulasova
Founded 1969, aims to bring together all arts and crafts organizations, establish links with similar organizations abroad, promote Czechoslovak craftsmanship at home and abroad, disseminate information. Organizes exhibitions and seminars.

Česky Fond Vytvárných Uměni
Narodní 37, CZ 111 59 Prague
☎ (+42) 2 22 43 35
Director: Ivan Stepanovsky
Czech Creative Art Fund. Aims to promote the arts, applied arts, design and architecture. Disseminates information, assists artists, publishes a newsletter, organizes exhibitions, seminars, commissions.

Slovensky Fond Vytvarnych Umeni
Trnavska cesta 112, CZ 821 01 Bratislava
☎ (+42) 7 22 02 13 or 7 22 58 63
Director: Miroslav Lindtner
Slovak Creative Art Fund. Aims to promote the arts, applied arts, design and architecture. Disseminates information, assists artists, publishes a newsletter, *Vytvarny Zivot*, ten times a year, organizes exhibitions, seminars and commissions.

Ústředi Lidové Umělecké Výroby
Národni třída 36, CZ 113 53 Prague
☎ (+42) 2–26 00 25
Director: Pavel Tojsl
Secretary: Alena Vondrušková
Central Office of Folk Art. Aims to preserve indigenous folk crafts, publishes a quarterly newsletter *Umeni a Remesla*, organizes exhibitions, fairs.

Ústředi Uměleckých Remesel
Myslikova 6, CZ 120 07 Prague
Tel (+42) 2 29 56 41 or 2 29 56 42
Director: Karel Augusta
Secretary: Antonín Hartmann
Arts and crafts centre. Promotes a wide range of crafts by organizing exhibitions, fairs, courses, workshops.

Ustředie Lidovej Umělecké Výroby
Obchodná 62, CA 816 11 Bratislava
☎ (+42) 7 51 24 0
Director: Jozaf Tkačik
Assistant Director: Pavel Schulz
Central Office of Folk Art. Aims to promote indigenous folk crafts, organizes exhibitions, fairs.

Ustredie Umeleckych Remesiel
Technicka 7, CZ 823 51 Bratislava
☎ (+42) 7 22 30 60 or 7 22 50 71 Fax (+42) 7 236 649
Director: Matej Turcer
Arts and crafts centre. Promotes a wide range of crafts and crafts conservation, organizes exhibitions, fairs, workshops.

DENMARK

Danske Kunsthandvaerkeres Landsammenslutning (DKL)
Linnesgade 20, DK 1361 Copenhagen K
☎ (+45) 33 15 29 40
Chairman: Birgit Krogh
Executive Secretary: Nina Linde
Danish Arts and Crafts Association.

Aims to promote and develop Danish arts and crafts. Disseminates information, organizes exhibitions at home and abroad and seminars and workshops. Publishes *Dansk Kunsthandvaerk* quarterly.

Danish Silversmiths
Guldsmedehojskolen, Vaerkstedvej 5, DK 2500 Valby
☎ (+45) 31 46 12 52
Chairman: Ib Andersen
Aims to promote the silversmith's craft, organizes exhibitions worldwide.

Guldsmedefagets Fallesrad
26 Ryvangs Alle, DK 2100 Copenhagen OE
Association representing gold- and silversmiths. Publishes a newsletter.

Kunsthandvaerkerradet
Amaliegade 15, DK 1256 Copenhagen K
☎ (+45) 31 12 36 76
Chairman: M.A.A. Bernt
Danish Crafts Council. Aims to promote and develop arts and crafts. Disseminates information, mediates between craftspeople and various organizations, organizes exhibitions, conferences, courses.

Selskabet Til Haandarbejdets Fremme
Glentevej 70 B, DK 2400 Copenhagen NV
☎ (+45) 31 10 20 88
Chairman: Erik Lassen
Executive Director: John Hansen
Danish Handcraft Guild. Organizes sales and exhibitions, educational courses. Publishes, quarterly, *Haandarbejdets Fremme*.

Stoftrykker og Vaeverlauget
Hvidkildevej 64, DK 2400 Copenhagen NV
☎ (+45) 31 12 36 76
Chairman: Nanna Nissen
Danish Printers and Weavers Guild. Aims to extend knowledge of traditional and modern crafts. Organizes courses and exhibitions, publishes a magazine bi-monthly for members.

World Crafts Council, National Committee Denmark
Vaerkstedvej 5, DK 2500 Valby
☎ (+45) 31 46 12 51 or 31 46 12 52
Executive Chairman: Ib Andersen
Founded 1979, aims to promote Danish crafts abroad. Disseminates information about Danish crafts abroad and foreign crafts at home, organizes exhibitions.

FINLAND

Artisaani
Unioninkatu 28, SF 00100 Helsinki
☎ (+358) 0 66 52 25

President: Malia Klemettinen-Nuutilainen
Helsinki craftspeople's cooperative. Aims to help craftspeople market their work. Organizes exhibitions in Finland and other Scandinavian countries, disseminates information.

Finlands Guldsmeds Forbund
Vuorikatu 3A, SF 00100 Helsinki 10
☎ (+358) 0 66 05 62
Director: Pekka Kaotto
Finnish gold- and silversmiths' association. Publishes a newsletter.

Finnish Handicraft Association
Kalevankatu 61, Box 186, SF 00181 Helsinki
☎ (+358) 0 694 9766
Founded 1913, a nationwide advisory organization serving handicraft industries. Funded by government grant and other contributions. Disseminates information, organizes an educational programme, aims to promote high-quality crafts and to help craftspeople sell their work.

Katsa Ry
c/o Leena Joninen, Kattuuni ky, Haapaniemenkatu 6 B, SF 00530 Helsinki
☎ (+358) 0 762 480
President: Jukka Tommila
Secretary: Karin Lilja-Makkonen
Aims to develop and support crafts, organizes exhibitions at home and abroad, educational events and trips abroad.

Katsa Ry
c/o Erik Kurtze, Tuulhattu, SF 25500 Pernio
President: Erik Kurtze
Secretary: Taina Pailos
Aims to support and develop crafts. Organizes exhibitions at home and abroad, educational events and study trips abroad.

Konsti
Hillaviita 2, SF 60150 Seinajoki
☎ (+358) 64 122 822
President: Paivi Rintaniemi
Secretary: Paula Hiltunen
Professional association for craftspeople and designers in the Vaasa province. Aims to promote design and craft in the area, organizes exhibitions, meetings and courses.

Ornamo
Kluuvikatu 1 D, SF 00100 Helsinki
☎ (+358) 0 175 977
Chairman: Yrjo Turka
Director: Karino Pohto
Founded 1911, a professional organization for Finnish designers and craftspeople, it aims to promote both industrial arts and design and crafts and applied arts. Provides links between member associations, protects the

interests of its members, gives advice, disseminates information, arranges exhibitions and seminars. Publishes a bulletin and a quarterly publication *Muoto* (Form).

Taiko
Kluuvikatu 1 D, SF 00100 Helsinki
☎ (+358) 0 175 338
President: Merja Wingvist
Secretary: Kaisa Viljo
Aims to promote crafts and craftspeople and maintain contact with similar organizations at home and abroad. Disseminates information, publishes *Ornamo* newsletter in conjunction with other member associations, organizes exhibitions, meetings and seminars.

Texo
Kluuvikatu 1 D, SF 00100 Helsinki
☎ (+358) 0 175 350
President: Liisa Poutanen
Secretary: Leena Kemppainen
Professional association of textile designers. Aims to advance textile design. Maintains contact with similar organizations at home and abroad, represents its members at home and abroad, disseminates information. Organizes the Nordic Textile Triennale, the Finnish Textile Triennale and other exhibitions.

FRANCE

L' Association des Potiers de la Borne
F 18250 Henrichemont
Organization of contemporary potters. Organizes exhibitions in the summer.

Association International du Nouvel Objet Visuel (INOV)
c/o Catherine Brelet, 27 rue de l'Université, Paris
☎ (1) 42 61 58 54
General Secretary: Anne Devinck
Founded 1965, a non-profit-making organization concerned with arts and crafts, brings creative artists together, disseminates information on the national and international context, produces a newsletter, collaborates with *L'Atelier*.

Centre des Métiers d'Art Contemporain
Musée des Arts Décoratifs, 107 rue de Rivoli, F 75001 Paris
☎ (+33) 1 42 60 56 58
Director: Marie-Laure Perrin
Organized by the 20th-Century Department of the Musée des Arts Décoratifs, it aims to encourage and promote contemporary craft of the highest quality, to establish contact with craftspeople nationally and internationally. Provides an information resource.

Centre National des Arts Plastiques
Ministère de la Culture, Bureau des Métiers d'Art, 27 avenue de l'Opéra, F 75001 Paris
☎ (+33) 40 15 73 00

Cirva
62 rue de la Joliette, F 13002 Marseille
☎ (+33) 91 56 11 50
Glass.

Société d'Encouragement aux Métiers d'Art (SEMA)
20 rue de la Boétie, F 75008 Paris
☎ (+33) 1 42 56 74 50
President: M. Vatelot
Amongst other things, education in the crafts at all levels.

Tee Pee
33 rue des Jeuneurs F 75002 Paris
☎ (+33) 1 40 26 03 50
Director: Jean François Mathieu
Library specializing in textiles, design and fashion.

Textile Art Centre
3 rue Felix Fauré, F 75015 Paris
☎ (+33) 1 45 58 23 91
President: Michel Thomas
International centre for textiles.

GERMANY

Bundesverband Kunsthandwerk e. V.
Bleichstrasse 38a, D 6000 Frankfurt
☎ (+49) 69 28 05 10
President: Reinhart Chr. Bartholomai
Federal association of various regional arts and crafts organizations, represents the interests of craftspeople, promotes and organizes exhibitions, publishes a newsletter three times a year. Illustrated directory of over 400 craftspeople in Germany published 1990.

Gesellschaft für Goldschmiedekunst e. V.
p.A. Deutsches Goldschmiedehaus, Altstadter Markt 6, D 6450 Hanau 1
☎ (+49) 6181 25 65 56
President: Walter Dennert
Director: Christianne Weber
Association of goldsmiths.

Gesellschaft für Keramikfreunde e. V.
p.A. Ulrich Gertz, Dambachtal 43, D 6200 Wiesbaden
☎ (+49) 6121 50 9 97
President: Paul Wilhelm Enders
Secretary: Ulrich Gertz
Ceramics.

Interessengemeinschaft Handweberer-Bundesverband e. V.
Obere Vorstadt 12, D 7030 Sindelfingen
☎ (+49) 7031 1178
Weaving.

Forum für Schmuck und Design e. V.
Lutticherstrasse 47, D 5000 Cologne 1
☎ (+49) 221 52 71 70
Manager: Wilhelm Mattar
Dynamic contemporary jewelry organization. Publishes information.

HOLLAND

Dutch Form
Waterlooplein 211, NL 1011 PG Amsterdam
☎ (+49) 20 38 11 20
President: Reinier Sinaasappel
Secretary: René var der Land
Founded 1989 to promote quality in applied arts, graphic and interior design. Organizes exhibitions and lectures, produces publications and acts as an information centre.

Federatie van Kunstenaarsverenigingen
Passeerdersgracht 32–1, NL 1016 XH Amsterdam
☎ (+31) 20 23 77 61 and 20 24 62 32
President: Rinus Haks
Secretary: Willem Woudenberg
Founded 1947, it aims to support artists in relation to government and the market, to bring together various artists' associations, to mediate between these organizations and the government. It covers the fine arts, design and crafts, is funded by government grant and produces a newsletter.

Genootschap van Samenwerkende Ambachtskunstenaars (GSA)
Bosdrift 275, NL 1214 JZ Hilversum
☎ (+31) 35 21 52 64 or 35 21 40 70
President: M.J. van der Sandt
Secretary: W.M. Bakker-Offerman
Guild of Craft Artists. Organizes exhibitions, runs a gallery.

Keramisch Werkcentrum Heusden
Pelsestraat 15, Postbus 15, 5256 ZG Heusden
☎ (+31) 41 62 16 94
Director: Adriaan van Spanje
Excellent organization for any artists/ architects/designers to realize a project or do research. Publishes catalogues. Converts to larger premises as the Europees Keramisch Werkcentrum in 's-Hertogenbosch end 1991.

Nederlandse Vakgroep Keramisten
c/o Netty Janssens, Wilhelminapark 68, NL 5041 ED Tilburg
☎ (+31) 13 43 58 76
President: Joop van Ulden
Secretary: Netty Janssens
Dutch Association of Ceramists. Aims to represent the interests of professional ceramists. Organizes exhibitions and publishes a newsletter, *Keramiek*.

Vereniging van Vormgevers en Sierraadontwerpers (VES)
c/o Arie Vijfvinkel, Postbus 791, NL 1000 AT Amsterdam
☎ (+31) 3465 67549
President: Lous Martin
Secretary: Arie Vijfvinkel
Association of Three-dimensional and Jewelry Designers. Aims to represent the interests of professional goldsmiths and jewelers. Liaises with other organizations, publishes a newsletter, organizes exhibitions at home and abroad.

World Crafts Council – Europe
Secretariat: Federati Van Kunstenaarsverenigingen, Passeeredersgracht 31–1, NL 1016 XH Amsterdam
☎ (+31) 20 23 77 61/24 62 32
Fax (+31) 20 20 82 14
Collates and disseminates information on the European crafts scene.

HUNGARY

Hungarian Association of Arts and Crafts
Vorosmarty ter 1, H Budapest V

Idea
PO Box 12, H 1440 Budapest
Applied Arts Association.

IRELAND

Crafts Council of Ireland
Powerscourt Townhouse Centre, South William Street, Dublin 2
☎ (+353) 1 679 7368 and 679 7383
Fax (+353) 1 679 7385
Chief Executive: Terry Kelly
Craft Development Officer: Sean O'Farrell
Aims to manage, fund and promote crafts of high quality through a series of exhibitions at its HQ Gallery. Disseminates information through its Information Office, organizes workshops and seminars and an annual Craft Trade Fair and publishes *Craft Review* and various booklets.

JAPAN

Craft Center Japan
Maruzen Building, Nihonbashi, Tokyo
Association of designers. Showroom for local and export sales.

Nihon Kohgei Kai
2 National Museum, Ueno Park, Daito-ku, Tokyo
Japanese National Arts Association, sponsored by the Ministry of Education.

Nihon Mingei Kyokai
c/o Japan Folk Crafts Museum, 4–3–
33 Komaba, Meguro-ku, Tokyo 153
☎ (+81) 3 467 4527
Japanese Folk Art Association.

Nippon Gendai Kohgei Bijutsu-Ka Kyokai
17–10 4-chome, Higashi-Ueno, Daito-ku, Tokyo
Japanese Contemporary Artist-Craftsmen Association.

Nitten
3-8-5 Sendagi Bunkyo-ku, Tokyo 113
☎ (+81) 33 822 3226
The biggest Japanese organization, with the longest history concerned with modern crafts, also painting and sculpture.

So-Dei-Sha
6-chome, Gojohashi, Higashiyama-ku, Kyoto
Experimental ceramists' group.

Zen Nihon Kohgei Bijutsu-Ka Kyokai
1–4, Kanda, Koji-cho, Chiyoda-ku, Tokyo
National Japanese Craftsmen's Association.

NEW ZEALAND

Crafts Council of New Zealand
22 the Terrace, Wellington, PO Box 498, Wellington 1 NZ
☎ (+64) 4 727 018 Fax (+64) 4 727 003
Executive Director: Margaret Belich
Information Director: Pamela Braddell
Established in 1977 to support craftspeople and crafts in New Zealand, a member association but also affiliated to craft guilds and associations. Aims to represent craftspeople and promote their interests, disseminate information, promote the image of New Zealand crafts abroad, promote training and education, organize lectures, workshops. Publishes *New Zealand Crafts*.

NORWAY

Foreningen Brukskunst
Stortorvets Basarer, Stortorvet 1 B, N 0155 Oslo 1
☎ (+47) 2 42 89 90
President: Bjorg Abrahamsen
Secretary: Esther Haukeland
Corporation of Craftspeople and Designers. Aims to promote design and function in Norwegian crafts and industry. Publishes a newsletter, *Brukskunst*, and organizes exhibitions at home.

Landsforbundet Norsk Bruskunst
Uranienborgveien 2, N 0258 Oslo 2
☎ (+47) 2 55 76 28
President: Arne Jon Jutrem

Secretary: Ulla Tarras-Wahlberg
Norwegian Society of Crafts and Design, founded in 1918 to promote Norwegian industrial design and crafts. Organizes exhibitions at home and abroad, often in collaboration with other Scandinavian design organizations.

Norges Gullsmedforbund
Storgaten 14, N 0184 Oslo 1
☎ (+47) 2 17 07 27 Fax (+47) 2 17 07 27
Director: Ingar M. Rebne
Norwegian gold- and silversmiths' association. Publishes a monthly magazine.

Norges Husflidslag
PO Box 3693 Gamlebyen, N 0135 Oslo 1
☎ (+47) 2 19 79 68
President: Per Evale
Secretary: Ingunn Saetervadet Christiansen
Norwegian Association of Handicraft. Aims to preserve traditional crafts and promote contemporary Norwegian crafts. Publishes a newsletter, *Norsk Husflid*, and organizes exhibitions, mostly at home, some abroad.

Norske Kunsthandverkere
Peder Claussensgt. 7, N 0165 Oslo 1
☎ (+47) 2 44 17 45
President: Bente Saetrang
Norwegian Association for Arts and Crafts, founded 1975 as the Norwegian Craftsmen's Union, it represents craftspeople's interests, organizes exhibitions at home and abroad, publishes a newsletter, *Kunsthandverk*, and organizes workshops and seminars.

SPAIN

AA-Fad
Brusi 45, SP 08006 Barcelona
☎ (+34) 209 11 55
President: Assumpcio Raventos
Secretary: Ramon Gausset i Vinos
Founded 1973 to promote arts and crafts, organizes conferences and exhibitions at home and abroad.

Associacion Andaluza para la Artesania
E1 Post 80, Arfe s/n, SP 41001 Seville
President: José Vazquez Hidalgo
Aims to promote crafts, traditional and contemporary, specifically in the region of Seville. Organizes exhibitions and courses, disseminates information, assists craftsmen.

Associacion d'Artesans Creatius de Catalunya
Wellington 29, SP 08018 Barcelona
President: Maria Narbon
Aims to promote the crafts and creative activities, organizes exhibitions.

Associacion de Ceramistes de Catalunya
Equador 2 2on 5a porta, SP 08029 Barcelona
President: Ingnasi Mayolas
Aims to promote traditional and contemporary ceramics, produced industrially and by craftsmen. Organizes exhibitions.

Associacion Galega de Artesanos
Claveles 9 1-A, SP 15008 La Coruna
President: Manuel Gonzalez Arias
Aims to promote both traditional and avant-garde crafts. Organizes exhibitions and fairs.

Centre del Vidro de Barcelona – FAD,
Comtes de Belloc, 192, SP 08014 Barcelona
☎ (+34) 490 28 86 and 490 16 56
Director: Pilar Munoz
Founded 1987 to promote creativity in the field of glass. Organizes workshops and exhibitions with international scope.

Fundacion de Gremios
Gardenal Herrera Oria 378, E 28035 Madrid
☎ (+34) 216 18 40
President: Enrique Moral Sandoval
Founded in 1941 to promote and conserve traditional crafts. Is concerned with conservation, organizes educational courses, disseminates information, organizes exhibitions.

SWEDEN

Blas och Knada
Hornsgatan 26, S 11720 Stockholm
☎ (+46) 8 42 77 67
Aims to bring together professional craftworkers and collectors, while maintaining the highest standards of technique and design. Disseminates information, organizes national and international exhibitions, runs seminars.

Centrum for Konst & Hantverk
Wallingatan 38, S 111 24 Stockholm
☎ (+46) 8 10 81 84
Information Officer: Asa Lindgren
Centre for Arts and Crafts.

Foreningen for Nutida Svenskt Silver
PO Box 5229, S 102 45 Stockholm
☎ (+46) 8 63 81 10
President: Ake Thorstensson
Secretary: Jorun Koch
Aims to promote Swedish silversmiths and their work, organizes exhibitions of Swedish silver at home and abroad, publishes a newsletter for members, organizes exhibitions in its own gallery and elsewhere.

Foreningen Svensk Form
Restiernas gata 12, S 116 31 Stockholm

☎ (+46) 8 644 33 03 Fax (+46) 8 644 22 85
Founded 1845, a non-profit-making, state-funded organization aiming to produce and disseminate good design, and provide a better public and private environment for the individual. Publishes a newsletter and *Form* magazine, organizes exhibitions, mainly abroad. Comprehensive information centre.

Foreningen Sveriges Konsthantverkare och Industriformgivare (KIF)
Wallingatan 38, S 11124 Stockholm
☎ (+46) 8 21 33 34
President: Conni Hultberg
Swedish Association of Craftsmen and Industrial Designers. Represents the interests of its members, disseminates information, publishes a quarterly newsletter, organizes exhibitions, seminars, courses.

Konsthantverkarna
M. Samuelsgatan 2, S 11144 Stockholm
☎ (+46) 8 11 03 60
President: Lars Flemming
Secretary: Ulla Parkdal
Association of craftspeople working in ceramics, glass, textiles, silver, wood and leather. Organizes six to seven exhibitions per year.

Lignum
Hornsgatan 29 c, S 11649 Stockholm
☎ (+46) 8 40 00 34
President: Hendrik Capanello
Secretary: Hanne Fultmann
Aims to develop technique and design in fine furniture and woodwork.

Metallum
Hornsgatan 30, S 11720 Stockholm
☎ (+46) 8 40 13 23
President: Marie Fernstrom
Secretary: Birgitte Sanitate
Aims to promote experimental work in metals and new materials and unorthodox methods of using them, to maintain high quality in regular exhibitions, to encourage exchange of ideas. Publishes a newsletter, *Metallumnytt*.

The National Association of Swedish Handicraft Associations
Sturegatan 29, S 114 36 Stockholm
☎ (+46) 8 21 63 84

Stok
Norrlandsgatan 18, S 111 43 Stockholm
☎ (+46) 8 10 03 77
A non-profit-making trade association for textile and clothing designers. Disseminates information, publishes a quarterly magazine, organizes exhibitions, seminars and debates.

Sveriges Juvelare-och Guldsmedsforbund
Gamia Brogatan 19, S 111 20 Stockholm
☎ (+46) 8 20 51 95 Fax (+46) 8 24 80 25
Director: Eric Gorm
Swedish gold- and silversmiths' association.

SWITZERLAND

Arbeitsgemeinschaft Schweizer Keramiker
CH 8607 Aathal-Seegraben
President: Markus Curau
Secretary: Irene Ott
Swiss Potters Association. Aims to promote professional work in ceramics in Switzerland. Publishes a newsletter for members, organizes a biennial exhibition of members' work in Switzerland.

Centre International de la Tapisserie Ancienne et Moderne
4 Avenue de Villamont, CH 1005 Lausanne
☎ (+41) 21 23 07 57
President: Paul René Martin
Secretary: Diana de Rham
Organizes the International Tapestry Biennale. Disseminates information and promotes contact between textile artists.

Crafts Council Schweiz, Suisse, Svizzera
Case Postale 898, CH 2501 Biel-Bienne
☎ (+41) 32 51 63 69
President: Antoinette Riklin
Secretary: Traute Stebler
Founded 1986 to promote the applied arts. Produces a quarterly bulletin, organizes exhibitions, disseminates information.

Iapma
Stockertstrasse 2, CH 4132 Muttenz
☎ (+41) 61 61 64 94 or 61 24 53 37
President: Dorothea Eimert
Secretary: Fred Siegenthaler
International Association of Hand Paper Makers and Paper Artists. Aims to promote handmade paper and paper artists, organizes exhibitions, workshops and seminars. Publishes a bi-annual newsletter in English.

L'Oeuvre
Case Postale 531, CH 1211 Geneva
☎ (+41) 22 36 11 88
President: Jean-Pierre Vorlet
Secretary: Josiane Tuescher
Aims to promote sculpture, the decorative arts, architecture and design. Publishes an information bulletin, organizes exhibitions.

Schweiz. Berufsverband für Handweben
T. Bider, Im Sesselacker 37, CH 4059 Basel
President: Annie Trieb
Secretary: Thérèse Bider
Professional Association of Swiss Handweavers. Publishes a quarterly newsletter *Textil-Forum-Textile*, organizes exhibitions and courses.

Schweizerische Arbeitsgemeinschaft Gestaltendes Handwerk
Eichwaldstrasse 15, CH 6002 Lucerne
☎ (+41) 41 42 90 90
President: Dieter Waeckerlin
Secretaries: Yvo Maller, Maya Hafliger, Judith Amstad
Founded 1950 to promote the creativity, high standards and financial betterment of craftspeople. Publishes a yearly newsletter and organizes exhibitions.

Segretario d'Animazione per l'Artigianato
Via Ronchetto 7, CH 6900 Lugano
☎ (+41) 91 52 13 86
Chairman: Marco Mumenthaler
Aims to promote arts and crafts of a high standard. Organizes exhibitions.

Vereinigung Schweizerischer Spitzenmacherinnen
Raubbulstrasse 11 C, CH 8600 Dubendorf
☎ (+41) 1 821 40 78
President: Griet van Houwe
Secretary: J. Wichser
Aims to promote handmade lace. Publishes a quarterly bulletin, organizes meetings and exhibitions.

UNITED KINGDOM

The Association of Guilds of Weavers, Spinners & Dyers
Green Close, Green Hammerton, York YO5 8BQ
Chairman: J.F.W. Searcy
Honorary Secretary: Rae Milne
Aims to encourage and maintain excellence of craftsmanship and design in this field. Collects and disseminates information, organizes workshops, demonstrations and lectures, maintains a library. Produces, quarterly, *The Journal for Weavers, Spinners and Dyers*.

British Artist Blacksmiths Association
c/o Sheply Dawson Architectural Engineering Ltd., Joseph Noble Road, Lillyhall, Workington, Cumbria CA14 4JX
☎ (+44) 900 68368
Honorary Secretary: Alan Dawson
Produces a newsletter, *The Blacksmith*.

British Artists in Glass
Broadfield House Glass Museum, Barnett Lane, Kingswinford,

West Midlands DY6 9QA
☎ (+44) 384 273011
Aims to collect and disseminate information, hold conferences, organize exhibitions, act as a central agency for the supply of equipment and materials, represent glass in the UK and liaise with similar organizations abroad.

Contemporary Applied Arts
43 Earlham Street, London WC2H 9LD
☎ (+44) 71 836 6993
Director: Tessa Peters
Professional association of craftspeople working in all fields. It aims to support its members by organizing exhibitions and selling their work and to stimulate excellence in the crafts environment by making the best of contemporary craft available to the public.

Crafts Council
44a Pentonville Road, London N1 9HF
☎ (+44) 71 278 7700
Director: Tony Ford
Britain's national crafts organization, set up as the Crafts Advisory Committee in 1971 to promote fine craftsmanship in the decorative and applied arts throughout England and Wales. Maintains links through regional arts associations and collaborates with local authorities, regional museums and art and craft centres. Disseminates information, has a slide index of over 500 British craftspeople, organizes exhibitions, has a major collection of English contemporary crafts, distributes grants and publishes *Crafts* magazine. Also Britain's WCC – Europe (World Crafts Council) base.

Craftsmen Potters' Association of Great Britain Ltd
William Blake House, Marshall Street, London W1V 1FD
☎ (+44) 71 437 7605
Aims to encourage creative ceramics. Members co-operate to sell and promote their work. The Association represents its members at national and international conferences and exhibitions. It runs Contemporary Ceramics shop and gallery and publishes, bi-monthly, *Ceramic Review*.

Designer Bookbinders
6 Queen Square, London WC1N 3AR
Secretary: Lester Bath
Organizes exhibitions and meetings and publishes *The New Bookbinder*.

Embroiderers Guild
Apartment 41A, Hampton Court Palace, East Molesey, Surrey KT8 9AU
☎ (+44) 81 943 1229
Director: Ann Joyce

Goldsmiths' Company
Worshipful Company of Goldsmiths, Foster Lane, London EC2V 6BN
☎ (+44) 71 606 7010

Aims to provide assistance in all areas of the industry in various ways, maintains a technical advisory service, organizes seminars and research activities. Has a collection of antique and modern plate, medals and jewelry; holds exhibitions and events.

Quilt Art
9 Old South Close, Hatch End, Pinner, Middlesex HA5 4TW
Contact: Christine Mitchell
Offshoot of The Quilters Guild; selective membership of the top quilters.

Society of Scribes and Illuminators
54 Boileau Road, London SW13 9BL
Secretary: Susan Cavendish
Aims to advance the crafts of writing and illumination. Encourages the production of wholly handmade books and documents. Publishes a newsletter, *The Scribe*.

UNITED STATES OF AMERICA

American Craft Council
72 Spring Street, New York NY 10012
☎ (+1) 212 274 0630 Fax (+1) 212 274 0650
President: Dan Keith Ray
Director, Craft Information Center: Linda Seckelson
Set up almost fifty years ago, aims to serves as a convenor for craftspeople, craft organizations and craft consumers dedicated to improving the craft economy by increasing public interest and understanding of crafts. Publishes *American Craft*, runs American Craft Enterprises Inc. (which markets craft through wholesale and retail fairs), American Craft Association (a national trade association for craftspeople and craft businesses) and American Craft Information Center (which coordinates and disseminates information through CraftNET, the Craft Registry and the Library's collections).

American Society of Furniture Artists (ASOFA)
PO Box 270188, Houston TX 77277

Artist-Blacksmith's Association of North America (ABANA)
PO Box 1181, Nashville IN 47448
☎ (+1) 812 988 6919

The Center for Tapestry Arts,
2nd Floor, 167 Spring Street (at West Broadway), New York NY 10012
☎ (+1) 212 431 7500
Director: Jean West
Founded 1989 as a non-profit-making organization to act as a resource center for artists working in tapestry and fiber-related media, through its exhibition, residency and educational

programmes. Mounts exhibitions in its own gallery, organizes workshops.

Embroiderers Guild of America
200 Fourth Avenue, Louisville KY 40202
☎ (+1) 502 589 6956

Glass Art Society
Box 1364, Corning NY 14830
☎ (+1) 614 487 8307

Handweavers Guild of America (HGA)
120 Mountain Avenue, B101, Bloomfield CT 06002
☎ (+1) 203 233 5124
President: Norma Smayda
Non-profit-making organization dedicated to promoting excellence in the textile arts and preserving textile heritage. Provides a forum for debate, encourages artists in fiber media. Publishes *Shuttle, Spindle and Dyepot*.

National Council on Education for the Ceramic Arts (NCECA)
PO Box 1677, Brandon OR 97411
☎ (+1) 503 347 4394

Society of American Silversmiths
PO Box 3599, Cranston RI 02910
☎ (+1) 401 461 3156

Society of North American Goldsmiths (SNAG)
5009 Londonderry Drive, Tampa FL 33647
☎ (+1) 813 977 5326

Surface Design Association (SDA)
4111 Lincoln Boulevard, Suite 426, Marina Del Ray CA 90292
☎ (+1) 614 756 9943
President: Lenore Davis
Secretary: Beverly Semmens
A non-profit-making educational organization. Aims to stimulate, promote and improve education in the area of surface design. Disseminates information, encourages debate. Publishes, quarterly, *Surface Design Journal*, and a quarterly newsletter.

Woodworking Association of North America (WANA)
Route 3 and Cummings Hill Road, PO Box 706, Plymouth NH 03264
☎ (+1) 603 536 3876

MUSEUMS

Art Gallery of South Australia
North Terrace, Adelaide SA 5000
☎ (+61) 85 207 7000 Fax (+61) 85 207 7070
Assistant Curator of Decorative Arts: Christopher Menz
Collection started 1884, comprehensive coverage of Australian crafts (emphasis on South Australia), some international items. All categories included, 5% on display at any one time. A contemporary craft exhibition every three years.

Art Gallery of Western Australia
Perth Cultural Centre, Perth WA 6000
☎ (+61) 9 328 7233 Fax (+61) 9 328 6353
Director: Paula Latos-Valier
Curator, craft and design: Robert Bell
Collection started 1969, international scope, all main categories, 25% on display, three exhibitions a year from the collection, an exhibition from national artists every 18 months, plus an international triennial.

Australian National Gallery
PO Box 1150, Canberra ACT 2601
☎ (+61) 6 2712411 Fax (+61) 6 271 2529
Director: Betty Churcher
Senior Curator, Australian art: John McPhee
Curatorial Assistant, international decorative arts: Roger Leong
Collection started 1982, international scope, concise collection of objects in all media by seminal artists and designers, emphasis on serial rather than one-off production, 60–80% is on display. Large glass collection. Outstanding national contemporary crafts collection.

City Art Gallery
PO Box 20, 40 Gurwood Street, Wagga Wagga NSW 2650
☎ (+61) 69 235 419 Fax (+61) 69 235 400
Director: Judy Le Lievre
Craft collection started 1979, international scope (mainly Australian, about 150 works by international artists), studio glass only, 95% on display. A triennial craft exhibition.

Curtin University of Technology
Bentley WA 6102
☎ (+61) 9 351 7347 Fax (+61) 9 351 2711
Director: Paul Thompson
Collection started 1968, mainly national scope, all main categories bar furniture represented, 98% on display, a contemporary craft exhibition is organized every two years. Substantial

jewelry collection (mainly Western Australian), also strong in fiber/textiles and ceramics. Work generally bought from graduating students and visiting artists-in-residence.

Museum of Contemporary Art
PO Box R1286, Royal Exchange, Sydney NSW 2000
☎ (+61) 2 252 4033 Fax (+61) 2 252 4361
Director: Leon Paroissien
Chief Curator: Bernice Murphy
Museum open to the public late 1991. Houses the Maningrida Weaving collection, comprising 600 pieces of work in fiber, representing the cultural activity of Aboriginal women in the communities of Western to Central Arnhemland in Australia.

National Gallery of Victoria
180 St Kilda Road, Melbourne VIC 3004
☎ (+61) 3 618 0222 Fax (+61) 3 614 4337
Director: James Millison
Senior Curator: Terence Lane
Curator, glass: Geoffrey Edwards
Curator, ceramics: Margaret Legge
Collection started 1861, national and international scope (emphasis on Australian craftwork 1945 onwards), all main categories represented, as much as 75% on display, generally one contemporary craft exhibition organized each year.

The Powerhouse
Museum of Applied Arts and Sciences, 500 Harris Street, Ultimo, Sydney NSW 2000
Postal address: PO Box K346, Haymarket, Sydney 2000
☎ (+61) 2 217 0111 Fax (+61) 2 211 0932
Director: Terence Measham
Assistant Director, collections: Jennifer Sanders
Senior Curator, Australian Decorative Arts, post 1945: Judith O'Callaghan
Curator: Grace Cochran
International Decorative Arts: Anne Watson
Collection started 1879, predominantly Australian ('comprehensive collection of Australian crafts since 1945 in all media'), some international items, all main categories, 40% on display, two contemporary craft exhibitions organized each year.

Queen Victoria Museum and Art Gallery
Wellington Street, Launceston TAS 7250
☎ (+61) 03 316777 Fax (+61) 03 371117
Director: Chris Tassell
Curator, craft: Glenda King
Collection started 1964, national scope, all main categories represented (broadly

based collection, strengths in ceramics and jewelry), 30% on display in the permanent craft gallery, contemporary craft exhibitions organized four or five times a year. A venue for touring exhibitions and tours some of its own exhibitions.

Queensland Art Gallery
PO Box 686, South Brisbane QLD 4101
☎ (+61) 7 840 7333 Fax (+61) 7 844 8865
Director: Doug Hall
Curator, decorative arts: Glenn R. Cooke
Collection started in the 1950s, regional scope only, mainly ceramics, glass, jewelry and textiles; small proportion on display, infrequent contemporary craft exhibitions. The major craft acquisition to date comprises the 175 items in the areas of ceramics, jewelry/metalwork and textiles/fiber acquired for the 1982 Survey of Contemporary Australian Craft.

AUSTRIA

Österreichisches Museum für Angewandte Kunst
Stubenring 5, A Vienna 1010
☎ (+43) 222 711 36 Fax (+43) 222 713 1026
Director: Peter Noever
Departmental Curators: Hanna Eggard, Verena Formanek, Ingrid Gazzari, Katharina Gsöllpointner, Regina Haslinger, Brigitte Huck, Ludwig Neustifter, Manfred Trummer, Waltraud Neuwirth, Elisabeth Schmuttermeier, Angela Völker, Johannes Wieninger, Christian Witt-Döring.
Contemporary craft collection started 1986, international scope, all main categories represented, contemporary craft exhibition organized once a year. Closed for renovation since spring 1989, the main building due to open to the public April 1991, with all construction work completed by 1992.

Steirisches Glaskunstzentrum und Glasmuseum
Hochtregisterstrasse 1, A 8572 Bärnbach
☎ (+43) 3142 62 9 50 or 62 1 41
Operator: Hans Martin Hittaller
Departmental Curators: Karl Neuhauser, Walter Kienreich
Collection started 1983, international scope, art glass and studio glass only, 50% on display, contemporary craft exhibition organized once a year.

BELGIUM

Musée de la Tapisserie
9 place Reine Astrid, B 7500 Tournai
Recently opened Museum displaying collections assembled by the Fondation de la Tapisserie, des Arts du Tissu et des Arts Muraux of the French-speaking community in Belgium. As well as its historical collection, the Museum promotes the work of contemporary textile artists from the international French-speaking community.

Musées d'Archéologie et d'Arts Décoratifs
Quai de Maastricht 10, B 54000 Liège
☎ (+32) 41 22 16 00 or 23 20 68
Contemporary craft collection started 1958, international scope, all main categories, 5% on display.

CANADA

The Canadian Craft Museum
1411 Cartwright Street, Vancouver BC V6H 3R7
☎ (+1) 604 687 8266 Fax (+1) 604 684 7174
General Manager: Ed Oscapella
Curatorial Consultant: Lloyd Herman
Collection started 1985, national scope only (postwar contemporary Canadian craft, non-traditional), all main categories represented bar furniture, items from the collection will be on display by the end of 1991. Four exhibitions a year of fine craft and folk art, traditional and contemporary, local, national and international.

Musée des Arts Décoratifs de Montréal
2929 Jeanne d'Arc, Montréal H1W 3W2
Postal address: CP 12000, Succursale A, Montréal (Québec) H3C 3P3
☎ (+1) 514 259 2575 Fax (+1) 514 284 0123
Director: Luc d'Iberville-Moreau
Collection started 1979, international scope, all main categories, 2% on display, exhibitions of contemporary craft organized.

Ontario Crafts Council
Chalmers Building, 35 McCaul Street, Toronto ON S7T 1V7
☎ (+1) 416 977 3551 Fax (+1) 416 977 3552
Director: John Foster
Curator: Alan C. Elder
A small but noteworthy collection of Canadian crafts.

CZECHOSLOVAKIA

Muzeum Skla a Bižuterie
Jiráskova v. 4, CZ 466 01 Jablonec nad Nisou
☎ (+42) 428 22522
Director: Antonín Langhamer
Curator, glass: Jana Urbančová
Curator, jewelry: Vera Maternová
Jewelry and glass collection started 1961. Industrially produced work and one-offs from Czechoslovakia only. Two exhibitions organized each year, 1% on display at any time.

Sklarské Muzeum
CZ 47114 Kamenický Šenov
☎ (+42) 425 92206
Contemporary glass collection.

Sklarské Muzeum
CZ 47301 Nový Bor
☎ (+42) 424 2196
Contemporary glass collection.

Umĕleckoprůmyslové Muzeum
Ulilce 17. Listopadu 2, CZ 110 01 Praguo 1
☎ (+42) 232 0051, 232 0017 and 232 8964
Director: Jaroslav Langr
Assistant Director: Helena Koenigsmarková
Curator, glass and ceramics: Olga Drahotová
Curator, contemporary crafts: Sylva Petrová
Curator, furniture and metalwork: Vera Vokacová
Curator, textiles: Eva Uchalová
Collection started 1885, mainly national in scope. All main categories, especially contemporary glass. No contemporary displays but exhibitions organized every one to two years.

DENMARK

Arhus Kunstmuseum
H. Guldbergsgade 2, DK 8000 Arhus C
Director: Jens Erik Sorenson

Glasmuseum
Strandvejen 8, DK 8400 Ebeltoft
☎ (+45) 86 34 17 99 Fax (+45) 86 34 60 60
Administrative Curator: Charlotte Sahl-Madsen
Collection started 1986, international scope, glass only, 30% on display, contemporary craft exhibitions organized three times a year. More than 500 international glass artists represented. Museum relies to some extent on donations/loans of work from glass artists.

Hjorring Kunstmuseum
Brinck Seidelinsgade 10, DK 9800 Hjorring

☎ (+45) 98 92 41 33 Fax (+45) 98 92 16 95
Director: Hanne Pedersen
Contemporary craft collection started 1981, regional scope (with an intention to broaden to international scope within the next few years), ceramics, jewelry, furniture and textiles only, 5–10% on display at present, two or three contemporary craft exhibitions organized each year.

Holstebro Kunstmuseum
Herningvej 1,
(Postal address: Sonderbrogade 2) DK 7500 Holstebro
☎ (+45) 97 42 45 18
Director: Jesper Knudsen
Contemporary craft collection started 1966, primarily national scope with some international items, ceramics and textiles only, 60–80% on display, a contemporary craft exhibition organized twice a year.

Kunstindustrimuseet
Bredgade 68, DK 1260 Copenhagen K
☎ (+45) 8814 9452
Director: Kristian Jakobsen
Danish Museum of Decorative Arts, established 1890, international scope (mostly Danish and Scandinavian, with a small selection from Japan and other countries), all main categories represented, approximately 15–20% on display, between five and seven contemporary craft exhibitions organized each year.

Kunstmuseet Trapholt
Aeblehaven 23, DK 6000 Kolding
☎ (+45) 75 542422
Director: Sven Jorn Andersen
Curator: Ane Hejlskov Larsen
Contemporary collection started in 1981, national scope only, ceramics, glass, furniture and textiles, 60% on display, four contemporary craft exhibitions organized each year.

FINLAND

Suomen Lasimuseo
Tehtaankatu 23, SF 11910 Riihimäki
☎ (+358) 914 741 494 Fax (+358) 914 741 700
Director: Heikki Matiskinen
Curator: Kaisa Koivisto
Collection started 1961, specializes in Finnish glass, both industrially produced and craftsman-made. The Museum also houses the Tapio Wirkkala collection, comprising objects in glass, wood, metal and ceramic.

Taideteollisuus Museo
Korkeavuorenkatu 23, SF 00130 Helsinki
☎ (+358) 0 174 455 Fax (+358) 0 626 733
Director: Jarno Peltonen

239

Chief Curator: Mariaane Aav
Curator: Ebba Brännback
Assistant Curator: Anna-Lisa Amberg
Collection started 1871, scope primarily national (aims to represent work by all major craftspeople in Finland) but with some international items, all main categories, only 1% on display at any time, at least four exhibitions of contemporary craftwork each year.

FRANCE

Musée Cantini
19 rue Grignan, F 13006 Marseille
☎ (+33) 91 54 77 75
Director: Bernard Blistene
Head Curator: Nicolas Cendo
Curator: Olivier Cousinou
Curator: Bernard Millet
Collection started 1950, international scope, 80% on display, six contemporary craft exhibitions organized each year.

Musée des Arts Décoratifs
Hotel de Lalande, 39 rue Bouffard, F 33000 Bordeaux
☎ (+33) 56 90 91 60 Fax (+33) 56 44 56 07
Curator: Jacqueline du Pasquier
Collection started 1980, no budget, international scope, ceramics, glass, jewelry, metalwork, furniture and clocks, 80% on display, approximately one contemporary craft exhibition organized a year. No 20th-century permanent gallery, but temporary exhibitions are organized regularly.

Musée des Arts Décoratifs
107 rue de Rivoli, F Paris 75001
☎ (+33) 1 42 60 32 14
Curator, contemporary craft (especially furniture): Guillemette Delaporte
Curator, glass: Jean-Luc Olivié
Curator, jewelry and metalwork: Chantal Bizot
Curator, textiles: Nadine Gasc
Curator, toys: Monica Burckhardt
Curator, wallpaper: Véronique de Bruignac
International scope, all main categories, plus wallpaper and toys, 50% on display, contemporary craft exhibitions organized.

Musée des Arts de la Mode
107 rue de Rivoli, F 75001 Paris
☎ (+33) 1 42 60 32 14
Costume collection.

Musée du Berry
4–6 rue des Arènes, F 18000 Bourges
☎ (+33) 48 700 41 92
Curator: Jean-Paul Le Maguet

Musée Jean Lurçat et de la Tapisserie Contemporaine
4 Boulevard Arago, F 49100 Angers
☎ (+33) 41 88 64 65

Director: Viviane Huchard
Curator: Françoise Estienne
Collection started 1967, tapestry only, international scope, 50% on display, contemporary craft exhibitions twice a year. Prominent in the collection is the *Chant du Monde* series of tapestries by Jean Lurçat.

Musée Municipal de Céramique
Place de la Mairie, F 06220 Vallauris
☎ (+33) 93 64 16 05

Musée National Adrien Dubouché
Place Winston Churchill, F 87000 Limoges
☎ (+33) 55 77 45 58
Collection started 1845, international scope, ceramics and glass only. All of the collection is currently in store, contemporary craft exhibitions organized occasionally.

Musée National de la Céramique
Place de la Manufacture, F 92310 Sèvres
☎ (+33) 45 34 99 05
Chief curator: Antoinette Halle

GERMANY

Badisches Landesmuseum
Schloss, D 7500 Karlsruhe 1
☎ (+49) 721 135 6542 Fax (+49) 721 135 6537
Director: Volker Himmelein
Curator: Peter Schmitt
Collection started 1960, international (mainly European) scope, all main categories included with the emphasis on contemporary ceramics and glass. Usually two exhibitions each year.

Deutsches Textilmuseum
Adreasmarkt 8, Krefeld 4150
☎ (+49) 2151 572046
Collection of 20,000 textiles spanning 2000 years. Venue for the Biennale der Textilkunst (European fibre art).

Glasmuseum Frauenau
Am Museumspark 1, D 8377 Frauenau
☎ (+49) 9926 718/719 Fax (+49) 9926 1799
Director: Alfons Hannes
Curator: Horst Weber
Collection started 1975, international scope, glass only, 30% of contemporary collection on display.

Glasmuseum Immenhausen
Am Bahnhof 3, D 3524 Immenhausen
☎ (+49) 5673 2060
Director: Friedrich-Karl Baas
Collection started 1981, international scope, glass only, 40% on display, contemporary glass exhibitions three or four times a year.

Glasmuseum Wertheim
Mühlenstrasse 24, D 6980 Wertheim

☎ (+49) 9342 6866
Director: Gertrud Löber
Collection started approximately 1960, international scope, glass only, 70 to 80% on display, contemporary craft exhibitions organized twice a year.

Hessisches Landesmuseum
Friedenplatz 1, D 6100 Darmstadt
☎ (+49) 6151 125434 Fax (+49) 6151 28942
Director: Wolfgang Beeh
Curator: Carl Benno Heller
Collection started before 1820, international scope, all categories represented, 50% on display, annual craft exhibition organized.

Hetjens-Museum
Deutsches Keramikmuseum, Palais Nesselrode, Schulstrasse 4, D 4000 Düsseldorf
Ceramics.

Keramikmuseum Westerwald
Deutsche Sammlung für Historische und Zeitgenössische Keramik, Lindenstrasse, D 5410 Höhr-Grenzhausen
☎ (+49) 2624 3666
Collection started 1976, international scope, ceramics only, 30% on display, special contemporary ceramic exhibitions organized two to four times a year, national and international in scope. Awards the Westerwald Prize for ceramics, and a special prize for German ceramics.

Keramion
Museum für Zeitgenössische Keramische Kunst, Bonnstrasse 12, D 5020 Frechen
Ceramics.

Kestner-Museum
Trammplatz 3, D 3000 Hanover 1
☎ (+49) 511 168 2120
Glass collection.

Kunstgewerbemuseum
Tiergartenstrasse 6, D 1000 Berlin 30
☎ (+49) 30 266 29 02 or 266 29 03
Director: Barbara Mundt
Curators: Stefan Bursche, Dietrich Kötzsce, Suzanne Netzer
Collection started 1867, international scope, all main categories represented, 85% of collection on display, one exhibition organized each year.

Kunstmuseum Düsseldorf
Ehrenhof 5, D 4000 Düsseldorf
☎ (+49) 211 899 2460 Fax (+49) 211 899 3575
Director: Hans Albert Peters
Curator for glass: Helmut Ricke
One of the most important glass collections in Europe, started c. 1936 and greatly enhanced by the acquisition of the Hentrich Collection in 1963. It comprises about 250 pieces made by

some 150 artists, 70% on display, and a contemporary craft exhibition is organized about once a year. Some contemporary furniture and textiles.

Kunstsammlungen der Veste Coburg
D 8630 Coburg
Director: Clementine Schack von Wittenau
Collection started c. 1960, international scope, ceramics and glass only. Presents the prestigious Coburg Glass Prize every eight years. Huge international collection of contemporary studio glass. The ceramics collection includes work by various Bavarian potters, with some work by national and international figures. Has a competition for young potters every seven years.

Museum des Kunsthandwerks
Grassimuseum, Johannisplatz, D 7010 Leipzig
☎ (+37) 41 29 15 43 or (+37) 41 29 15 45
Director: A. Grzesiak
Collection started 1874, national scope only, all main categories included plus books, 1% on display at any one time, craft exhibitions organized. Bauhaus, Wiener Werkstätte, etc.

Museum für Angewandte Kunst
An der Rechtschule, D 5000 Cologne 1
☎ (+49) 221 2213860 Fax (+49) 221 2213885
Director: Brigitte Klesse
Collection started 1888, international scope, all main categories represented, 30% on display, contemporary craft exhibitions organized once or twice a year. Represents 20th-century crafts and design and industrially produced items. Ceramics, the largest part of the collection, are displayed separately.

Museum für Kunst und Gewerbe
Steintorplatz 1, D 2000 Hamburg 1
☎ (+49) 40 2486 2732 Fax (+49) 40 2486 2834
Director: W. Hornbostel
Curator: Rudiger Joppien
Collection started 1877, all main categories represented, 20% on display. Exhibitions of the work of individual artists are organized, as well as an annual craft fair for Northern Germany which was started in 1879.

Museum für Kunsthandwerk
Schaumainkai 17, D 6000 Frankfurt am Main 70
☎ (+49) 69 2121 21201 Fax (+49) 69 7500 2613
Curator: Sabine Runde
Collection started 1900, international scope, all categories represented (with emphasis at present on ceramics and glass), 35% on display, a contemporary craft exhibition every two years.

Museum für Zeitgenössische Glasmalerei Langen
Altes Rathaus, Wilhelm-Leuschner-Platz 3, D 6070 Langen
The only museum in Germany devoted to painting on glass. Recently established, international scope, modest as yet, no state funding.

Schleswig-Holsteinisches Landesmuseum
Schloss Gottorf, D 2380 Schleswig
☏ (+49) 4621 18130 Fax (+49) 4621 81355
Director: Heinz Spielmann
Curator, 20th-century art: Christian Rathke
Curator, cultural history: Paul Zubek
Collection started 1974, national scope only, all main categories represented, 90% on display, a contemporary craft exhibition organized every two years.

Schmuckmuseum Pforzheim im Reuchlinhaus
Jahnstrasse 42, D 7530 Pforzheim
☏ (+49) 7231 392126
Director: Fritz Falk
Collection started 1961, international scope, jewelry only, 60% on display. Major contemporary craft exhibitions organized (for example, Ornamenta I in 1990). Ornamenta 2 is in 1993.

Vitra Museum
Charles-Eames-Strasse 1, D 7858 Weim am Rhein
Director: Rolf Fehlbaum
International furniture collection, including commissioned new works.

Württembergisches Landesmuseum
Altes Schloss, Schillerplatz 6, D 7000 Stuttgart 1
☏ (+49) 711 279 3400 Fax (+49) 711 279 3499
Director: Claus Zoege von Manteuffel
Curator, ceramics: Hans-Ulrich Roller
Curator, textiles: Rainer Y
Curator, glass, jewelry, metalwork, woodwork, furniture: Heike Schröder
Collection started 1851. International scope. All main categories represented. 25% on display. Contemporary craft exhibition organized every two years.

HOLLAND

Centraal Museum
Agnietenstraat 1, NL 3512 XA Utrecht
☏ (+31) 30 315541
Curator: Ida van Zijl
Collection started 1838, mainly national scope (aims to represent all major Dutch craftsmen and women), all main categories represented (objects designed for, and to be used in, the home), up to 25% on display, one contemporary craft exhibition each year.

Gemeentemuseum Arnhem
Utrechtseweg 87, NL 6812 AA Arnhem
☏ (+31) 85 512431 Fax (+31) 85 51 48
Director: L. Brandt Corstius
Curator: H.E.D. Martens
Collection started 1920, national scope only, all main categories represented bar textiles, 5% on display, three to four exhibitions organized each year.

Haags Gemeentemuseum
Stadhouderslaan 41, NL 2517 HV 's-Gravenhage
☏ (+31) 70 338 1111 Fax (+31) 70 355 7360
Curator, modern applied art and design: Marjan Boot
Decorative arts collection started at the end of the 19th century, national and international scope, all main categories represented, one-off and serial items.

Museum Boymans-Van Beuningen
Mathenesserlaan 18–20, NL 3015 CK Rotterdam
☏ (+31) 10 441 9400 Fax (+31) 10 436 0500
Director: W.H. Crouwel
Head of department, decorative arts and design: J.H. ter Molen
Collection started in the 1920s, international scope, all main categories represented (from domestic to luxury items), contemporary craft exhibitions organized frequently.

Museum voor Hedendagse Kunst het Kruithuis
Citadellaan 7, NL 5211 XA Den Bosch
☏ (+31) 73 122188
Director: Yvonne G.J.M. Joris
Contemporary craft collection started 1960, international scope, ceramics and jewelry only, 10% on display, half of all exhibitions are of international contemporary craftwork. Purchases made from the exhibitions.

Museum het Princessehof
Nederlands Keramiekmuseum, Grote Kerkstraat 11, NL 8911 DZ Leeuwarden
☏ (+31) 58 127438
Curator, ceramics: A.H. Hidding

Nederlands Kostuummuseum
Stadhouderslaan 41, NL 2517 HV The Hague
☏ (+31) 70 338 1111 Fax (+31) 70 355 7630
Director: Rudi Fuchs
Curator, costume and jewelry: Ietse Meij
Collection started 1951, international scope, jewelry and textiles only (modern Dutch jewelry from 1960 onwards, designer knitwear and accessories). Museum closed in 1990, due to open 1991 or 1992. Some items from the permanent collections are usually on display and a special jewelry or textile

exhibition is organized every one to two years.

Nederlands Textielmuseum
Goirkestraat 96, NL 5046 GN Tilburg
☏ (+31) 13 367475 Fax (+31) 13 363240
Curator: Carolien Boot
Collection started 1983, national scope only, textiles only (Dutch textile design from 1890 to present day, both hand- and industrially made), approximately three contemporary textiles exhibitions a year. Produces a publication, Textuur.

Stedelijk Museum
Paulus Potterstraat 13, NL 1071 CX Amsterdam
☏ (+31) 20 5732 911 Fax (+31) 20 752716
Director: W.A.L. Beeren
Curator, ceramics and textiles: Liesbeth Crommelin
Contemporary craft collection started 1923. International scope. All main categories represented. Small percentage on display. Ten to twelve contemporary craft exhibitions organized each year.

Stichting National Glasmuseum
Lingedijk 28, NL 4142 LD Leerdam
☏ (+31) 3451 12714
Curator: Annet van der Kley-Blehxtoon
Collection started 1953, mainly national scope, glass only, 60% on display, one contemporary craft exhibition each year.

HUNGARY

Baranyai Alkotolepek
Baranyai Creative Colonies, Vajda Janos ter 2, H 7800 Siklós
☏ (+36) 73 21736 and 73 21257
Director: Komor Istvan
Curator: Imre Schrammel
Collection started 1968, ceramics only. Sixteen international ceramics symposia organized since 1968 and two-thirds of the work generated at these symposia remains in the permanent collection, 5% of which is on display.

Ferenczy Museum
Ulastagh Gy. u. 1, H 2000 Szentendre
☏ (+36) 26 10 244
Director: József Bihari
Curator: Lea Schenk
Ceramics, largely the work of Margit Kovacs, some international purchases, 80% on display. A contemporary craft collection for Pest province organized every four years.

Iparmuvészeti Muzeum
Ulloi út 33–37, PO Box 3, H 1450 Budapest
☏ (+36) 1175 222 and 1175 635 Fax (+36) 1175 880
Director: Gyula Rózsa
Curator, furniture: Ferenc Batári

Curator, ceramics and glass: Imre Katona
Curator, textiles: Emoke László
Curator, metalwork and jewelry: Éva Békési
Contemporary collection started 1972, national scope only, all main categories represented plus design and packaging, 8% on display, about two contemporary craft exhibitions each year.

Szombathelyi Képtár Textilcollection
Rákóczi Ferenc U1. 12, H 9700 Szombathely
☏ (+36) 94 14 096
Director: Salamon Nándor
Curator: Torday Aliz
Contemporary textile collection started 1970, Hungarian textiles comprise 5/6th of the collection, the remaining 1/6th consists of miniature textiles from international sources. Contemporary textile exhibition organized every two years. Directory of 1,200 textile artists and a slide library.

ITALY

Museo Internazionale delle Ceramiche
Via Campidori 2, I 48018 Faenza
☏ (+39) 0546 21240 Fax (+39) 0546 27141
Director: Gian Carlo Bojani
Curator, Italian maiolica: Carmen Ravanelli Guidotti
Librarian: Guiseppina Valgirnigli
Collection started 1908, historical Italian and international contemporary ceramics, 30% on display. Organizes major international ceramics biennial and presents the 'Faenza' awards.

Museo Vetrario
Fdm. Giustinian 8, I 30124 Murano
☏ (+39) 041 73 95 86
Director: Giandomenico Romanelli
National glass collection started 1840, 100% on display; exhibition of contemporary glass organized once a year.

JAPAN

Aichi Prefectural Ceramic History Museum
234 Minami Yamaguchicho, Seto City, Aichi Prefecture
☏ (+81) 561 84 7474
Japanese ceramics from the Jomon period to the present.

Costume Museum
5th Floor, Izutsu Building, Horikawa-Dori, Shin-Hanayacho-kado, Shimogyo-ku, Kyoto 600
☏ (+81) 75 351 6750
Japanese costume, from ancient to modern times.

Crafts Gallery, National Museum of Modern Art
1 Kitanomaru-koen, Chiyoda-ku, Tokyo 102
☎ (+81) 3 211 7781
Curator: Mitsuhiko Hasebe
Outstanding national collection of contemporary Japanese crafts.

Hiroshima Museum of Art
3–2 Motomachi, Naka-ku, Hiroshima 730
☎ (+81) 82 223 2530

Hokkaido Museum
N.I.W. 17 Chuo-ku, Sapporo 060
☎ (+81) 11 644 6881

Hyogo Prefectural Museum of Modern Art
8–30 Harada-dori 3-chome, Nada-ku, Kobe 657
☎ (+81) 78 801 1591
Contemporary crafts, national and international scope. Venue for major international craft exhibitions.

Ishikawa Prefectural Museum of Art
2–1 Dewamachi, Kanazawa, Ishikawa Prefecture 920
☎ (+81) 762 31 7580
Collection includes lacquerwork, textiles and Kutani ware.

Japan Folk Crafts Museum
4–3–33 Komaba, Meguro-ku, Tokyo 153
☎ (+81) 3 467 4527
Folk crafts from Japan and Korea, also international.

Kawai Kanjiro's House
569 Kanei-cho, Gojozaka, Higashiyama-ku, Kyoto 605
☎ (+81) 75 561 3585
The ceramics of Kawai Kanjiro and crafts objects used in his traditional Japanese house.

Kurashiki Folkcraft Museum
1–4–11 Chuo, Kurashiki, Okayama Prefecture 710
☎ (+81) 864 22 1637
Folk crafts, national and international scope.

Kure City Museum
Irifune Yama Park, 4-9 Saiwaicho, Kure 737
☎ (+81) 823 25 2007

Kyoto National Museum of Modern Art
Enshojischo, Okazaki, Sakyo-ku, Kyoto 606
☎ (+81) 75 761 4111
Curator, contemporary arts: M. Uchiyama
A major collection of contemporary craft, national and international scope.

Mashiko Reference Collection Museum
3388 Mashiko, Mashiko-machi, Haga-gun, Tochigi Prefecture 321–42, Northeastern Honshu
☎ (+81) 2857 2 5300
Ceramics by Shoji Hamada and his collection of Eastern and Western ceramics, textiles, furniture, etc.

MOA Museum of Art
26–2 Momoyama-cho, Atami, Shizuoka Prefecture 413
☎ (+81) 557 84 2511
Japanese and Chinese works.

Ohara Museum of Art
1–1–15 Chuo, Kurashiki, Okayama Prefecture 710
☎ (+81) 864 22 0005
Contemporary Japanese crafts, including ceramics and textiles.

Okinawa Prefectural Museum
1–1 Onakacho, Shuri, Naha, Okinawa Prefecture 903
☎ (+81) 988 84 2243
Ceramics, textiles, lacquerwork.

Osaka Japan Folk Crafts Museum
10–5 Senri-Banpaku-Koen, Suita, Osaka Prefecture 565
☎ (+81) 6 877 1971
Japanese folk crafts.

Seishi Hakubutsukan
Paper Museum, 1–1–8 Horifune, Kita-ku, Tokyo 114
☎ (+81) 3 911 3545
Japanese papers, also products and tools used in the production of handmade paper.

Shigaraki Ceramic Cultural Park
Museum of Contemporary Ceramic Art, 2188–7 Chokushi, Shigaraki, Kohga-gun, 529–18 Shiga Prefecture
☎ (+91) 748 83 0969 Fax (+81) 748 83 1195
Curator: Tomio Sugaya
Exceptional new, purpose-built ceramics complex, including museums with historical Japanese and contemporary international collections, exhibition galleries, workshops and residential accommodation.

Suntory Museum of Art
11th Floor, Suntory Building, 1–2–3 Moto-Akasaka, Minato-ku, Tokyo 107
☎ (+81) 3 470 1073
Collection includes Japanese lacquer, ceramics, glass, costume masks.

Wakayama Prefecture Museum
Wakayama Park, 1 Ichiban, Wakayama 640
☎ (+81) 734 23 2467

NEW ZEALAND

Dowse Art Museum
45 Laings Road, Lower Hutt
Postal Address: PO Box 30–396, Lower Hutt
☎ (+64) 4 660 502 Fax (+64) 4 694 290
Director: Bob Maysmor
Collection started 1971, predominantly national scope. All main categories represented bar furniture, up to 10% on display, half of all exhibitions presented (thirty-five a year) have a 'craft edge'.

National Art Gallery
Buckle Street, PO Box 467, Wellington
☎ (+64) 4 859 609 Fax (+64) 4 857 157
Curator-in-charge: Tim Walker

NORWAY

Kunstindustrimuseet
St Olavs gate 1, N 0165 Oslo 1
☎ (+47) 2 29 35 78 Fax (+47) 2 11 39 71
Director: Anniken Thue
Curator, textiles: Anne Kjellberg
Curator, glass and ceramics: Randi Gaustad
Collection started 1876, international scope (mainly Norwegian and Scandinavian), all main categories, 10% on display. Two to four contemporary craft exhibitions a year.

Nordenfjeldske Kunstindustrimuseum
Munkegt. 5, N 7013 Trondheim
☎ (+47) 7 52 13 11
Director: Jan-Lauritz Opstad

Nordnorsk Kunstmuseum
PO Box 1009, Muségaten 2, N 9001 Tromsø
☎ (+47) 83 80 090
Director: Frode Ernst Haverkamp
Collection started 1986, mainly national in scope (with an emphasis on northern Norway), all main categories represented bar furniture, 40% on display, contemporary craft exhibitions organized. Special interests are textiles, glass and jewelry.

Vestlandske Kunstindustrimuseum
Nordahl Bruns gt. 9, N 5014 Bergen
☎ (+47) 5 325108
Director: Peter Anker

POLAND

Centralne Muzeum Włókiennictwa
Ul. Piotrkowska 282, Łódź
Director: Norbert Zawisza
Central Museum of Textiles, founded 1960. Major textile collection and exhibitions, including the International Triennale of Tapestry.

Museum Ceramiki
Ul. Adama Mickiewicza 13, P 59–700 Boleslawiec
☎ (via operator) 3857
Director: Teresa Wolanin
National collection of ceramics started 1967, mostly domestic stoneware, 1950–80, 20% on display, one contemporary craft exhibition a year.

SPAIN

Museo de Cerámica de Manises
C/ Sagrario 22, E 4690 Manises (Valencia)
☎ (+34) 154 51 16 ext. 31
Director: Josep Pérez Camps
Collection started 1967, regional scope only, exclusively ceramics ('an excellent representative collection of contemporary ceramic art'), 45% on display, one exhibition organized each year.

Museo Nacional de Cerámica y de Las Artes Suntuarias González Marti
Poeta Querol 2, E 46002 Valencia
☎ (+34) 351 63 92 Fax (+34) 351 65 01
Director: Paz Soler Ferrer
Curator: Jaime Coll Conesa
Regional ceramics collection started 1950, mainly donations. Two or three exhibitions a year. No figurative ceramics. Artists represented include Picasso.

Museu de Ceràmica
Palau de Pedralbes, Avgda Diagonal 686, E 08034 Barcelona
Director: Maria Dolors Giral
Collection started 1989, international scope, ceramics only, about 50% on display. Occasional contemporary ceramic exhibitions.

SWEDEN

Rohsska Konstslojdmuseet
PO Box 53178, Vasagatan 37–39, S 40014 Gothenburg
☎ (+46) 031 200505 Fax (+46) 031 184692
Director: Christian Axel-Nilsson
Curator, exhibitions and library: Thomas Baagøe
Curator, education: Inger Cavallius
Collection started 1906, international scope, all main categories represented. A new contemporary craft gallery will open in 1991. About twenty contemporary craft exhibitions organized each year. The principal museum in Sweden specializing in arts and crafts and industrial design.

SWITZERLAND

Kornhaus
Kantonales Amt für Wirtschafts- und Kulturausstellungen, Postfach 3116, Zeughausgasse 2, CH 3007 Bern
☎ (+41) 31 22 31 61
Director: Max Werren
National collection started 1980 with emphasis on the Canton of Bern. Ceramics, textiles and all main categories represented bar woodwork and furniture, also paper arts and silhouettes, 20% on display. Two or three contemporary craft exhibitions organized each year.

Musée Ariana
10 Avenue de la Paix, CH 1202 Geneva
☎ (+41) 022 734 29 50
Director: Claude Lapaire
Curator: Marie-Thérèse Coullery
Collection started 1870, national and international scope, ceramics and glass only. New galleries for 20th-century ceramics and applied arts exhibitions. The only museum of its type in Switzerland.

Musée des Arts Décoratifs
4 Avenue Villamont, CH 1005 Lausanne
☎ and Fax (+41) 21 23 07 21
Curator: Rosmarie Lippuner
Collection started 1971, international scope, ceramics, glass, textiles and jewelry plus paper, leather and theatrical masks. Strengths are 20th-century glass from Europe, Japan and the USA and 20th-century jewelry and works in paper. Acquisitions are made from the Museum's five to eight annual exhibitions. One tenth on display.

Musée Bellerive
Sammlung des Kunstgewerbemuseums Zürich, Postfach 323, CH 8034 Zürich
☎ (+41) 01 383 4376
Curator: Sigrid Barten
Collection started 1875, historical and contemporary, with priority now given to the 20th century. International scope (mainly European, some American and Japanese artists represented), all main categories plus musical instruments and puppets. Small proportion on display, exhibitions changed three times a year.

UNITED KINGDOM

Aberdeen Art Gallery & Museum
Schoolhill, Aberdeen AB9 1FQ
☎ (+44) 224 646333 Fax (+44) 224 632133
City Arts Officer: Ian McKenzie
Keeper, applied art: Christine Rew
National collection started 1978 with a regional emphasis. All main categories, particularly metalwork, jewelry and tapestry, also leather- and basketwork; 65–70% on display, generally ten contemporary craft exhibitions each year.

Aberystwyth Arts Centre
University College of Wales, Aberystwyth (Dyfed) SY23 3DE
☎ (+44) 0970 623 339
Curator, ceramics: Moira Vincentelli
Collection started in the 1920s, international scope, ceramics only (bought from the Ceramic Series exhibitions and the International Pottery Festival). Also has a special interest in traditional ceramics from the non-Western world. About 50% on display and the remainder may be viewed by appointment. The bi-monthly Ceramic Series exhibitions feature the work of individual contemporary ceramists. Organizes a Biennial International Potters Competition and an annual summer exhibition devoted to a particular area of craft and design.

Art Gallery & Museum
Kelvingrove, Glasgow G3 8AG
☎ (+44) 41 357 4537 Fax (+44) 41 357 3929
Director: Julian Spalding
Keeper, decorative art: Brian Blench
Collection started 1970, international scope, all main categories represented, up to 10% on display, two or three exhibitions of contemporary craft organized each year.

Birmingham Museum & Art Gallery
Chamberlain Square, Birmingham B3 3DH
☎ (+44) 21 235 2839 Fax (+44) 21 236 6227
Director: Michael Diamond
Keeper: Glennys Wild
Deputy Keeper: Martin Ellis
Assistant Keeper: Helen Spencer
Collection started 1885, mainly national and regional, all main categories plus fashion, mixed media and stained glass, 50% on display, sometimes more, contemporary craft exhibitions organized occasionally.

Broadfield House Glass Museum
Barnett Lane, Kingswinford, West Midlands DY6 9QA
☎ (+44) 384 273011 Fax (+44) 384 453576
Director: Charles Hajdamach
Curator: Roger Dodsworth
Collection started 1974, mainly national with some international pieces, glass only, 60% on display, one or two contemporary glass exhibitions organized each year.

City Museum and Art Gallery
Hanley, Stoke-on-Trent ST1 3DW
☎ (+44) 782 2021 73 Fax (+44) 782 4040 93
Senior Assistant Keeper of Ceramics: Kathy Niblett
Collection started 1979, currently comprises works by over seventy contemporary ceramists, exclusively national scope, work acquired from in-house exhibitions, donations from potters and by purchase. Some of the collection is always on display. Occasional exhibitions.

Cleveland Crafts Centre
57 Gilkes Street, Middlesbrough (Cleveland)
☎ (+44) 0642 226351 Fax (+44) 642 326983
Craft Officer: Barry Hepton
Collection comprises British studio pottery and international contemporary jewelry. 80% of the ceramic collection is on display, 30% of the jewelry. It is hoped that one touring exhibition and two in-house exhibitions will be organized each year.

Crafts Council
44a Pentonville Road, London N1 9HF
☎ (+44) 71 278 7700
Director: Tony Ford
Curator, collection: Amanda Fielding
The pre-eminent national collection of contemporary British crafts, Government-funded, started in 1972. All main categories plus toys and automata, bookbindings and lettering. Over one thousand items in the collection, providing a national loan source. Generally six exhibitions are organized a year. No permanent galleries, about a third of the collection is on loan, the rest in storage at any one time. Over 800 works, documented and illustrated in the book *Building a Crafts Collection*.

Crafts Study Centre
Holburne of Menstrie Museum, Great Pulteney Street, Bath
☎ (+44) 225 66669
Director: Barley Roscoe
Important, selective collection of postwar contemporary crafts and study archives especially relating to ceramics, textiles and lettering. Most of the collection has been donated.

Paisley Museum & Art Gallery
High Street, Paisley (Scotland)
British ceramics collection started c. 1958, 20% on display, but any piece can be viewed by arrangement. No exhibitions.

The Scottish Development Agency
Rosebery House, Haymarket Terrace, Edinburgh EH12 5EZ
☎ (+44) 31 337 9595 Fax (+44) 31 337 9318
Head of Crafts Division: Helen Bennett
Government-funded collection started 1980 to represent craftspeople living and working in Scotland. Occasional commissions, traditional and avant-garde work, all main categories represented, touring exhibitions organized. Purchasing suspended temporarily in 1990, pending a decision on funding by the Scottish Office.

Shipley Art Gallery
Prince Consort Road, Gateshead NE8 4JB
☎ (+44) 91 477 1495
Museum Officer, contemporary craft: Helen Joseph
Collection started in the 1970s, national scope only, all main categories represented, traditional and avant-garde work collected. One of the major contemporary craft collections in the UK. Provides a venue for major crafts exhibitions.

Sudbury Pots Foundation
Sudbury Hall, Sudbury, Derbyshire
☎ (+44) 28 378305
Chairman: D.S. Sorrell
Collection started 1936, collection comprises exclusively 20th-century British ceramics, 80% on display; a contemporary crafts exhibition is organized every two to three years. The Rollo Ballantyne collection of ceramics by Rie, Coper and Cardew has been augmented with work by contemporary ceramists.

Ulster Museum
Botanic Gardens, Belfast BT9 5AB
☎ (+44) 232 381251 Fax (+44) 232 665510
Curator, applied art: Michael Robinson
Collection started 1982, British and European scope, until recently comprising only ceramics and glass, now extending into media such as wood and metal. The glass collection will tour the UK during 1991 and 1992.

Victoria and Albert Museum
South Kensington, London SW7 2RI
☎ (+44) 71 938 8282 and 938 8283 Fax (+44) 71 938 8341
Director: Elizabeth Esteve-Coll
Curator, ceramics and glass: Oliver Watson
Curator, metalwork collection: Richard Edgcumbe
Curator, furniture and woodwork: Christopher Wilk
Curator, textiles: Valerie Mendez
Deputy Curator, textiles, care and access: Lindy Parry
The principal applied arts museum in Great Britain, started collecting in 1844, houses the National Art Library.
Ceramics – international scope (75% from the UK, the remainder from non-British artists), one third on display, temporary exhibitions organized in the ceramics galleries.
Glass – international scope, one-quarter to one-third on display, temporary exhibitions in the glass galleries organized very rarely.
Furniture and woodwork – donations solicited from craftspeople, international scope, occasional exhibitions organized, nothing acquired since 1989.
Metalwork – international scope,

extensive collection of jewelry from the UK, Continental Europe, the USA and Australia, significant collections of silver and ironwork, 80–90% on display. Exhibitions of contemporary metalwork and jewelry organized occasionally. Textiles – one of the most comprehensive collections in the world, international scope, fashion (couture clothes) and textiles (commercially- and craftsman-produced). Aims to have as representative a collection of the most interesting and original textiles from the Western world (no ethnic textiles collected) as is possible within the financial limits. No regular contemporary textile exhibitions organized, but all recent acquisitions (where feasible) displayed in the textile galleries within a year of their acquisition.

UNITED STATES OF AMERICA

American Craft Museum

40 West 53rd Street, New York NY 10019
☎ (+1) 212 956 3535 Fax (+1) 212 459 0926
Director: Janet Kardon
Senior Curator: John Perreault
Curator, travelling exhibitions: Frances Kelly
Assistant Curator: Nina Stretzler
Curator, education: Egle Zyglas
Collection started 1958, national scope only, all main categories, over 300 artists represented, 12% on display at any time, about ten exhibitions of contemporary craft organized each year. The museum aims to exhibit, document, collect and conserve craft art and other art disciplines as they intersect with craft.

Cooper-Hewitt Museum

National Museum of Design, Smithsonian Institution, 2 East 91st Street, New York NY 10128
☎ (+1) 212 860 6868 Fax (+1) 212 860 6909
Director: Dianne H. Pilgrim
Curator, decorative arts: David McFadden
Curator, textiles: Milton Sonday
Assistant Curator, wallcoverings: Joanne Warner
Collection started 1897, craftwork collected regularly. Donations solicited from artists, dealers, collectors and patrons. International scope, all main categories plus lighting, wallcoverings, books and bookbinding. Strengths in the collections include textiles (both studio and production), ceramics, glass and metalwork. No permanent collection galleries but special installations and thematic exhibitions organized.

Corning Museum of Glass

1 Museum Way, Corning NY 14830
☎ (+1) 607 937 5371 Fax (+1) 607 937 3352
Director: Dwight Lanmon
Curator, 20th century: Suzanne Frantz
Curator, American: Jane Spillman
Collection started 1850, international scope, glass, jewelry and furniture. The 'largest international collection in the world documenting the art and history of glass. Contemporary glass includes all techniques and current approaches to glass art and design.' An annual exhibition organized and their juried annual *New Glass Review* of work by 100 glass artists published in *Neues Glas* magazine.

Craft & Folk Art Museum

Fourth Floor, 6067 Wilshire Boulevard, Los Angeles CA 90036
☎ (+1) 213 937 5544 Fax (+1) 213 937 5576
Director: Patrick Ela
Collection started 1975, international and national scope (mostly South Californian and Japanese), all main categories plus toys and plastic food. Exhibitions organized.

Everson Museum of Art

401 Harrison Street, Community Plaza, Syracuse NY 13202
☎ (+1) 315 474 6064
Director: Ronald A. Kuchta
Curator, ceramics: Terrie White
Ceramics collection started 1916, international scope, 95% on display, one or two exhibitions organized a year. Over 3,000 works of ceramic art, more than half of which are American, ranging from 1000 AD to the present.

Leigh Yawkey Woodson Art Museum,

700 North 12th Street, Wausau WI 54401
☎ (+1) 715 847 7010 Fax (+1) 715 845 7103
Director: Kathy Kelsey Foley
Curator, collections: Jane Weinke
Glass and prorcelain collections.

Los Angeles County Museum of Art

5905 Wilshire Boulevard, Los Angeles CA 90036
☎ and Fax (+1) 213 931 7347
Director: Earl A. Powell III
Assistant Curator, decorative arts: Martha Drexler Lynn
International scope, all main categories except jewelry (with the focus on one-off and production works in ceramic, glass, metal and furniture), relies on donations to augment collection, 10% on display, yearly exhibitions of contemporary craft.

Metropolitan Museum of Art

1000 Fifth Avenue, New York NY 10028
☎ (+1) 212 879 5500 Fax (+1) 212 570 3879

Director: Philippe de Montebello
Curator, American decorative arts: Morrison Heckscher
In addition to its comprehensive collection of world art, the Museum has a special interest in American decorative arts.

Museum of American Textile History

800 Massachusetts Avenue, North Andover MA 01845
☎ (+1) 508 686 0191
Director: Thomas A. Leavitt
Curator, textiles: Diane Fagan Affleck
Collection started 1964, American textiles only, 1% on display, no contemporary textiles exhibitions organized.

Museum of Fine Arts

465 Huntingdon Avenue, Boston MA 02115
☎ (+1) 617 267 9300 ext. 215 Fax (+1) 617 267 0280
Director: Alan Shestack
Curators: Jonathan Fairbanks, Katherine Lane Weems
Department formed 1971, national scope only, all main categories bar textiles, only a small proportion of the contemporary craft collection is on display. Contemporary craft exhibitions organized occasionally.

Museum of Modern Art

11 West 53rd Street, New York NY 10019
☎ (+1) 212 708 9480
Director: Richard E. Oldenburg
Curator, architecture and design: Stuart Wrede
Collection started 1932, international scope, all main categories bar furniture, 5% on display, occasional small exhibitions based on a theme organized in the department gallery.

Renwick Gallery of Contemporary Crafts

Smithsonian Institution, Pennsylvania Avenue at 17th Street NW, Washington D.C. 20560
☎ (+1) 202 357 1300
Director: Joshua Taylor
Collection started 1972, national scope only, all main categories, 25% on display, four exhibitions of contemporary craft organized each year. Work acquired through donation of work from craftspeople or funds for their purchase.

Textile Museum

2320 'S' Street NW, Washington D.C. 20008
☎ (+1) 202 667 0441
The Museum buys ethnographic textiles only and has contemporary textiles from Asia and South/Central America. Less than 1% on display. A contemporary craft exhibition organized every two to three years.

Toledo Museum of Art

PO Box 1013, Toledo OH 43697
☎ (+1) 419 255 8000 Fax (+1) 419 255 5638
Director: David Steadman
Curator, 19th- and 20th-century glass: Davira S. Taragin
Studio glass collection started 1962, recently augmented by items from the Saxe Collection, international scope, entire collection on display in the Art in Glass Gallery or in the Glass Study Room. The Museum gives major commissions from time to time and is to organize a major exhibition of work in all craft media from the Saxe Collection in 1993.

GALLERIES

AUSTRALIA

Gary Anderson Gallery
13 McDonald Street, Paddington NSW 2021
☎ (+16) 2 331 1524 Fax (+61) 2 332 2344
Ceramics.

Australian Craftworks
127 George Street, Sydney NSW 2000
☎ (+61) 2 247 7156
Ceramics.

Beaver Galleries
81B Denison Street, Deakin ACT 2600
☎ (+61) 62 825 294
Ceramics, glass, furniture.

Contemporary Jewellery Gallery
162A Queen Street, Woolahra NSW 2025
☎ (+61) 2 321 611
Jewelry.

Crafts Council Centre Perth
1st Floor, Perth City Railway Station, Wellington Street, Perth WA 6000
☎ (+61) 9 325 2799 Fax (+61) 9 325 1221
All media.

Crafts Council of ACT Gallery
1 Aspinal Street, Watson ACT 2602
☎ (+61) 6 241 2373
All media.

Cuppacumbalong Craft Centre
Naas Road, Tharwa ACT 2620
☎ (+61) 6 375 116
Ceramics.

Distelfink Gallery
43 Burwood Road, Hawthorn VIC 3122
☎ (+61) 3 818 2555 Fax (+61) 3 819 2499
Ceramics, furniture, glass.

Robin Gibson Gallery
278 Liverpool Street, Darlinghurst NSW 2010
☎ (+61) 2 331 6692 Fax (+61) 2 331 1114

Greenhill Galleries
140 Barton Terrace West, North Adelaide SA 5006
☎ (+61) 8 267 2887 Fax (+61) 8 239 0148
and at 20 Howard Street, Perth WA 6000
☎ (+61) 9 321 2369

Jam Factory Crafts Centre
169 Payneham Road, St Peters SA 5069
☎ (+61) 8 362 5661 Fax (+61) 8 363 0551
All media.

Maker's Mark Gallery
85 Collins Street, Melbourne VIC 3000
☎ (+61) 3 654 8488 Fax (+61) 3 650 7940
Jewelry, metalwork.

Meat Market Craft Centre
42 Courtney Street, North Melbourne VIC 3051
☎ (+61) 3 329 9966 Fax (+61) 3 329 2272
All media.

Roslyn Oxley Gallery
Sudan Lane, Paddington NSW 2021
☎ (+61) 2 331 1919

AUSTRIA

Galerie Slavik
Himmelpfortg. 17, A Vienna 1
☎ (+43) 1 513 48 12
International jewelry.

Glasgalerie Klute
Franziskanerplatz 6, A 1010 Vienna
☎ (+43) 1 513 53 22
Glass.

Keramic Studio
Krugerstrasse 18, A 1010 Vienna
Ceramics.

V & V
Bauernmarkt 19, A 1010 Vienna
☎ (+43) 1 535 63 34
International jewelry.

BELGIUM

Argile
Rue de Neufchâtel 5A, B 1050 Brussels
Ceramics.

Atelier 18
Rue du Président 18, B 1050 Brussels
☎ (+32) 2 511 93 49
Director: Eric Lemesre
Ceramics.

Capricorne
39 rue des Frépiers,
B 7000 Mons
☎ (+32) 65 35 27 65
and at 10 rue de Mons, B 74000 Soignies
☎ (+32) 67 33 46 81
Director: Monique Bruneau
A variety of crafts.

Espace Marianne Hoffdummer
Place Stephanie 18, B 1050 Brussels
All media.

Espace-Partenaires
Route de Liège, B 5360 Hamois
☎ (+32) 83 61 25 51
Occasional jewelry shows.

Galerie Desko
Hoogledestraat, B 8110 Kostermsark
Ceramics.

Galerie La Main
215 rue de la Victoire, B 1060 Brussels
☎ (+32) 2 538 54 66
Directors: Yves Bical and Christine
Debras
Ceramics, textiles.

Galerie Neon
19 rue Defacqz, B 1050 Brussels
Owner: Bernard François
Jewelry, clothing, accessories.

Galerie Le Volcan
13 rue Charles Dupret, B 6000
Charleroi
☎ (+32) 71 32 99 10
Director: M. Rousseau
Ceramics.

Galerie Transparence
Rue Sainte-Anne 28, B 1000 Brussels
☎ (+32) 2 513 9865
Director: Christine Wacquez-Ermel
International glass.

Provinciaal Museum Sterckshof
160 Hooftvunderlei, B 21000 Antwerp
☎ (+32) 3 324 0207 or 3 324 7176
Director: Sam Walgrave
Contemporary craft exhibitions.

CANADA

Ashton's
267 Queen Street East, Toronto ON
M5A 1S6
☎ (+1) 416 366 6846
Director: Bruce Somers
Ceramics, jewelry.

Bounty
York Quay Centre at Harbourfront, 235
Queen's Quay West, Toronto ON M5J
2G8
☎ (+1) 416 973 4993
Director: Virginia Wright
Contemporary craft in all media.

Canada's Four Corners
93 Sparks Street, Ottawa ON K1P 5B5
☎ (+1) 613 236 2322
Director: Jack Cook
Wide variety of objects in all media.

The Craft Gallery and Craftworks
35 McCaul Street, Toronto ON M5T
1V7
☎ (+1) 416 977 3551
Director: Alan C. Elder
Wide variety of objects in all media.

Discovery
320 Davenport Road, Toronto ON M5R
1K6
☎ (+1) 416 924 0929
Director: Rhona Slomovic
Ceramics, glass.

Galerie Design Métiers d'Art
29 rue Notre-Dame, Place Royale, G1K
4E9 Quebec
☎ (+1) 418 694 0267
A variety of crafts.

Galerie Elena Lee Verre d'Art
1518 Sherbrooke Street West,
Montreal PQ H3G 1L3
☎ (+1) 514 932 3896
Glass.

The Glass Art Gallery Inc.
21 Hazelton Avenue, Toronto ON M5R
2E1
☎ (+1) 416 968 1823
Director: J. Khendry
Ceramics, glass.

The Guild Shop
140 Cumberland Street, Toronto ON
M5R 1A8
☎ (+1) 416 921 1721
Director: Sandra McBurney
Wide variety of objects in all media.

Mariposa Glassworks
312 College Street, Toronto ON M5T
1S3
☎ (+1) 416 923 2085
Director: Wayne Howell
Glass.

Museum of Textiles
55 Centre Avenue, Toronto ON M5G
2H5
Venue for contemporary textile
exhibitions.

Prime Canadian Crafts
229 Queen Street, Toronto ON M5V
1Z4
☎ (+1) 416 593 5750
Director: Suzann Greenaway
Ceramics, furniture, jewelry.

Quest Gallery
105 Banff Avenue, Banff Alberta
and at 1023 Government Street,
Victoria BC
Ceramics.

Uncommon Objects
York Quay Centre, 235 Queen's Quay
West, Toronto ON M5J 2G8
☎ (+1) 416 973 4963
Director: Jean Johnston
Wide variety of objects in all media.

Susan Whitney Gallery
2220 Lorne Street, Regina S4P 2M7
☎ (+1) 306 569 9279

DENMARK

Bla Form Textil Studie
Radhusstraede 8, DK Copenhagen K
☎ (+45) 33 13 08 88
Director: Pia Hedegaard
Textiles and fashion design.

Damhuset Kunsthandvaerk,
Lyngby Hovedgade 1 C, DK 2800
Lyngby
Ceramics.

Dansk Kunsthandvaerk
Danish Arts and Crafts, Amagertorv 1
DK 1160
Copenhagen K
Ceramics.

Galerie Metal
Nybrodgade 26, DK 1203
Copenhagen K
☎ (+45) 33 14 55 40
Director: Jan Lohmann
Danish and international jewelry and
metalwork.

Galleri Egelund
Ny Ostergade 11, DK 1101
Copenhagen K
☎ (+45) 33 93 92 00
Director: Jorgen Egelund
Danish and international glass and
ceramics.

Gallerie Q
Store Kongens Gade 96, DK 1264
Copenhagen K
Ceramics.

Hans Hansen Solv
Amagertorv 16, DK 1160
Copenhagen K
☎ (+45) 33 15 60 67
Silver holloware by contemporary
Danish silversmiths.

Selskabet Til Handarbejdets Fremme
Danish Handicrafts Guild, Tranevej 15,
DK 2400 Copenhagen NV
Ceramics.

Selskabet Til Handarbejdets Fremme
Lyngby Stottcenter 42, DK 2800
Lyngby
Ceramics.

Strandstraede Keramik
Lille Strandstraede 12, DK 1254
Copenhagen K
☎ (+45) 33 11 99 46
Ceramics (stoneware and porcelain).

FINLAND

Artisaani
Unioninkatu 28, SF 00100 Helsinki
Ceramics.

Design Forum,
Vientitalo, Etelaesplanedi 8A, SF 00130
Helsinki
Furniture, textiles.

Galleria 25
Kasarmikatu 25, SF 00130 Helsinki
Textiles.

Helsky
Unioninkatu 27, SF 00170 Helsinki
Finnish crafts.

Lapponia Jewelry OY
PO Box 72, SF 00511 Helsinki
Fax (+358) 0 712 878
Contact: Miss Erja-Riitta Pellinen
Jewelry.

Pot Viapori
Suomenlinna B 45, SF 00190 Helsinki
Ceramics.

FRANCE

Avant-Scène
4 place de l'Odéon, F 75006 Paris
☎ (+33) 1 46 33 12 40 Fax (+33) 1 46
33 92 78
Director: Elisabeth Delacarte

Carpe Diem
60 boulevard Beaumarchais, F 75011
Paris
☎ (+33) 1 43 57 77 03
Director: Maryvonne Chollet
Ceramics, glass.

Galerie d'Amon
28 rue Saint Sulpice, F 75006 Paris
☎ (+33) 1 43 26 96 60
Directors: J.P. and M. Maffre
Glass and ceramics.

Galerie Suzel Berna
24 rue Georges Clemenceau, F 06600
Vieil Antibes
☎ (+33) 93 34 89 93 Fax (+33) 93 34
10 62
International glass.

Galerie Capazza
Le Grenier de Villâtre, F 18330 Nançay
☎ (+33) 48 51 80 22
Directors: Sophie Capazza, Gérard
Capazza
Fine craft, glass.

Galerie Caroline Corré
14 rue Guénégaud, F 75006 Paris
☎ (+33) 1 43 54 57 67
Jewelry.

Galerie Christel
16 boulevard Louis Blanc, F 87000
Limoges
☎ (+33) 55 34 23 36
Glass, ceramics, enamelling,
metalwork.

Galerie Différences
11 rue du Roi Doré, F 75003 Paris
☎ (+33) 1 48 87 38 13
Ceramics, furniture, metalwork, textiles.

Galerie L'Éclat du Verre
12 passage Véro-Dodat, F 75001 Paris
☎ (+33) 1 42 21 34 48
Glass.

Galerie Épona
40 rue Quincampoix, F 75002 Paris
☏ (+33) 1 42 77 36 90
Director: Odette Watel
Ceramics and glass.

Galerie International du Verre
Verrerie de Biot, Chemin des Combes,
F 06410 Biot
☏ (+33) 93 65 03 00 Fax (+33) 93 65
00 56
Director: Serge Lechaczynski
Contemporary glass.

Galerie Mostra
12 rue Brisemiche, F 75004 Paris
☏ (+33) 1 48 04 37 16
Furniture.

Galerie Gladys Mougin
30 rue de Lille, F 75007 Paris
☏ (+33) 1 40 20 08 33
Director: Gladys Mougin
Contemporary furniture.

Galerie Nadir
15 rue Filaterie, F 74000 Annecy
☏ (+33) 50 45 20 60
Director: Jean-Pierre Postaire
Glass and ceramics.

Galerie Nestor Perkal
8 rue des Quatre-Fils, F 75003 Paris
☏ (+33) 1 42 77 46 80
Director: Nestor Perkal
Furniture, glass, ceramics, metalwork.

Galerie Place des Arts
8 rue de l'Argenterie, F 34000
Montpellier
☏ (+33) 67 66 05 08
Director: Franklin Polack
Glass.

Galerie Place des Arts
3 rue Romiguières, F 31000 Toulouse
☏ (+33) 61 21 87 87
Director: Patricia de Rivery
Glass and ceramics.

Galerie D.M. Sarver
99 rue Quincampoix, F 75002 Paris
☏ (+33) 1 48 04 50 51
Directors: Daniel and Michèle Sarver
Ceramics, glass, metalwork.

Galerie Terra Viva
Maison de la Terre, F 30700 St Quentin
La Poterie
☏ (+33) 66 22 48 78
Director: Serge Tribouillois
Glass, ceramics.

Galerie Via
10 place Saint-Opportune, F 75001
Paris
☏ (+33) 1 42 33 14 33
Director: Jean-Claude Maugirard
Furniture.

Galerie Marie Zisswiller
61 rue d'Auteuil, F 75016 Paris
☏ (+33) 1 45 24 32 59
Jewelry.

Le Grand Magasin
24 rue de la Commune, F 13210 Saint
Rémy de Provence
☏ (+33) 90 92 18 79
Director: Francis Braun
Ceramics, glass, furniture, jewelry.

Inov
32 allée Darius-Milhaud, F 75019 Paris
☏ (+33) 1 42 39 55 65
Director: Régine Canaux
Glass, ceramics, metalwork.

Magasin de la Manufacture de Sèvres
Place André Malraux, F 75001 Paris
☏ (+33) 1 47 03 40 20
Sèvres porcelain.

Maison de la Céramique
25 rue Josué Hofer, F 68200 Mulhouse
☏ (+33) 89 43 32 55
Director: Jean-Luc Gerhardt
Ceramics, six exhibitions per year,
permanent exhibition of thirty
contemporary ceramists.

Néotu
25 rue de Renard, F 75004 Paris
☏ (+33) 1 42 78 96 97
Director: Pierre St Audenmeyer
Furniture, glass, ceramics.

Objet Insolite
32 rue des Blancs-Manteaux, F 75004
Paris
☏ (+33) 1 48 87 92 36

Le Rond Dans L'Eau
6 rue Victor Hugo, F 64200 Biarritz
☏ (+33) 59 24 35 48
Director: Michèle Crouau
Ceramics, furniture, glass.

Clara Scremini Gallery
39 rue de Charonne (new address: rue
des Tournelles, 1991), F 75011 Paris
☏ (+33) 1 43 55 65 56
Director: Clara Scremini
Glass.

GERMANY

Anthologie Quartett
Schloss Huennefeld, D4515
Bad Essen 1
☏ (+49) 5472 41 40/39
36 Fax (+49) 5472 43 40
Director: Rainer Krause
Furniture exhibitions, and production.

CCAA Glasgalerie Köln
Auf dem Berlich 24, D 5000 Cologne
91
☏ (+49) 221 86 46 76
Glass.

Essener Glasgalerie
Annastrasse 74, D 4300 Essen 1
☏ (+49) 201 77 36 12 or 201 79 10 10
Director: Gerd Kruft
Glass (some fifty international glass
artists).

First Glas Galerie
Hessstrasse 58, U2 Theresstrasse, D
8000 Munich
☏ (+49) 89 5 23 62 08
Glass.

Galerie Art du Feu
Weinhofberg 5, D 7900 Ulm
☏ (+49) 7 31 61 04 89
Directors: Anette Fischer, Ute Simm
Ceramics.

Galerie b 15
Baaderstrasse 15, D 8000 Munich 5
☏ (+49) 89 2 02 10 10
Director: Renate Wunderle
International ceramics.

Galerie Bergmann
Kirchweg 29, D 3100 Celle
☏ (+49) 5141 54983
Director: Karin Bergmann

Galerie Blau
Dorfgasse 8, D 7801 Freiburg
Ceramics, jewelry.

Galerie Monica Borgward
Parkstrasse 73, D 2800 Bremen
☏ (+49) 421 3 47 90 35
Glass.

Galerie Bowig
Am Rathaus, Friedrichstrasse 2A, D
3000 Hanover 1
☏ (+49) 511 81 55 25 or 511 32 07 02
International ceramics.

Galerie Cebra
Franklinstrasse 46, D 4000 Düsseldorf
30
☏ (+49) 211 44 56 34
Jewelry.

Galerie Ewers an Gross St Martin
An Gross St Martin 6, D 5000
Cologne 1
☏ (+49) 221 23 19 83
Ceramics, glass.

**Galerie für Englische Keramik
Marianne Heller**
Allmenstrasse 31, D 6902 Sanhausen/
Heidelberg
☏ (+49) 6224 3317
Ceramics.

Galerie für Modernen Schmuck
Weckmarkt 3, D 6000 Frankfurt 1
☏ (+49) 69 29 22 88
Jewelry.

Galerie für Schmuck
Grosser Burstah 38, D 2000
Hamburg 1
☏ (+49) 40 36 55 74
Jewelry.

Galerie Glashart
Am Marstall 23, D Hanover 1
☏ (+49) 511 32 40 00
Glass.

Galerie Gottschalk-Betz
Oeder Weg 29, D 6000 Frankfurt am
Main
☏ (+49) 69 59 11 45
Director: M. Gottschalk-Betz
International glass.

Galerie Charlotte Hennig
Rheinstrasse 18, D 6100 Darmstadt
☏ (+49) 6151 24617
Ceramics, glass, jewelry (5–6
exhibitions a year).

Galerie Herrmann
Tgl. 9–12 u. nach Vereinbarung, D
8371 Drachselsried
☏ (+49) 9945 395
Glass.

Galerie Kunsthandwerk
Pariserstrasse 12, D 1000 Berlin 12
☏ (+49) 30 8 22 28 02
Director: Sybille Voormann
Ceramics, glass, furniture, textiles, toys.
Seven exhibitions a year.

Galerie L
Elbchaussee 31, D 2000 Hamburg 11
☏ (+49) 40 3 90 30 11
Director: Charlotte van Finckenstein
Ceramics, glass.

Galerie Pande
Hinterer Brühl 1, D3200 Hildesheim
☏ (+49) 5121 127 42
Fax (+49) 5121 1321 72
Directors: Peter Schmitz and Bernard
Herkenrath
Various crafts, latest trends.

Galerie Smend
Mainzer Strasse 31, D 5000 Cologne 1
☏ (+49) 221 31 20 47 or 221 31 51 63
Textiles.

Galerie Treykorn
Savignyplatz 13, D 1000 Berlin 13
☏ (+49) 30 3 12 95
Jewelry.

Galerie Und
Huttenstrasse 40, D Düsseldorf
Furniture.

Glas des 20. Jahrhunderts
Augsburger Strasse 50, D 8870
Gunzberg
☏ (+49) 8221 9 33 22 or 8221 9 32 23
Director: Christiane Waldrich-Mengele
Glass.

Kunsthaus am Museum Carola van Ham
Drususgasse 1–5, D 5000 Cologne
☎ (+49) 221 23 81 37 or 221 23 75 41
Glass.

Muffendorfer Keramikgalerie
Muffendorfer Haupstrasse 39, D 5300
Bonn 2 (Bad Godesberg)
☎ (+49) 2 28 33 42 76
Director: Horst Heidermann

Pavé
Bilkserstrasse 4, D 4000 Düsseldorf 1
☎ (+49) 211 32 75 53
Jewelry.

Spektrum
Turkenstrasse 96, D 8000 Munich 40
☎ (+49) 89 28 45 90
Jewelry.

HOLLAND

Binnen Collectie
Keizersgracht 82, NL 1015 CT
Amsterdam
☎ (+31) 20 25 96 03 Fax (+31) 20 27
26 54
Director: Helen van Ruiten
Ceramics, jewelry.

Braggiotti Gallery
Landswerf 220, NL 3063 GG
Rotterdam
☎ (+31) 10 41 26 095
Directors: Christian Braggiotti, P.J.
Amtsberg
International glass.

Galerie Amphora
Van Oudenallenstraat 3, NL 6862 CA
Oosterbeek
☎ (+31) 85 33 36 85
Ceramics.

Galerie Beeld en Ambeeld
Walstraat 13, NL 7511 GE Enschede
☎ (+31) 53 30 03 57
Directors: Martha Haveman, Karel
Betman
Jewelry.

Galerie Tom Berends
Westeinde 22, NL 2512 HD The Hague
☎ (+31) 70 46 19 98
Director: Tom Berends
Jewelry.

Galerie Rob van den Doel
Anna Paulownastraat 195A, NL 2518
BD The Hague
☎ (+31) 70 36 46 239
Director: Rob van den Doel
Glass (chiefly Dutch and
Czechoslovakian).

Galerie de Fiets
Oude Delft 195, NL 2611 HD Delft
☎ (+31) 15 13 18 49
Directors: Will Lutz, Germaine
Knipscheer
Ceramics.

Galerie Inart
Paulus Potterstraat 22–24 NL 1071 DA
Amsterdam
☎ (+31) 20 66 41 881
Directors: Indoor BV, Carla Koch
Ceramics, glass, work in precious
metals.

Galerie Het Kapelhuis
Breestraat 1, NL 3811 BH Amersfoort
☎ (+31) 33 63 19 84
Directors: M. Blitterswijk, H.A.
Koopmans
Applied arts, textiles, ceramics.

Galerie Marzee
Ganzenheuvel 33, NL 6511 WD
Nijmegen
☎ (+31) 80 22 96 70
Director: Marie-Jose van den Hout
Furniture, jewelry.

Galerie Puntgaaf
Stoeldraaierstraat 56a, NL 9712 BX
Groningen
☎ (+31) 50 18 28 78
Director: Cor de Nobel
Furniture, textiles.

Galerie Ra
Vijzelstraat 80, NL 1017 HL Amsterdam
☎ (+31) 20 26 51 00
Diector: Paul Derrez
International jewelry.

Galerie Louise Smit
Prinsengracht 615, NL 1016 HT
Amsterdam
☎ (+31) 20 25 98 98
Director: Louise Smit
Jewelry.

Galerie Summat To Wear
Zeedijk 39a, NL 1012 AR Amsterdam
☎ (+31) 20 38 28 21
Director: Tine Withagen
Clothing, textiles.

Galerie de Witte Voet
Kerkstraat 149, NL 1017 GG
Amsterdam
☎ (+31) 20 25 84 12
Director: Annemie Boissevain
Ceramics, glass.

Kunst en Keramiek
Korte Assenstraat 16, NL 7411 JP
Deventer
☎ (+31) 5700 13004
Directors: R and L. Van de Voorde
Ceramics, glass.

Terra Keramiek
Nieuwstraat 7, NL 2611 HK Delft
☎ (+31) 15 14 70 72
Directors: Joke Doedens, Simone Haak
Ceramics.

Trits/Sieraden
Nieuwstraat 11–13, NL 2611 HK Delft
☎ (+31) 15 13 26 97
Directors: Laura Bakker, Gert
Boekestein
Jewelry.

HUNGARY

Galerie Jozsefvarosi Kiaaitoterme
Josef Jorut 70, H 1085 Budapest
Ceramics.

Pecsi Galeria
Szechenyi ter 11, H 7632 Pecs
Ceramics.

IRELAND

HQ Gallery
Powerscourt Townhouse Centre, South
William Street, Dublin 2
☎ (+353) 1 797 368
Run by Crafts Council of Ireland.

ITALY

Galleria d'Arte Moderna
Via Nzario Sauro 58a, I 41100 Modena
☎ (+39) 59 243455
Director: Emilio Mazzoli
Contemporary furniture.

Galleria Forni
Via Farini 26, I 40124 Bologna
Ceramics.

Galleria Il Gabbiano
Via della Frezza, I Rome
Ceramics.

Il Giardino dell' Arte
Via Santo Vitale 7A, I 40125 Bologna
☎ (+39) 51 22 06 42 Fax (+39) 51 22
30 54
Director: Pier Francesco Ferroni
Ceramics.

Studio d'Arte Contemporanea
Via Baldini 15, I 47037 Rimini
Director: Miroslav Krsul

JAPAN

Akasaka Green Gallery
1F Ito Building, Minato-ku, Tokyo 107
☎ (+81) 3 3401 5255
Director: M. Ito

Gallery Gallery
Kyoto
Fiber art

Gallery Haku
Senpuku Building, 4–6–14 Nishi
Temma, Kita-ku, Osaka 530
☎ (+81) 6 363 0493
Director: M. Toriyama

Gallery Isogaya
Nagao Building 7F, 1-4-12
Nishishinbashi, Minatoku, Tokyo
☎ (+81) 33 3591 8797

Gallery Iteza
B Fujita Building, Sanjo Kobashi
Higashi, Nakagyo-ku, Kyoto 604
☎ (+81) 75 211 7526
Director: Kazuko Fujita

Gallery Koyanagi
1–7–5 Ginza, Chuo-ku, Tokyo
☎ (+81) 3 3561 1896
Director: Atsuko Koyanagi

Gallery Mori
1F Takahashi Building, 7–10–8 Ginza,
Chuo-ku, Tokyo 104
☎ (+81) 3 3573 5327 or 3 3573 5328
Director: Kunihiko Mori

Gallery Muu
Ayanishikoennai, Nishiotoin-Ayakoji
Sagaru, Shimogyo-ku, Kyoto
☎ (+81) 75 343 6658
Textiles.

Gallery Nakamura
2F Anekoji-dori Kawara-machi Higashi-
ira, Nakagyo-ku, Kyoto 604
☎ (+81) 75 231 6632
Director: M. Nakamura

Gallery Pousse/Ichikawa Gallery
Ginza Abitasion 202, 5–14–16 Ginza,
Chuo-ku, Tokyo 104
☎ (+81) 3 5565 3870

Gallery Tenjiku
2-22-15 Tokiwadai, Itabashi-ku, Tokyo 174
☎ (+81) 33 5994 3441

Gallery Ueda
B1 Asahi Building, 6–6–7 Ginza,
Chuo-ku, Tokyo 104
☎ (+81) 3 3574 7553 or 3 3574 7554
Director: Akira Ueda

Inui Gallery
Tokodo Building 7F, 3-21-12 Akasaka,
Minatoku, Tokyo

Isetan Art Gallery
Isetan department store, 3–14–1
Shinjuku, Shinjuku-ju, Tokyo 160
☎ (+81) 3 3352 1111

Kandori
Hotel New Otani, 4-1 Kioicho, Chiyoda-
ku, Tokyo
☎ (+81) 33 3239 0146

Kasahara Gallery
5–30 Koraibashi, Higashi-ku, Osaka 541
☎ (+81) 6 227 5137
Director: Rynnosuke Kasahara

Kuroda Toen
7–8–6 Ginza, Chuo-ku, Tokyo 104
☎ (+81) 3 3571 3223

Maronie
Kyoto
Director: Kyoji Tsuji
Ceramics.

Maruzen Craft Centre Gallery
Maruzen, 23–10 Nihonbashi, Chuo-ku, Tokyo 103
☎ (+81) 3 3272 7211

Masuda Studio
2-20-17 Hyakunincho, Shinjuku-ku, Tokyo 169
☎ (+81) 33 3368 0054

Matsuya Craft Gallery
Matsuya department store, 3–6–1 Ginza, Chuo-ku, Tokyo 104
☎ (+81) 3 3567 1211

Miharudo Gallery
3-14-18 Mejiro, Toshima-ku, Tokyo 171
☎ (+81) 33 952 7977
Fax (+81) 33 952 7977
Director: Miharu Ando
Various crafts.

Mitsukoshi Art Gallery
Mitsukoshi department store, 1–4–1 Nihonbashi Muromachi, Chuo-ku, Tokyo 103
☎ (+81) 3 3241 3311
Director: M. Kuroda

The Office
Kyoto
Director: Kyoji Tsuji

Seibu Art Forum
1–28–1 Minami Ikebukuro, Toshima-ku, Tokyo 171
☎ (+81) 3 3981 0111

Senbikiya Gallery
1-1-9 Kyobashi, Chuo-ku, Tokyo
☎ (+81) 33 3281 0320

Shibuya Craft Gallery
Seibu department store, 21–1 Udagawa-cho, Shikuya-ku, Tokyo 150
☎ (+81) 3 3462 0111

Takashimaya Gallery
Takashimaya department store, Shijokawara-machi, Shimogyo-ku, Kyoto 600
☎ (+81) 75 221 8811

Takashimaya Gallery
Takashimaya department store, 2–4–1 Nihonbashi, Chuo-ku, Tokyo 103
☎ (+81) 3 3211 4111

Wacoal Ginza Art Space
B1 Daiichi Miyuki Building, 5–1–15 Ginza, Chuo-ku, Tokyo 104
☎ (+81) 3 3573 3798

Wako
4–5–11 Ginza, Chuo-ku, Tokyo 104
☎ (+81) 3 3562 2111

NEW ZEALAND

Crafts Council Gallery
22 the Terrace, Wellington,
☎ (+64) 4 727 018
Ceramics, glass, jewelry, textiles, wood.

NORWAY

Brudd
Markvejen 42, N 0554 Oslo 5
☎ (+47) 2 382398
Ceramics.

Galleri Nikolai
Bryggen 7, N 5000 Bergen
☎ (+47) 5 317315

Galleri NK
Posboks 1745 Nordnes, N 5024 Bergen
☎ (+47) 5 900140
Director: Lise Jonette Gjertsen
Ceramics.

Galleri Villvin
N 4950 Risør
☎ (+47) 41 50508

Kunsthåndverkeren
Dronningensgt. 29, N 7000 Trondheim
☎ (+47) 7 516803

Kunsthåndverkerne Kongensgate
Rådhusgt. 24, N 0158 Oslo 1
☎ (+47) 2 422361

Kunstnerfobundet
Kjrell Stubsgt. 3, N 0161 Oslo 1
☎ (+47) 2 414029
Director: Gina Stang
Ceramics, crafts in general.

Lille Øvregaten Kunsthåndverk
Lilleø øvregt. 17, N 5000 Bergen
☎ (+47) 5 317466

Ram-Galleri
Kongensgt. 3, N 0153 Oslo 1
☎ (+47) 2 335992
Director: Lotte Sandberg
Ceramics, glass, metalwork, textiles.

Rebella
Torshovgata 2, N 0476 Oslo 4
☎ (+47) 2 373482
Jewelry.

Verkstedsutsalget
Gabelsgt. 47, N 0262 Oslo 2
☎ (+47) 2 443157
Ceramics.

SPAIN

Espai Positura
Marques de Sentmenat, 89, SP 08029 Barcelona
☎ (+34) 3 3 22 43 65

Galeria Ambit
Conseil de Cent 28e, SP 08007 Barcelona
Ceramics.

Galeria Ceramo
Correia 38, SP 0100 Vitoria-Gasbetz
Ceramics.

Galeria Hipotesi
Rambla de Catalunya, 105, SP 08008 Barcelona
☎ (+34) 3 2 15 02 98
Jewelry.

Galeria Réné Metras
Conseil de Cent 331, SP 08007 Barcelona
Ceramics.

Galeria Sargadelos
Calle Zurbano 46, SP Madrid
☎ (+34) 1 4104830
and at C/ rue Nova, SP Santiago de Compostela
Ceramics.

SWEDEN

Blas & Knada
Hornsgatan 26, S 117 20 Stockholm
☎ (+46) 8 42 77 67
Ceramics and glass.

Galleri Orrefors
Strandvagen 15, S 114 56 Stockholm
☎ (+46) 8 662 73 20
Glass.

Galleri Ratatosk
Haga Nygata 27 a-b, S 413 01 Gothenburg
☎ (+46) 31 11 36 46
Glass, textiles.

Galleri Rocade
Skeppargatan 29, S 114 52 Stockholm
☎ (+46) 8 660 99 70
Textiles.

Kao-Lin
Hornsgatan 50B, S 117 21 Stockholm
☎ (+46) 8 44 46 00
Ceramics.

Konsthantverkshuset
Slussgatan 1, S 411 06 Gothenburg
☎ (+46) 31 15 13 80 and (+46) 31 15 13 85
Ceramics, glass, textiles.

Loftet
Lilla Torg 7, S 211 34 Malmo
☎ (+46) 40 12 30 19
Ceramics.

Nielsen Gallery
Vastergatan 40, S 211 21 Malmo
☎ (+46) 40 30 24 41
Glass, ceramics.

SWITZERLAND

Galerie de l'Amiral Duquesne
6 rue de l'Amiral Duquesne, CH 1170 Aubonne
Swiss ceramics.

Galerie Atrium
Kanonengasse 35, CH 4051 Basel
☎ (+41) 61 22 65 40

Galerie Maya Behn
Neumarkt 24, CH 8001 Zürich
☎ (+41) 1 252 65 25
Director: Maya Behn
International ceramics, glass, jewelry, textiles.

Galerie Desinfarkt
Belpstrasse 47, CH Bern
Ceramics, jewelry.

Galerie Farel
Place du Marché 1, CH 1860 Aigle
International jewelry, textiles and paper objects.

Galerie Filambule
Rue des Terreaux 18 bis, CH 1003 Lausanne
Fiber arts.

Galerie Leonelli
Rue Charles Vuillermet 6, CH 1005 Lausanne
☎ (+41) 21 312 24 48
Ceramics.

Galerie Midi Pile
Rue du Midi 12, CH 1003 Lausanne
☎ (+41) 21 23 12 14
Director: Micheline Schenker
Ceramics, glass.

Galerie No
6 rue Enning, CH 1003 Lausanne
Jewelry.

Galerie Sanske
Stampfenbachstrasse 6, CH 8001
Zürich
☎ (+41) 1 261 60 64
International glass.

Galerie Heidi Schneider
Lowengasse 5, CH 8810 Horgen
☎ (+41) 725 30 53
Ceramics, glass.

Galerie Tragart
Spalenvorstadt 5, CH 4051 Basel
☎ (+41) 61 25 40 70

Galerie Trois
2 place de la Taçonnerie, CH 1204
Geneva
☎ (+41) 22 28 45 07
Directors: Georgette Strobino, Lionel
Latham
International glass.

Galerie Michèle Zeller
Kramgasse 30, CH 3000 Bern 8
☎ (+41) 31 22 93 88
International jewelry.

Galerie zum Oberen Schwamen
Hauptstrasse 28, CH Zurzach

Rennweg Galerie
Schweizer Heimatwerk, Rennweg 14,
CH 8001 Zürich
☎ (+41) 1 221 35 73
Ceramics, jewelry, furniture.

Schmuckforum
Zollikerstrasse 6, CH 8001 Zürich
☎ (+41) 1 3 83 66 79
Director: Alban Hürlimann
International jewelry.

UNITED KINGDOM

Aberystwyth Arts Centre
Penglais Hill, Aberystwyth SY23 3DE
☎ (+44) 970 4277
Major venue for crafts exhibitions,
ceramics, glass, jewelry, wood.

Amalgam
3 Barnes High Street, London SW13
☎ (+44) 81 878 1279
Ceramics, glass, jewelry.

Artizana
The Village, Prestbury, Cheshire SK10
4DG
☎ (+44) 625 827582
Glass, ceramics, furniture, jewelry,
metalwork, textiles, toys.

Beaux Arts Ceramics
York Street, Bath BA1 1NG
☎ (+44) 225 64850
Director: Reg Singh
Ceramics.

Bluecoat Display Centre
School Lane, Liverpool
☎ (+44) 51 709 4014
Ceramics, glass, jewelry, metalwork,
textiles.

The Collier Campbell Shop
45 Conduit Street, London W1R 9FB
☎ (+44) 71 287 2277
Directors: Susan Collier, Sarah
Campbell
Jewelry, textiles.

Contemporary Applied Arts
43 Earlham Street, London WC2H 9LD
☎ (+44) 71 836 6993
Director: Tessa Peters
Major exhibition venue, all crafts
represented, membership association,
shop and gallery. Receives a grant from
the Crafts Council of England and
Wales.

**Contemporary Ceramics (formerly
Craftsmen Potters Shop)**
William Blake House, 7 Marshall Street,
London W1V 1SD
☎ (+44) 71 437 7605
Run by the Craftsmen Potters
Association. Large selection of
contemporary British ceramics.

Contemporary Textiles Gallery
Vigo Galleries, 6a Vigo Street,
London W1
☎ (+44) 71 439 9071
Director: Gillian McKinlay
Specializes in contemporary British
textiles for interiors. Most textile media
represented.

Courcoux and Courcoux
90–92 Crane Street, Salisbury SP1
2QD
☎ (+44) 722 333471
Ceramics.

The Craft Centre and Design Gallery
City Art Gallery, The Headrow, Leeds
LS1 3AB
☎ (+44) 532 462485
International ceramics and jewelry.

Crafts Council Gallery
44a Pentonville Road, London N1 9HF
☎ (+44) 71 278 7700
Major, government-funded venue for
contemporary craft exhibitions.

Crafts Council Shop at the V & A
Victoria and Albert Museum, South
Kensington, London SW7 2RL
☎ (+44) 71 589 5070
Work selected from Crafts Council
slide-index members, Crafts Council
grant recipients and craftsmen and
women represented in the Crafts
Council collection. All media.

Peter Dingley
8 Chapel Street, Stratford-upon-Avon
☎ (+44) 789 205001
Director: Peter Dingley

Electrum
21 South Molton Street, London W1Y
1DD
☎ (+44) 71 629 6325
Director: Barbara Cartlidge
International jewelry.

Galerie Besson
15 Royal Arcade, 28 Old Bond Street,
London W1X 3HD
☎ (+44) 71 491 1706
Director: Anita Besson
International ceramics.

The Glasshouse
65 Long Acre, London WC2 9JH
☎ (+44) 71 836 9785
British studio glass.

Godfrey and Twatt
7 Westminster Arcade, Parliament
Street, Harrogate HG1 2RN
☎ (+44) 423 525300
Directors: Mary Godfrey, Alex Twatt
Ceramics, glass, jewelry, metalwork,
textiles.

The Hart Gallery
23 Main Street, Linby, Nottingham
NG15 8AE
☎ (+44) 602 638707
Directors: Katharine A. Hart, John L.
Hart
Contemporary ceramics.

New Ashgate Gallery
Wagon Yard, Farnham GU9 7JR
☎ (+44) 252 713208
Ceramics, furniture, glass, jewelry,
metalwork, textiles, toys.

New Craftsman
24 Fore Street, St Ives, Cornwall TR26
1HE
☎ (+44) 736 795652
Ceramics, glass, jewelry, textiles.

Nexus
14 Broad Street, Brighton BN2 1TJ
☎ (+44) 273 684480
Director: Cynthia Cousens
Ceramics, jewelry, metalwork, textiles.

Anotol Orient
239A Ladbroke Grove, London W10
6HG
☎ (+44) 81 960 9262
Director: Anatol Orient
Ceramics, viewing by appointment only.

Oxford Gallery
23 High Street, Oxford OX1 4AH
☎ (+44) 865 242731
Ceramics, glass, jewelry, metal, wood.

Primavera
10 Kings Parade, Cambridge IB2 1SJ
☎ (+44) 223 357708
Ceramics, glass, jewelry, metal, textiles,
wood.

Paul Rice
60 Blenheim Crescent, London W11
1NY
☎ (+44) 71 229 8241
Director: Paul Rice
Ceramics exhibitions, viewing by
appointment.

Royal Exchange Craft Centre
Royal Exchange Theatre, St Ann's
Square, Manchester M2 7DH
☎ (+44) 61 833 9333
Ceramics, glass, jewelry, textiles, toys,
wood.

The Scottish Gallery
94 George Street, Edinburgh EH2 3DF
☎ (+44) 31 225 5955
Jewelry, studio ceramics, wood,
metalwork.

Themes and Variations
231 Westbourne Grove, London W11
☎ (+44) 71 727 5331
Director: Liliane Fawcett
Furniture and glass.

**Andrew Usiskin Contemporary Art
Gallery**
11 Flask Walk, London NW3
☎ (+44) 71 431 4484
Director: Andrew Usiskin
Various crafts.

Wilson & Gough
106 Draycott Avenue, London SW3
☎ (+44) 71 823 7082 Fax (+44) 71
581 3499
Director: Julie Wilson Dyer Gough
International ceramics, glass,
metalwork, textiles.

UNITED STATES OF
AMERICA

The Allrich Gallery
251 Post Street, San Francisco CA
94108
☎ (+1) 415 398 8896

American Crafts Gallery
1310 Larchmere Boulevard, Cleveland
OH 44120
☎ (+1) 216 231 2008
Director: Sylvia Ullman
Ceramics.

Anderson and Anderson
#240, 4001 Avenue North, Dulwich
MN 55401

Archon
6H, 525 West 49th Street, New York
NY 10019

Art et Industrie
594 Broadway, New York NY 10012
☎ (+1) 212 431 1661 Fax (+1) 212 925 5762
Director: Rick Kaufman
Furniture.

Artwear
456 West Broadway, New York NY 10012
☎ (+1) 212 673 2000
Jewelry.

Artworks Gallery
155 South Main, Seattle WA 98104
☎ (+1) 206 625 0932

Bellas Artes
#406, 584 Broadway, New York NY 10012
☎ (+1) 212 274 1116

Rena Bransten Gallery
77 Geary, San Francisco CA 94108
☎ (+1) 415 982 3292

Center for Tapestry Arts
2nd Floor, 167 Spring Street (at West Broadway), New York NY 10012
☎ (+1) 212 431 7500
Director: Jean West
Textiles.

Christy/Taylor Gallery
Crocker Center, Suite 243, 5050 Town Center Circle, Boca Raton FL 33486
☎ (+1) 407 394 6303
Glass.

Garth Clark Gallery
24 West 57th Street, New York NY 10019
☎ (+1) 212 246 2205
Director: Mark del Vecchio
and at 170 South la Brea Avenue, Los Angeles CA 90036
☎ (+1) 213 939 2189
and at Kansas City by appointment
☎ (+1) 816 735 5299
International ceramics.

Connell Gallery/Great American Gallery
333 Buckhead Avenue, Atlanta GA 30305
☎ (+1) 404 261 1712
Woodwork, textiles.

Contemporary Crafts Gallery
3934 S.W. Corbett Avenue, Portland OR 97201
☎ (+1) 503 223 2654
Ceramics.

Contemporary Porcelain
105 Sullivan Street (SoHo), New York NY 10012
☎ (+1) 212 219 2172
Ceramics.

Cowles Gallery
420 West Broadway, New York NY 10012
☎ (+1) 212 925 3500
Director: Charles Cowles
Ceramics, glass.

Craft Alliance
6640 Delmar, St Louis MI 63130
☎ (+1) 314 725 1151
Ceramics.

Susan Cummins Gallery
12 Miller Avenue, Mill Valley CA 94941
☎ (+1) 415 383 1512
Director: Susan Cummins
Ceramics, jewelry.

Del Mano Gallery
11981 San Vicente Boulevard, Los Angeles CA 90049
☎ (+1) 213 476 8508
and at 33 E. Colorado Boulevard, Pasadena CA 91105
☎ (+1) 818 793 6648

Helen Drutt Gallery
1721 Walnut Street, Philadelphia PA 19103
☎ (+1) 215 735 1625
Director: Helen Drutt
Ceramics, furniture, jewelry.

Aaron Faber Gallery
666 Fifth Street, New York NY 10019
☎ (+1) 212 586 8411
Director: Edward Faber
Jewelry.

Ferrin Gallery
179 Main Street, Northhampton MA 01060
☎ (+1) 413 586 4509

Foster/White Gallery
3112 Occidental South, Seattle WA 98104

Katie Gingrass Gallery
714 North Milwaukee Street, Milwaukee WI 53202
☎ (+1) 414 289 0855
Director: Katie Gingrass
Ceramics, jewelry, paper, textiles.

The Glass Gallery
4720 Hampden Lane, Bethesda MA 20814
☎ (+1) 301 657 3478
Glass.

The Greenberg Gallery
44 Maryland Plaza, St Louis MO 63108
☎ (+1) 314 361 7600
Fax (+1) 314 361 7743
Director: Sissy Thomas
Ceramics.

Habatat Gallery
32255 Northwestern Highway, Suite 45, Farmington Hills MI 48018
☎ (+1) 313 851 9090

and at 608 Banyan Trail, Boca Raton FL 33432
☎ (+1) 407 241 4544
Director: Ferdinand Hampson
Glass.

Handworkshop
1812 West Main Street, Richmond VA 23220

Heller Gallery
71 Greene Street, New York NY 10012
☎ (+1) 212 966 5948
Director: Douglas Heller
Glass.

Hibbard McGrath Gallery
Box 7638, 101 North Main Street, Breckinridge CO 80424

Hokin Kaufman Gallery
210 West Superior Street, Chicago IL 60610
☎ (+1) 312 266 1211
Artist-designed furniture.

Holsten Galleries
206 Worth Avenue, Palm Beach FL 33480
☎ (+1) 407 833 3403
Glass.

Jewelers Werk
2000 Pennsylvania Avenue NW, Washington D.C. 20006

Peter Joseph Gallery
4th Floor, 745 5th Avenue, New York NY 10151

Julie: Artisans Gallery
687 Madison Avenue, New York NY 10021

Leo Kaplan Limited
969 Madison Avenue, New York NY 10021
☎ (+1) 212 535 2407
Furniture, glass.

Kentucky Art and Craft Gallery
609 West Main Street, Louisville KY
☎ (+1) 502 589 0102

Klein Art Works
400 North Morgan, Chicago IL 60622
☎ (+1) 312 243 0400
Director: Paul Klein

Kurland/Summers Gallery
8472A Melrose Avenue, Los Angeles CA 90069
☎ (+1) 213 659 7098
Director: Ruth Summers
Glass.

Leedy-Voulkos Gallery
1919 Wyandotte, Kansas City MI 64108
☎ (+1) 816 474 1919
Ceramics.

Maurine Littleton Gallery
1667 Wisconsin Avenue NW, Washington D.C. 20007
☎ (+1) 202 333 9307
Director: Maurine Littleton
Glass.

The London Gallery
563 Lincoln Avenue, Winnetka IL 60093
☎ (+1) 708 869 2272
Director: Pat Barnes
Ceramics, metalwork, textiles.

Nancy Margolis Gallery
367 Fore Street, Portland ME 04101
☎ (+1) 207 775 3822
Ceramics, glass, furniture, jewelry, textiles.

Marx Gallery
208 West Kinzie Street, Chicago IL 60610
☎ (+1) 312 464 0400
Glass.

Maveety Gallery
Salishan OR
☎ (+1) 503 764 2318
Woodwork, textiles.

Meredith Gallery
805 N. Charles Street, Baltimore MD 21201
☎ (+1) 301 837 3575
Furniture.

Miller Gallery
9 Church Street, Montclair NJ 07042
☎ (+1) 201 744 2553
Directors: Kenneth Miller, Eleinore Miller
Glass.

Thomas Moser Cabinetmarkers
210 West Washington Square, Philadelphia PA 19106
and at 415 Cumberland Avenue, Portland ME 04101

Néotu
133 Greene Street, New York NY 10012
☎ (+1) 212 982 0210
Director: Pierre St Audenmeyer
Furniture, glass, ceramics.

Northwest Gallery of Fine Woodworking
202 1st Avenue South, Seattle WA 98104

Anne O'Brien
2114 R Street NW, Washington D.C. 20008

Objects Gallery
230 West Huron Street, Chicago IL 60610
☎ (+1) 312 664 6622
Director: Ann Nathan
Ceramics, furniture, wood.

Franklin Parrasch Galleries
2114 R Street NW, Washington D.C.
20008
☎ (+1) 202 328 8222
Director: Franklin Parrasch
Ceramics, textiles, wood.

Perimeter Gallery
356 West Huron Street, Chicago IL
60610
☎ (+1) 312 266 9473
Director: Frank Paluch
Ceramics, fiber.

Plum Gallery
3762 Howard Avenue, Kensington MD
20895

Pritam & Eames
27–29 Race Lane, East Hampton NY
11937

Pro-Art
5595 Pershing, St Louis MI 63112
☎ (+1) 314 361 4442
Ceramics.

Max Protetch Gallery
560 Broadway, New York NY 10012
☎ (+1) 212 966 5454
Director: Max Protetch
Various crafts.

**Joanne Rapp Gallery/The Hand and
the Spirit**
4222 North Scottsdale Road,
Scottsdale AR 85251
☎ (+1) 602 949 1262
Director: Joanne Rapp
Ceramics.

Rezac Gallery
2nd Floor, 301 West Superior, Chicago
IL 60610
☎ (+1) 312 751 0481

Joan Robey Gallery
939 Broadway, Denver CO 80203
☎ (+1) 303 892 9600

Betsy Rosenfield Gallery
212 West Superior, Chicago IL 60610
☎ (+1) 312 787 8020
Director: Betsy Rosenfield
Glass.

Esther Saks Gallery
311 West Superior, Chicago IL 60610
☎ (+1) 312 751 0911
Director: Esther Saks
Ceramics.

**San Francisco Craft & Folk Art
Museum**
Building A, Fort Mason Center, San
Francisco CA 94563
☎ (+1) 415 775 0990
Director: J. Weldon Smith
Important venue for contemporary craft
exhibitions.

Sansar
Tenley Mall, 4200 Wisconsin Avenue
NW, Washington D.C. 20016
☎ (+1) 202 244 4448
Furniture.

Schneider/Bluhm/Loeb Gallery
230 West Superior, Chicago IL 60610
☎ (+1) 312 988 4033
Director: Martha Schneider
Ceramics, jewelry, metalwork.

Signature Gallery
Dock Square, North Street, Boston MA
02109

Snyderman Gallery
317 South Street, Philadelphia PA
19147
☎ (+1) 215 238 9576
Glass, furniture.

Bernice Steinbaum Gallery
132 Greene, New York NY 10012
☎ (+1) 212 431 4224

The Sybaris Gallery
301 W. Fourth Street, Royal Oak MI
48067
☎ (+1) 313 544 3388
Furniture.

Brendan Walter Gallery
1001 Colorado Avenue (at 10th Street),
Santa Monica CA 90401
☎ (+1) 213 395 1155

Dorothy Weiss Gallery
256 Sutter Street, San Francisco CA
94108
☎ (+1) 415 397 3611
Director: Dorothy Weiss
Ceramics.

The Works Gallery
319 South Street, Philadelphia PA
19147
☎ (+1) 215 922 7775
Ceramics, jewelry, etc.

Judy Youens Gallery
2631 Colquitt Street, Houston TX
☎ (+1) 713 527 0303

PUBLICATIONS

We have indicated where publications may be of interest to collectors.

AUSTRALIA

Ceramics – Art and Perception
35 William Street, Paddington NSW 2021
☏ (+61) 2 361 5286 Fax (+61) 2 361 5402
Editor: Janet Mansfield
Quarterly
Started 1990, a critical assessment of international contemporary ceramics. Collector.

Craft Arts International
PO Box 363, Neutral Bay NSW 2069
☏ (+61) 2 908 4797 Fax (+61) 2 953 1576
Editor: Ken Lockwood
Quarterly
Covers all craft media, news, reviews, profiles, debate, primarily national in focus with some international perspective, exhibition listings. Collector.

Fibre Forum
Australian Forum for Textile Arts, Sturt Crafts Centre, PO Box 192, Mittagong NSW 2575
☏ (+61) 48 711 291 Fax (+61) 48 713 169
Editor: Janet de Boer
Three times a year
Covers all fiber media and techniques, news, reviews, profiles, mainly national with some international perspective. Collector.

Pottery in Australia
2/68 Alexander Street, Crows Nest, Sydney NSW 2065
☏ (+61) 2 436 1681 Fax (+61) 2 906 4703
Editor: Leonard Smith (new editor to be appointed 1991)
Quarterly
Published by the Potters' Society of Australia. Principally concerned with promoting the work of Australian potters working in all techniques. News, reviews, profiles, international perspective only where directly applicable to the Australian scene.

BELGIUM

Artisanat de Création
c/o I.E.S.C.M., rue du Congrès 33, B 1000 Brussels (new address not yet available)
Editor: Anne Dessaintes
Bi-monthly
French-language publication, black and white, all disciplines, news, reviews, debate, information, profiles, features, national scope with some international perspective.

Tamat
82 boulevard des Combatants, B 7500 Tournai
☏ (+32) 69 23 42 85
Quarterly
French-language bulletin produced by the Fondation de la Tapisserie, des Arts du Tissu et des Arts Muraux of French-speaking Belgium. Principally national with some international coverage. News, reviews, exhibitions calendar.

CANADA

Ontario Craft
Ontario Crafts Council, Chalmers Building, 35 McCaul Street, Toronto ON M5T 1V7
☏ (+1) 416 977 3551
Editor: Marianne C. Kearney
Quarterly
Association publication, news, reviews, profiles, articles, exhibitions calendar, principally regional in scope with some international perspective. Also produce *Craft News*, edited by Gail Crawford, eight times a year. Collector.

CZECHOSLOVAKIA

Glass Review
c/o Artia, Ve Smečkách 30, CZ 11127 Prague 1
☏ (+42) 2 267941
Editor-in-Chief: Zdenka Kalabisova
Monthly
Published in Czech, English-language edition available. Covers glass and china, but with an emphasis on glass. Focuses on glass artists from Czechoslovakia, on industrial design, some articles with historical perspective. Collector.

Umění a Remesla
Sňemovní 9, CZ 118 00 Prague 1
☏ (+42) 2 536802
Editor: Dr Karel Fabel
Quarterly
Czech-language publication with abstracts in English, German and Russian, covering folk art and artistic crafts as well as fine arts, architecture, design, etc. Articles on historical background, profiles of contemporary craftsmen and women, national and international scope. Collector.

DENMARK

Dansk Kunsthandvaerk
Herredsvejen 7, DK 8581 Nimtofte
☏ (+45) 863 98464
Editor: Merete Erbou Laurent
Quarterly
Danish-language publication covering all craft disciplines. News, reviews, profiles, articles, exhibitions calendar,

mainly national with some international scope. Collector.

Guldsmedebladet
Ryttervej 1, DK 4894 Øster-Ulslev
☏ (+45) 53 86 55 66
Editor: Bendich Bech-Thostrup
Eleven times a year
Danish-language association publication (also subscribed to by non-members worldwide), the official organ of the goldsmiths', jewelers' and silversmiths' trades in Denmark. News, reviews, articles, international perspective, black and white photographs.

FINLAND

Design in Finland
The Finnish Foreign Trade Association, PO Box 908, SF 00101 Helsinki
Editor-in-Chief: Jussi Sipila
Annual
English-language, glossy, trade-oriented publication, special issue of the *Finnish Trade Review*, covers design and crafts. A showcase for Finnish products, some articles and profiles.

Form-Function Finland
Korkeavuorenkatu 19A, SF 00130 Helsinki
☏ (+358) 0 171 621
Editor-in-chief: Barbro Kulvik
Quarterly
Finnish-language publication (English-language translation), covering architecture, industrial arts, crafts, product design and graphics. Articles, news, exhibitions and book reviews, profiles. Collector.

Kotiteollisuus
PO Box 186, SF 00181 Helsinki
☏ (+358) 0 694 0012 Fax (+358) 0 694 0067
Editor: Marketta Luutonen
Bi-monthly
Finnish-language publication, copies available with Swedish translations. News, reviews, articles on professional craftsmen and -women and questions of general interest.

Muoto
Kustannusosakeyhtio Tietopuu, Orionintie 18, SF 02200 Espoo
☏ (+358) 0 452 1688 Fax (+358) 0 427 877
Editor: Juhani Keppo
Three times a year
Finnish-language publication (some English translations), produced by the Finnish Association of Designers. Emphasis on design, some coverage of crafts.

FRANCE

L'Atelier
41 rue Barrault, F 75013 Paris
☏ (+33) 1 45 67 67 21 Fax (+33) 1 43 06 42 69
Editor-in-Chief: Colette Save
Bi-monthly
French-language publication (some English translations), covering architecture, industrial arts, crafts and design. News, reviews, articles, profiles, national emphasis with some international perspective. Collector.

La Céramique Moderne
22 rue le Brun, F 75013 Paris
☏ (+33) 1 45 87 17 48
Editor: Milutin Krstic
Eleven times a year
French-language publication. Ceramics only. Product information, technical advice, some reviews, principally national with some international perspective.

Les Dossiers d'Argile
Hameau de Vière, La Rochegiron, F 04150 Banon
☏ (+33) 92 76 20 10
Editor: Camille Virot
Irregular, approximately once a year
French-language only. Beautifully produced 'booklets' intending to present, in the course of time, 'various studies on the art of present-day ceramics'. Collector.

La Revue de la Céramique et du Verre
61 rue Marconi, BP 3, F 62880 Vendin-le-Viel
☏ (+33) 21 42 82 01 Fax (+33) 21 43 63 20
Editor: Sylvie Girard
Bi-monthly
French-language publication, covering all aspects of ceramics and glass. News, reviews, articles, profiles, exhibitions calendar, national emphasis, international perspective. Collector.

GERMANY

Art Aurea
Karlstrasse 4, Postfach 3060, D 7900 Ulm/Donau
☏ (+49) 731 1520 67 Fax (+49) 731 152071
Editor: Reinhold J. Ludwig
Quarterly
German/English-language publication of five years' standing, covering interior design, jewelry, ceramics and studio glass. News, reviews, articles, profiles, debate, exhibitions calendar, international scope. Collector.

Gold + Silber – Uhren + Schmuck
Postfach 10 02 52, D 7022 Leinfelden-Echterdingen
☏ (+49) 711 75 94 0

Fax (+49) 711 75 94 3 90
Editor: Dr Klaus Hallwass
Monthly
German-language, trade-oriented publication for clocks and watches, gold- and silverware, precious stones and costume jewelry. Its main editorial subjects are product information, selling advice and sales.

Keramik Magazin
Postfach 18 20, D 5020 Frechen 1
☏ (+49) 22 34 5 70 01 Fax (+49) 22 34 5 70 05
Editor: Peter R. Aumann
Bi-monthly
German-language ceramics magazine with product information, news, reviews, profiles, exhibitions calendar. National scope mainly, with some European-wide information.

Kunst + Handwerk
Hauptstrasse 13, D 4006 Erkrath 2
☏ (+49) 2104 3 63 86 Fax (+49) 3 2104 3 62 86
Editor: Karl Günter Nicola
Bi-monthly
German-language edition only. Covers ceramics, metalwork, jewelry, textiles, bookbinding, art, glass, etc. News, reviews, profiles, articles, national and international scope, national exhibitions calendar with some international entries. Collector.

Neue Keramik
Unter den Eichen 90, D 1000 Berlin 45
☏ (+49) 30 831 2953 Fax (+49) 30 831 6281
Editor: Gustav Weiss
Bi-monthly
German-language magazine covering ceramics and glass, national and international scope, news, reviews, product news, calendar of exhibitions at home and abroad. Collector.

Neues Glas/New Glass
Hauptstrasse 13, D 4006 Erkrath
☏ (+49) 2104 3 63 86 Fax (+49) 2104 3 32 86
Editor-in-Chief: Karl-Günter Nicola
Quarterly
German/English glass magazine. Incorporates Corning Museum of Glass's annual *New Glass Review*. International scope, all aspects of studio glass production and design. News, reviews, profiles, articles. Collector.

Textil Forum
Friedenstrasse 5, Postfach 5944, D 3000 Hanover 1
☏ (+49) 511 81 51 20
Editor: Beatrijs Sterk
Quarterly
German-language only. International scope, all textile media. News, reviews, profiles, articles on historical aspects, international exhibitions calendar. Collector.

Textilkunst
Brabeckstrasse 38, D 3000 Hanover 71
☏ (+49) 511 52 36 48 Fax (+49) 5181 80 09 33 (subscriptions)
Editor: Barbara Koch-Munchmeyer
Quarterly
German-language edition only. Specialist textiles publication, covering all techniques. International scope. News, reviews, profiles, articles giving historical perspective. Collector.

HOLLAND

Bijvoorbeeld
Postbus 145, NL 3640 AC Mijdrecht
☏ (+31) 2979 84421
Editor: Herman Langmuur
Quarterly
Dutch-language publication covering crafts and applied arts. Principally national with some international perspective, news, reviews, profiles, exhibitions calendar. Collector.

IRELAND

Craft Review
HQ, Crafts Council of Ireland, South William Street, Dublin 2
☏ (+353) 1 797368 or 797383
Editor: Terry Kelly
Three times a year
Published by the Crafts Council of Ireland, principally national scope, news, reviews, some international perspective.

ITALY

Abitare
Corso Monforte 15, I 20122 Milan
☏ (+39) 2 76004251 Fax (+39) 2 791904
Editor: Franca Salti Gualteri
Eleven times a year
Italian/English. Covers architecture and design, crafts marginally. News, reviews, articles, some with historical perspective. Selective exhibitions mentioned. Collector.

Arte Tessile
Via Fiume 8, I Florence 50123
☏ (+39) 50 289639 Fax (+39) 50 289478
Editor: Alessandra Mottola Molfino
Annual
Started 1990. Italian-language edition, abstracts in English. Textile art, emphasis on historical textiles with some reference to the contemporary scene. Book reviews, international scope. Scholar, collector.

Domus
Via Achille Grandi 5/7, I 20089 Rozzano/Milan
☏ (+39) 2 824721 Fax (+39) 2 26863123

Editor: Mario Bellini
Monthly
Italian/English publication covering architecture, interiors, design, art, and craft principally where it intersects with design. News, reviews, articles, profiles. Collector.

Modo
Via Salomono 61, I 20138 Milan
☏ (+39) 2 449 1149 Fax (+39) 2 440 5544
Editor: Andrea Branzi
Monthly
Architecture, art and design.

JAPAN

Glass Work
Teramachidori, Ebisugawaagaru, Nakagyo-ku, Kyoto
☏ (+81) 75 223 5036
Editor: Koji Matano
Quarterly
Japanese-language publication with English abstracts, news, reviews, profiles, technical features, exhibitions calendar, international perspective, traditional and avant-garde. Collector.

Honoho Geijutsu
4-30-12 Kamimeguro, Meguro-ku, Tokyo 153
☏ (+81) 33 3715 2036
Editor: Yasufumi Morishita
Monthly
Japanese-language ceramics magazine. Excellent photography featuring the full gamut of contemporary ceramicists.

Katachi
2-14-27-501 Asagayaminami, Suginami-ku, Tokyo 166
Quarterly
Editor: O.H. Sasayama
The main general crafts magazine in Japan.

NEW ZEALAND

New Zealand Crafts
Crafts Council of New Zealand, PO Box 498, Wellington
☏ (+64) 4 727 018
Editor: Alan Loney (new editor to be appointed)
Three times a year
Covers all crafts; news, reviews, articles, profiles, focus on local activity, some international perspective. Local exhibitions only.

Threads
9 Montana Road, Totara Park, Upper Hutt
☏ (+64) 4 266 771
Editor: Jean Parnell
Bi-annual
Magazine of the Association of New

Zealand Embroiderers' Guilds. News, reviews, product information, local exhibitions calendar, national scope only.

NORWAY

Brukskunst
Stortorvets Basarer, Stortorvet 1 B, N 0155 Oslo 1
☏ (+47) 2 428990 Fax (+47) 2 426162
Editor: Sidsel Aarflot
Norwegian-language crafts association publication, black and white, crafts and design, news, reviews, profiles, mainly national in scope.

Kunsthåndverk
Kongensgt. 3, N 0153 Oslo 1
☏ (+47) 2 33 59 90
Editor: Kirsten Waarli
Quarterly
Norwegian-language publication (some English translations), profiles, book and exhibition reviews, exhibitions calendar, mainly national in scope with some international overview. Collector.

Norsk Husflid
Postboks 3693, Gamlebyen, N 0135 Oslo 1
☏ (+47) 2 17 39 75 Fax (+47) 2 17 37 83
Editor: Ingrid Lie
Five times a year
Norwegian-language publication, wide range of crafts represented, news, book reviews, product information, debate, articles giving historical perspective, mainly Scandinavian in scope with some international overview.

POLAND

Projekt
U1. Wspolna 32–46, P 00 679 Warsaw
☏ (through operator) 28 54 01
Editor: Jerzy Wasniewski
Bi-monthly
Polish-language publication (English, German and Russian translations) covering the visual arts and design.

SPAIN

Ceramica
Paseo Acacias 9, E 28005 Madrid
☏ (+34) 91 884 30 73
Editor: Antonio Vivas Zamorano
Quarterly
Spanish-language publication, ceramics only, news, reviews, profiles, product information, international scope. Collector.

SWEDEN

Form
Foreningen Svensk Form, Renstiernas gata 12, S 116 31 Stockholm
☏ (+46) 8 44 33 03 Fax (+46) 8 44 22 85
Editor-in-chief: Ulf Beckman
Eight times a year, one edition in English
Swedish-language publication (English translations) covering all aspects of design and crafts; news, reviews, profiles, articles, national emphasis. Scandinavian exhibitions calendar. Collector.

SWITZERLAND

Crafts Council Bulletin
Case Postale 898, CH 2501 Bienne
☏ (+41) 32 516369
Editor: Antoinette Riklin
Quarterly
Crafts Council bulletin, black and white, French and German text, specifically relating to crafts in Switzerland with information on museums and galleries, national exhibitions calendar, some international perspective.

UNITED KINGDOM

Animations
The Puppet Centre, Battersea Arts Centre, Lavender Hill, London SW11 5TN
☏ (+44) 71 228 5335
Editor: Penny Francis
Bi-monthly
Black and white publication dedicated to the arts of animation in theatre, film and television. News, reviews, profiles, debate, exhibition listings, international scope.

Ceramic Review
21 Carnaby Street, London W1V 1PH
☏ (+44) 71 439 3377 Fax (+44) 71 287 9954
Editors: Eileen Lewenstein, Emmanuel Cooper
Bi-monthly
Ceramics publication, news, reviews, articles, technical advice, product information, national and international scope, national exhibitions calendar. Collector.

Crafts
Crafts Council, 44a Pentonville Road, London N1 9HF
☏ (+44) 71 278 7700
Editor: Geraldine Rudge
Bi-monthly
Published by the Crafts Council of England and Wales. Comprehensive coverage of all the crafts, international scope, news, reviews, profiles, articles. Collector.

Crefft
Craft Department, Welsh Arts Council, 9 Museum Place, Cardiff CF1 3NX
Editor: Roger Lefevre
Quarterly
Newsletter, black and white, specifically for Welsh craftsmen and -women. News, reviews, profiles, regional scope only.

Embroidery
PO Box 42B, East Molesey, Surrey KT8 9BB
☏ (+44) 81 943 1229
Editor: Valerie Campbell-Harding
Quarterly
Published by the Embroiderers' Guild, textiles only, news, reviews, articles, profiles, historical perspective, exhibitions calendar, mainly national in scope.

Journal for Weavers, Spinners and Dyers
Association of Guilds of Weavers, Spinners & Dyers, BCM 963, London WC1N 3XX
Editor: Hilary Turner
Quarterly
Association publication, textiles, news, reviews, articles, profiles, technical features, mainly national in scope with some international perspective.

The New Bookbinder
Published by Designer Bookbinders, 6 Queen Square, London WC1N 3AR
Authoritative coverage of international bookbinding.

The Scribe
Society of Scribes and Illuminators, 54 Boileau Road, London SW13 9BL
Editor: Margaret Daubney
Three times a year
Association publication but 'membership is open to all who support its aims of encouraging the practice and influence of calligraphy and fine lettering'. Collector.

Stained Glass
Plait Hall, High Street, Ashwell Nr Baldock, Herts. SG7 5NP
☏ (+46) 274 2577
Editor: Phillida Shaw
Bi-annual
Published by the British Society of Master Glass Painters. Articles, news, book reviews, historical perspective, national scope.

Textiles
The Textile Institute, 10 Blackfriars Street, Manchester M3 5DR
☏ (+46) 61 834 8457 Fax (+46) 61 835 3087
Editor: Maureen Sawbridge
Quarterly
Trade publication aimed at 'those professionally committed to the design,

manufacture, use, understanding or marketing of textiles or any end-product derived from fibers'. Product information, technical features, historical perspective, book reviews.

Woodturning
166 High Street, Castle Place, Lewes BN7 1XU
☎ (+44) 273 477374 Fax (+44) 273 478606
Editor: Bernard C. Cooper
Quarterly
'A new professional journal for woodturning', founded 1990. Product information, features on international craftsmen and -women, reviews, technical advice.

Woodworking
166 High Street, Castle Place, Lewes BN7 1XU
☎ (+44) 273 477374 Fax (+44) 273 478606
Editor: Eric Bignell
Bi-monthly
News, book reviews, profiles, articles, technical advice, product information, historical perspective, mainly national, some international overview.

The World of Interiors
234 King's Road, London SW3 5UA
☎ (+44) 71 351 5177 Fax (+44) 71 351 3709
Editor: Min Hogg
Monthly
Interior-design magazine, covers crafts related to interior design (textiles, glass, ceramics, furniture), international scope, selective national and international exhibitions calendar.

UNITED STATES OF AMERICA

American Ceramics
9 East 45th Street, New York NY 10017
☎ (+1) 212 309 6886
Editor: Michael McTwigan
Quarterly
Major American ceramics publication. Profiles, news, reviews, debate, national exhibitions calendar. Collector.

American Craft
American Craft Council, 72 Spring Street, New York NY 10012
☎ (+1) 212 274 0630 Fax (+1) 212 274 0650
Editor: Lois Moran
Bi-monthly
Major American publication, produced by the American Craft Council, covering all craft media, news, reviews, profiles, debate, national and international exhibitions calendar. Collector.

Ceramics Monthly
1609 Northwest Boulevard, Box 12448, Columbus OH 43212
☎ (+1) 614 488 8236 Fax (+1) 614 488 4561
Editor: William C. Hunt
Monthly, except for July and August
Ceramics. News, reviews, technical information, profiles, product information, national and international exhibitions calendar. International perspective. Collector.

Fiberarts
50 College Street, Asheville NC 28801
☎ (+1) 704 253 0467
Editor: Ann Batchelder
Bi-monthly, except for July and August
Covers all disciplines related to fiber ('Surface Design, Tapestry, Handmade Paper, Basketry, Needlework, Wearables, Quilting, Weaving'). News, reviews, profiles. Principally national scope with some international perspective.

Fine Woodworking
The Taunton Press, Box 5506, Newtown CT 06470
☎ (+1) 203 426 8171
Editor: Dick Burrows
Bi-monthly
Furniture and woodwork. Product information, technical details. News, reviews, national exhibitions calendar, some international events listed.

Glass Art
PO Box 1507, Broomfield CO 80038
☎ (+1) 303 465 4965
Editor: Shawn Waggoner
Bi-monthly
Stained and decorative glass. Articles, news, reviews, profiles, technical features, international scope, exhibitions calendar. Collector.

Handwoven
201 East 4th Street, Loveland CO 80537
☎ (+1) 303 669 7672
Editor: Jane Patrick
Five times a year
Weaving and knitting, news, book reviews, articles, product information, technical features, national exhibitions calendar.

Metalsmith
5009 Londonderry Drive, Tampa FL 33647
☎ (+1) 813 977 5326
Editor: Sarah Bodine
Quarterly
Major U.S. publication for metalsmithing and jewelry.

Ornament
PO Box 2349, San Marcos CA 92079
☎ (+1) 800 888 8950
Editor: Dr Robert K. Liu
Quarterly

'Ancient, contemporary, ethnic' jewelry and clothing. News, reviews, profiles, international scope. Specialist articles. Collector.

Shuttle, Spindle and Dyepot
Handweavers' Guild of America, 120 Mountain Avenue B 101, Bloomfield CT 06002
☎ (+1) 203 242 3577
Editor: Judy Robbins
Quarterly
Textiles, news, reviews, profiles, technical advice, principally national focus.

Surface Design Journal
PO Box 20799, Oakland CA 94620
☎ (+1) 415 567 1992
Editor: Charles Talley
Quarterly
Surface Design Association publication, covering 'the coloring, patterning/designing of fabric, fiber and other materials'. News, reviews, articles, profiles, debate, technical advice, mainly national scope, some international and historical perspective. Collector.